GOD

SOME CONVERSATIONS

The Hafner Library of Classics

[Number Ten]

JOHANN GOTTFRIED HERDER

GOD

SOME CONVERSATIONS

A Translation with a
Critical Introduction and Notes

BY

FREDERICK H. BURKHARDT

President of Bennington College

1949
HAFNER PUBLISHING COMPANY
NEW YORK

PRINTED IN THE UNITED STATES OF AMERICA

FOREWORD

THE rise of modern religious ideas, the development of modern philosophy, and certain living issues of contemporary thought all receive a significant focus and clarification in the work of Herder translated in this book.

Thirty-five years ago in the *Hibbert Journal* for July, 1905, Dr. Arthur Cushman McGiffert published an article on "The God of Spinoza as Interpreted by Herder," and it was in Dr. McGiffert's lectures on the history of Christian thought at Union Theological Seminary that I myself about twenty years ago first heard mention of Herder's *Gott*. Dr. McGiffert thought "the doctrine of divine immanence contained in Herder's little book one of the most intelligent as well as purest and loftiest to be found in modern literature." Now in his Introduction to the present translation Dr. Burkhardt does well to question critically the argument by which Herder endeavors to reconstrue Spinoza's system as "teaching divine immanence instead of pantheism." For without doubt Herder's attempt to conceive a dynamic and evolutionary universe with God as its immanent and sustaining life belongs to a main current of modern religious thought. To scrutinize its bases is, therefore, not only required in the interest of historical criticism, but also contributes to understanding and testing important forms of the living religious consciousness.

Philosophy in the time of Kant and Goethe will also be better understood with the help of the present work. To elaborate on this point is, however, superfluous, since Dr. Burkhardt has admirably explained in his Introduction in how remarkably comprehensive a manner Herder's essay illumines

vii

the intellectual relations in the German classical period. He shows Herder's Neo-Spinozism to have been one of the several chief developments in German thought during the last half of the eighteenth century in criticism of the Aufklärung world-view, a development indispensable for understanding both Goethe and the speculative idealism of the nineteenth century. Keen students who necessarily experience difficulty in comprehending the transition from pre-Kantian to post-Kantian thought in terms of Kant alone will come upon many of the missing links which they need through this consciously syncretistic essay of Herder's. They will find its relations to numerous contemporaries, and to Leibniz, to Kant, to natural science and *Naturphilosophie* scarcely less illuminating than its connections with Spinoza.

It has not been part of Dr. Burkhardt's purpose in this work to carry his consideration of Herder's influence further than to Schelling and Hegel. Yet the question may fairly be raised whether Herder's interest for our own time is bounded by either speculative idealism or the liberal theology of immanence, neither of which enjoys the ascendency today which once it did. The growth of modern naturalism, the increased awareness of oriental religion and philosophy, the insistent need of relating science and religion — such factors of recent culture open new and wider perspectives in terms of which Herder's theme and spirit may speak further to the contemporary mind. It should be emphasized that he resolutely embraced a religious faith which welcomed without reservation, as an intrinsic part of its own cultivation, the development of scientific knowledge. In this respect the general position Herder took may represent a lasting type of great potential benefit.

Herder, who so assiduously sought out the spiritual expressions of all peoples, would certainly—were he alive today—

take interest in the further meeting of oriental and occidental thought. In these very Conversations about God, it may be noted, he introduced some excerpts from eastern literature. One or more of these excerpts refer to the absorption of the individual in God, and thus drive into the open the charge so generally urged against monism that it threatens to submerge the sense in which western civilization has for a long time regarded and cherished the individual personality. Certainly there are capital issues to be joined at this point, and considerations to be urged from more than one side. But it is not too much to say for Herder in this connection that he was centrally occupied with this problem of combining his monism with that powerful affirmation of individuality he so fully shared with his time. At the end of this work he wishes us to see

"the one and eternal principle of individuation . . . . developed along a line which leads into our innermost self. The more life and reality, that is, the more rational, powerful and perfect energy a being has for the maintenance of a whole which it feels belongs to itself, to which it imparts itself inwardly and entirely, the more it is an individual, a self." [575]

It is easy to recognize in this way of conceiving the individual and his relations a principle central to the world-view of Goethe as well as to the speculative idealism of Schelling and of Hegel. Yet this aspect of Herder's thought is not exhausted in its significance for nineteenth century speculation. It remains a powerful idea with important implications for the present and the future comprehension of man.

HORACE L. FRIESS

COLUMBIA UNIVERSITY
    JANUARY, 1940

TRANSLATOR'S PREFACE

THOUGH Herder's *Gott* has been a classic in Germany for over a century and a half and has been reprinted many times in that country, it has to my knowledge never before been translated into English. Because it is one of Herder's most important contributions to philosophical literature, and because, as I have attempted to show in the Introduction, it occupies a significant place in the development of German thought, it seemed worth while to make it available to English and American students of philosophy and religion.

The needs of the student of ideas have been uppermost in my mind in making the translation. It is consequently literal rather than literary, and I fear that most of the considerable grace and artistry of the original have been lost in the process. I trust, however, that the reader will find that the clarity of the text will make some small amends for this loss.

As for the Introduction, its purpose is primarily to place the work in its historical setting, to appraise its value as a contribution to the development of German idealism and to assist the student in the criticism of Herder's ideas.

Whatever merit the work possesses would have been considerably less had it not been for the kind assistance of friends and teachers. Most of all Professor Horace L. Friess guided me through the entire work, gave me the benefit of his own experience in translation, and in innumerable instances supplied me with criticisms which were unfailingly constructive. Professor J. H. Randall Jr. and Dr. James Gutmann gave generously of their time and scholarship. From the former's discussions in an undergraduate course in the history of philosophy at Columbia University, I derived my initial interest in Herder. Both read over the entire manuscript and gave me many valuable suggestions. To Dr. Gutmann I am especially indebted for assistance in the translation of some of the poetry. Canon L. W. Grensted of Oriel College, Oxford, directed me in my B. Litt. dissertation on Spinozistic influences in German philosophy when I attended that university, and the Introduction of this work has derived a good deal from his guidance. In a more general though no less important way, I have gained much inspiration from three remarkable teachers: Professors Edman, Schneider and Woodbridge, all of Columbia University.

Finally my thanks are due to Mrs. J. A. Ross, Mr. John P. Langston and especially to my wife for their great assistance in stylistic and mechanical matters.[1]

FREDERICK H. BURKHARDT

UNIVERSITY OF WISCONSIN
JANUARY 2ND, 1940

---

[1] Since the proofs of this work have been corrected, I have had the opportunity to examine an advance copy of F. McEachran's *The Life and Philosophy of Johann Gottfried Herder,* published by the Oxford University Press. I should not like this volume to go to press without at least mentioning this welcome addition to the Herder literature in our language, and recommending it to all who wish to become further acquainted with the author of *God, Some Conversations.*

Table of Contents

TABLE OF CONTENTS

INTRODUCTION

The bold face numerals in brackets, i.e. [**364**] in the text of the translation, refer to the corresponding pages in Volume XVI of the Suphan Edition of *Herders Werke*.

In the text, the following notation has been used:

* (asterisks) refer to Herder's own notes.

(A1) (A2) etc., refer to the notes in Appendix A, which contains the variations in the second edition. These variations have been listed according to the bold face numerals in brackets in the text.

(B1) (B2) etc., refer to the translator's notes which will be found in Appendix B. These notes are also listed according to the bold face numerals in brackets in the text.

Herder's Development and the Place of the "Conversations" in it

THE CLOSING years of the eighteenth century in Germany saw the beginning of a period of intellectual and literary activity which has rarely been equalled in the history of the human mind. No better introduction to the intellectual climate of these times could be desired than Johann Gottfried Herder's *God, Some Conversations*. In its pages are reflected the enthusiasm, the controversy and confusion of those transitional years, their criticism of the past, their search for new values in religion and philosophy, and the seeds which were being sown for the harvest of post-Kantian Idealism and Romanticism.

The clearness and the liveliness with which these main issues are presented, is due largely to the personality and the vision of the author. Herder's interests were above all else broad and diversified. Indeed, their diversity was such that he often could not complete all the plans which he had in mind, and a final judgment on his works must always make an invidious comparison with the deeper and more integrated works of some of his more famous contemporaries. It is no exaggeration to say, however, that he enriched more different fields of knowledge than any man of his time. Literature, education, philosophy, history, theology, philology, jurisprudence and biblical criticism all received fruitful and lasting contributions from his pen.

Possessing this extraordinary variety of interests, Herder drew his ideas from many and often disparate sources. As he

3

tells the reader in the Preface to the "Conversations,"[1] he took the inspiration for their doctrines from Spinoza, Leibniz, Shaftesbury and others. This does not mean to say that like Bayle whom he criticizes in the First Conversation, he merely "skimmed over all systems." He so fuses and develops the varied sources that the resultant ideas are his alone. Herder stands on his own merits as a creator and thinker, though he often built with materials which had been used before.

In seeking to understand the work of a thinker of this kind, it is especially rewarding to investigate his intellectual development. Even the briefest account reveals how he combined in rare degree an avidity for ideas with a keen perception for what was significant in the culture of his day.[2]

In 1762, Herder left his native town of Mohrungen in East Prussia,[3] to enter the University of Königsberg. He matriculated in the faculty of Theology, and attended the required lectures in the dogmatic and apologetic thought which dominated the universities of that day. Most of his education, however, was derived from his independent studies, and from the influence of two great men, Immanuel Kant and J. G. Hamann (1730–88), the so-called "Wizard of the North." Herder became a favorite pupil of the former, and the lifelong friend of the latter.

At that time, Kant's thought was undergoing a transition. His doctrines in logic, morals, and metaphysics show only hints

[1] *Herders Werke* (Suphan Ed.), XVI, 403. This edition is hereafter referred to as Su. In the translation, the pagination of the Suphan edition appears in bold-faced numerals in brackets in the text. (All subsequent references to the "Conversations" will be in terms of this pagination.)

[2] The best treatments of Herder's life and work are R. Haym, *Herder nach seinem Leben und seinen Werken,* 2 Vols. (Berlin, 1877–85); and E. Kühnemann, *Herder* (München, 1927). In English, H. Nevinson, *A Sketch of Herder and His Times* (London, 1884) is a good biography giving an interesting picture of Herder's age.

[3] He was born there in 1744.

of the critical philosophy which he was to develop in later years. His influence on Herder, therefore, consisted not so much in positive doctrine, as in the opposition to the school metaphysics of the eighteenth century which his skeptical attitude fostered in his young pupil.

Königsberg, like most German universities in the 1760's, was still a stronghold of the philosophy of Christian Wolff (1679–1754) and his followers. The members of this philosophical school regarded themselves as systematizers and elaborators of the doctrines of Leibniz, and represented the more pedantic and dogmatic temper of the German Aufklärung or Enlightenment.[4] That self-styled Age of Reason had as its predominant characteristics, a thorough-going practical outlook and an optimistic faith in the ability of human reason to understand the universe. Nature was conceived as a great teleological mechanism arranged for the benefit of man who, endowed with the divine light of reason, stood at its center. Its religion was Deism, with its "watchmaker" God existing outside the world He had created, and whose chief relation to it was to spruce up its machinery occasionally and to see that it continued its regular and mechanical course. The religious norm was a Christianity in terms of reason, with an almost exclusive emphasis upon morality as its core. All else was considered superstition and priestcraft. Essentially unhistorical, the age conceived itself to be the culminating point in the development of reason, the goal finally reached after ages of blundering in the fog of half-truth. It seemed that for the first time, the ideal philosophy had been realized. As Wolff ex-

[4] The term is here used only in its narrower sense as practically synonymous with the Leibniz-Wolffian and Deistic views. Cf. C. von Brockdorff, *Die deutsche Aufklärungsphilosophie* (München, 1926) for a fuller treatment. J. G. Hibben, *The Philosophy of the Enlightenment* (N. Y., 1910), and E. Cassirer, *Die Philosophie der Aufklärung* (Tübingen, 1932), treat the movement in its more general aspects in England, France, and Germany.

pressed it, that ideal was to explain "all possible things" by means of logical analysis and systematization.

Herder was to struggle all his life against the unwavering dogmatism and optimism of this superficial world-view. The "Conversations" bear frequent witness to the bitterness of his feelings toward this manner of philosophizing. Apart from his attacks upon its popular notion of a God "who plays with the world as a child plays with soap-bubbles," perhaps his severest criticisms are directed at the barren teleology with which the "enlighteners" thought to explain the universe.[5] The seeds of this revolt against shallow rationalism had been planted in him by a pietistic upbringing, for his parents, like many of the inhabitants of Morhrungen, were participants in that religious movement which spread among the lower middle classes during the eighteenth century. Pietism cherished a religion completely out of sympathy with the Deism of the Aufklärung. It was based upon the heart rather than the mind, and stressed a mystical personal communion with the Deity which was derided by the "reasonable" theologians of the time. As a movement it soon became submerged in the flood-tide of enlightenment, but it nevertheless left important traces upon the mind of a younger generation, which was to perpetuate its influence in the great period of philosophical and religious speculation which opened the new century.

With such an origin, it was natural that Herder should lend willing ears to Kant's skeptical thrusts at the prevailing rationalism of the Wolffian metaphysics. But he was even more receptive to the brilliant, oracular views of Hamann, who likewise inveighed against that school, though for different reasons. Unlike Kant, who attacked the Wolffians because their reasoning was poor, Hamann attacked them for the exaggerated place which they assigned to that power. For him the intellect was

[5] Cf. p. 132, [492] ff.

the least important possession of man. True knowledge was based upon belief and feeling, and the foundation and epitome of all truth was the Bible. He considered most of the problems of metaphysics to be entirely verbal, and their solutions empty word-formulae, or, as he liked to put it, mere "school dust."

Thus, early in his development, Herder was encouraged by these two men to rebel against the popular brand of rationalism. In later years, however, both of these teachers were to renounce their pupil, and he them, for although impressionable, Herder was no abject disciple, and the path which he afterward pursued led him in a direction altogether different from that of his mentors and older contemporaries. Their ways began to part even before he left Königsberg, for his study of Plato, Bacon, Shaftesbury and Rousseau opened up new vistas which fired his imagination and exposed him to influences which complemented and transformed those of Kant and Hamann. Rousseau's love of nature and humanity, his ideas on society, the state, and education exercised a profound and enduring effect. His enthusiasm was such that he once wrote with youthful fervor, "Come, Rousseau, be my leader!"[6] This devotion can be plainly seen in his early writings, which are permeated with Rousseauesque atmosphere and pursue lines of interest which have close kinship with the French philosopher. Though it is easy to exaggerate its importance, there is no doubt that Herder's humanistic leanings owed a great deal to this early stimulation.

Shaftesbury's influence was even more persistent, especially in the growth of Herder's religious outlook. The attraction which the English thinker offered can best be seen in a letter

[6] Su., XXIX, 265. Hettner, in his *Literaturgeschichte des 18. Jahrhunderts* (Braunschweig, 1881), sees Rousseau as the greatest influence of Herder's youth, as does O. Pfleiderer in *The Philosophy of Religion since Spinoza* (London, 1886–7). Most other critics give this place to Hamann, and, when Herder's development is considered as a whole, they would seem to be more nearly right.

which Herder wrote in 1770, defending Shaftesbury against the charge of atheism which had been made by a French critic:

"An atheist who preaches nothing so much as order, harmony and highest wisdom in the structure of the whole world. . . . that atheist, with his great World-Spirit (for me the sublimest name for God) is more to me than ten such 'pettifoggers' (*Kleinmeister*) in philosophy."[7]

In a large sense, Herder made Shaftesbury's world-view his own, and his religious writings are always more or less colored by it. In the "Conversations," for instance, the influence is easily discernible in the persistent emphasis upon the order, harmony and wisdom of the universe, as well as in the rhapsodic mood and general aesthetic attitude toward God and nature which pervade the entire work.[8]

At the end of 1764 Herder left Königsberg for Riga, where he was soon to achieve local fame as a teacher in the cathedral school. While at that post, he began his study of another philosopher whose thought had an important influence upon him— Leibniz. In 1765, the *Nouveaux essais sur l'entendement humain* were published for the first time, revealing a Leibniz whose doctrines were radically different from those which the Wolffian system had made popular. As a result of the publication of that work a complete reinterpretation of Leibniz became necessary, for it was obvious that not only had the schools based their systems upon a comparatively unimportant part of Leibniz's thought, but also that Wolff and his followers had,

---

[7] To Merck Sept. 12, 1770. In *Herders Lebensbild* (E. G. von Herder, ed.), Erlangen, 1846, III, 110 ff.

[8] The early date of Shaftesbury's influence, and its important place in Herder's thought has prompted F. J. Schmidt in *Herders Pantheistische Weltanschauung* (Berlin, 1888), to make him the sole source of Herder's monism. But as will appear below, there were other influences which greatly strengthened this view of Herder's, and gave it a fresh turn.

as Herder later said, dissected his system until at last, "it stood there like a tree on which caterpillars and beetles had left on each leaf a metaphysic of dry threads, so that the dryad of the tree wept for mercy—'Leibniz, Leibniz! Where is thy spirit!' "[9]

The tree, once he had cleared it of the cob-webs, yielded much fruit for Herder, for a great many of the ideas on the nature of the universe, its continuity and development, which play such an important role in his later thought, are results of his rediscovery of the truer Leibniz.[10]

Most of these philosophical notions were only fermenting during the Riga period, for Herder's interests were at that time more inclined to aesthetics and theology than to philosophy. His first published works were mainly concerned with criticisms of the somewhat artificial literature of the time. He also published an excellent critique of Lessing's *Laokoon* and a first attempt at biblical criticism.[11] Most of what he had to say on philosophy and religion was in the vein of Kant, Hamann and Rousseau, but his own views were gradually taking shape. His interest became focused more and more upon the history of the development of man, and in 1769 he was already making plans for a "universal history of the education of mankind." Although he never executed it in any systematic manner, all of his subsequent works may be regarded as parts of this youthful design.

In 1769 he left Riga, and for two years he traveled through

[9] *Teutscher Merkur.* 1776 Su. IX, 500. (A similar view is expressed in the "Conversations." p. 126 [**483–4**].)

[10] It should be noted, however, that the rediscovery was by no means complete. A great many of the important writings of Leibniz, such as the *Discourse on Metaphysics* and the correspondence with Arnaud and Hessen-Rheinfels were discovered only during the 19th century.

[11] *Fragmente über die neuere deutsche Literatur,* 1766 Su. I; *Kritische Wälder.* 1768–9 Su. III, IV.

France and Germany. During that time his work on "The Origin of Language" was crowned by the Berlin Academy.[12] It was the first product of the genetic method which he was later to apply to many other fields. This method and the theme of the unity of man and nature which runs through the work were in those days comparatively novel. Unlike the "enlightened" minds for whom the origin of speech was convention, and unlike the devout such as Hamann and Süssmilch for whom it was divine, Herder found it unnecessary to rely upon a speech-making, or any other occult faculty, in explaining the mystery of language. His method led him to the conclusion that both its origin and development could be explained in terms of a natural growth from primitive imitative and interjectional cries. These speculations on the theory of language and especially his views on the intimate relationship between the development of speech and man's reflective capacity, were undoubtedly very influential in later years, when he so forcefully opposed Kant's *a priorism* in epistemology.

His conception of the unity of man and nature heralded a period during which Herder's thought increasingly turned towards a unified, monistic world-view. In 1771, he became pastor of Bückeburg, and in the five years which he spent there, he became an important religious leader in Germany. His works of this time, too numerous to be individually examined here, are predominantly concerned with theological questions. Their general tone is emotional and mystical, and opposed to reason as the path to knowledge of God. The following passage from one of his writings of this period, is typical:

"(If) we weaken ourselves through abstraction, separate and split up our senses, and shred our whole feeling into little threads which no longer feel anything wholly and purely,—

[12] *Abhandlung über den Ursprung der Sprache,* Su. V. 1–156.

(then) naturally the great sense of 'God, the Omnipresent in the world' must thereby become weakened and dulled."[13]

This attitude to abstract reasoning he later softened, but he retained the conception of God as "Omnipresent in the world" and developed it into the form in which it appears in the "Conversations." In this Bückeburg period the conception of divine immanence is couched mainly in aesthetic terms, and is apparently most influenced by Shaftesbury. He regards the Deity as the World-Soul, and nature as His beautiful garment. In the "Conversations," however, although the aesthetic aspect remains, he expresses a reluctance to conceive God as the soul of the universe, considering it a facile and dangerous image. In general, too, his later view has a greater emphasis upon the moral revelations of the Deity—the world-order becomes "good" and "wise" as well as "beautiful."

These years at Bückeburg, between 1771 and 1776 correspond almost exactly with his period of *Sturm und Drang*.[14] As is characteristic of that movement, his works in poetry and religion are all imbued with the spirit of rebellion against artificiality and "reasonableness." The stress is always upon the personal and inner life, upon lyricism in poetry and mysticism in religion. Above all it is stamped with a temper of *Schwärmerei* or "enthusiasm," which to the Aufklärung was a term of the utmost derogation. The intensity of the revolt often carried him and his contemporaries to extremes of sentimentality and mawkishness, extremes against which Herder himself was soon to turn and enter upon a more calm and lucid period. Even during this Bückeburg time, his works in other less emotional fields such as history and psychology, show signs

---

[13] *Älteste Urkunde des Menschengeschlechts*, Su. VI, 273.
[14] Herder is generally regarded as the initiator of this movement in German literature.

of a more considered and scientific appraisal of contemporary intellectual currents. The spirit of reaction to the Aufklärung is still strong and his antagonism to cut and dried solutions is as virile as ever, but the reaction is less unbridled, and the attack more pointed and constructive.

This is apparent in his "Another Philosophy of History,"[15] the object of which, as Herder put it, was "to heap fire and hot coals upon the skull of our century." The word "another" in the title is an ironic comment upon the hosts of philosophies of history which were appearing at that time, all in the Aufklärung tradition, and all making the eighteenth century the goal of universal history. In contrast to them, Herder finds no such goal but only an eternal progress in history. He treats the development of mankind as part of the continual progress of nature, and points out the intimate interrelationship between man and his environment in the course of his natural development. He gives up the traditional distinction between God and the world, and finds all history to be the revelation of God in the process of the universe.[16]

In his "Of Perception and Feeling,"[17] a work half psychological and half religious, Herder sought to bridge the traditional distinctions between body and soul, emotions and intellect, knowledge and will. He maintained that there are no distinct and isolated soul-faculties, but only grades of a single force. He stresses the relation between perception and feeling, and especially the importance of the latter in human knowledge. The body is a complex of forces of different grades; the

[15] *Auch eine Philosophie der Geschichte,* 1774. Su. V, 475–594.

[16] Some of these ideas were later developed by Lessing in his *Die Erziehung des Menschengeschlechts* (1780), Werke XVIII (Hempel). (The debt of Lessing to Herder is usually seen the wrong way round.) This early work is also the basis of Herder's chief historical work, *The Ideas Toward a Philosophy of the History of Mankind.*

[17] *Vom Erkennen und Empfinden der menschlichen Seele,* 1774, 5, 8. Su. VIII, 165–333 (three versions).

soul is a force of the highest grade. Since the connection which it has with the bodily forces is the most intimate possible, there can be, he says, no psychology without a physiology.

This same psychological theory, which obviously depends upon the doctrines of the *Nouveaux essais* appears again in the "Conversations" where it is applied to solving the problem of thought and extension as attributes of God.[18] There, however, he is more inclined to emphasize the rational powers. Although he still stresses the part of feeling in knowledge, reason now plays a role of cardinal importance, particularly in the knowledge of God.

In the first version of "Perception and Feeling" which Herder wrote in 1774, a new influence appears, which is very enlightening in view of his growing confidence in the powers of reason and his tendency toward monism. In his discussion of the freedom of the will (which he condemns as an illusion), Herder fortifies what he has said with a most appreciative reference to the philosophy of "the holy Spinoza."[19]

Direct references to this thinker are rare in Herder's works of this period. But it is known from a letter to a friend that he was an enthusiastic reader of the *Ethics* during the year 1774.[20] His published writings show only the beginning of a study, the fruits of which were to be harvested in the "Conversations" more than a decade later. The paucity of his references is, however, no indication of the significance which Spinoza's doctrines had for Herder. The circumstances of the

[18] See below, Introduction, p. 44 ff., and text, p. 101–104 [**447–453**].

[19] Su. VIII, 201–2.

[20] To Gleim. *Von und an Herder* (ed. Düntzer), I, 35 ff. The actual date of Herder's first knowledge of Spinoza is uncertain. Haym op. cit. p. 269 puts it at 1774–5. W. Vollrath, *Die Auseinandersetzung Herders mit Spinoza* (Darmstadt, 1911), sets it as early as 1769. (There is a single reference to Spinoza's *Ethics* in that year, in the *Archäologie des Morgenlandes*. Su. VI, 109.) However the Spinozistic tendencies become clear-cut only after 1774, and this is perhaps the more accurate date.

time were such as to make an appreciative student of these doctrines (especially if he were a theologian), reluctant to make the fact public. Since Spinoza's death, his doctrines had become almost universally feared, hated, and the subject of much vituperation.[21] He was known chiefly at second hand through Bayle's article in his philosophical *Dictionnaire* (1696) which, as Herder says in the "Conversations,"[22] completely misinterpreted his views. After being maligned as an atheist by theologians and philosophers alike, his system was submitted to the critical appraisal of Christian Wolff in his *Theologia naturalis* (1737). After every attempt to be unbiased, Wolff nevertheless came to the conclusion that Spinozism was fatalistic, "not far from a denial of God, and just as harmful as this. Indeed, to a certain degree, it is even more harmful than atheism."[23]

By reason of Wolff's influence, this verdict settled Spinoza's case in Germany for a long time to come. From then on, with few exceptions,[24] no serious attention was given him. Though still hated, fear gave place to neglect and ignorance, and Spinoza was treated, as Lessing put it, "like a dead dog."[25]

During the late sixties and early seventies however, a hand-

[21] For the fortunes of Spinozism in Germany during the first half of the 18th century, see M. Krakauer, *Zur Geschichte des Spinozismus in Deutschland während der ersten Hälfte des 18. Jahrhunderts* (Breslau, 1881). M. Grunwald, *Spinoza in Deutschland* (Berlin, 1897), and E. Altkirch, *Maledictus und Benedictus* (Leipzig, 1924), are compilations of references to Spinoza in Germany from his death to modern times.

[22] See p. 76, [413] ff.

[23] The complete critique is printed in H. Scholz, *Die Hauptschriften zum Pantheismusstreit* (Berlin, 1916). The above quotation is from page LVIII.

[24] Among them was Moses Mendelssohn in his *Philosophische Gespräche* (1755). His standpoint is still very "enlightened" and he too regards Spinoza as an atheist, but he nevertheless desires to credit Spinoza with important contributions to speculation. He finds, for instance, that Spinoza anticipated Leibniz's "Pre-established Harmony."

[25] He made this statement in a conversation about Spinoza with Jacobi. It is reproduced in Jacobi's *Über die Lehre des Spinoza in Briefen an den Herrn Moses Mendelssohn* (Breslau, 1785). See also below, Introduction, p. 28.

ful of men, Lessing, Herder, Goethe, and Friedrich Jacobi, all independently became interested in the doctrines of the notorious lense-grinder. The first three became his enthusiastic admirers. Jacobi, though he paid homage to the precision and consistency of Spinoza's mind, regarded his system as an example of what to him were the terrible consequences of all thorough-going rational demonstration: atheism and fatalism.

The character and significance of this Spinozistic revival will be dealt with subsequently.[26] It is sufficient here to have noted that Herder was one of the few men of his day to be attracted by Spinozism and to make of it a source of fruitful inspiration. After 1774 the monistic tendencies of his thought became more sharply defined. His aesthetic and emotional views in religion became on the whole more calm and rational, and his thought took a more ethical turn than before. A good deal of this development was, of course, merely the natural maturing of Herder's ideas. Nevertheless, a comparison of the "Conversations" with the works of the Bückeburg period, makes it evident that the changes are almost invariably in a Spinozistic direction. Moreover, the fact that he chose Spinoza as the basis of the later work, in itself argues for a decided influence from this source.

During the period in which this transformation of his views took place, Herder was at Weimar. In 1776, through the influence of his friend Goethe, he had been appointed General Superintendent of the Clergy in that Duchy. He had met Goethe in Strasburg some six years earlier, and a firm friendship between the two men had begun. During the months which they spent there together Herder exercised a tremendous influence upon the young poet, and he is generally credited with having helped Goethe's genius to expression at a crucial time in its development. Now, however, the two men were on

[26] See below, Introduction, p. 28 ff.

more equal terms. At Weimar they studied and discussed natural science and philosophy, and especially the works of Spinoza. In the understanding of the latter, however, Goethe confessed himself to have but little talent for cold and abstract metaphysics, and seems to have been content to follow the lead of his friend.

Partly the result of these mutual studies and conversations, and partly the product of his whole development, were Herder's two finest works, the "Ideas Toward a Philosophy of History of Mankind"[27] and the "Conversations." Taken together these writings form a summary and expansion of Herder's best ideas in almost every field.

The "Ideas" are a philosophy of nature, history, and humanity all in one. Their great thesis is, that in order to understand man properly it is first necessary to understand the universe in its larger aspect. Herder accordingly begins his history of mankind with the statement, "The earth is a star among stars," and descends through considerations of the astronomical and geographical conditions of the world, its animal and vegetable kingdoms and the relation of man to them, to a treatment of the various races and cultures which inhabit the globe and their history up to modern times. The last volume was to have dealt with the latter, but Herder never completed it.

In his method, Herder's determination to avoid the besetting sin of contemporary philosophies of history is clear when he says: "We will put aside all metaphysics and confine ourselves to experience and physiology." From the observation of the particular, however, nothing is more clear to him than that it is necessary to arrive at general laws which organize the universe into a great unity, into an animated system of

[27] *Ideen zur Philosophie der Geschichte der Menschheit,* Su. XIII, XIV. It was translated into English by T. Churchill, *Outlines of a Philosophy of the History of Man,* 2 vols. (London, 1803).

forces which are arranged in a graduated series. Though he denies particular, final causes, a grand development and progress is evinced in the world as a whole. Man is an integral part of this whole, a particular organization of the forces which pervade it everywhere. He too has developed in the same manner,[28] and he too is progressing toward a far-distant goal where all the capacities and potentialities of humanity will be realized.[29] Moreover, this living drama of creation is like a great book containing the thoughts of God, a book which Herder, "like some schoolboy" is engaged in spelling out.

"Everywhere," he says, "the great analogies of nature have led me to religious truths which, though I find it difficult, I must suppress since I would not prematurely anticipate, but faithfully follow step by step, that light, which everywhere beams upon me from the hidden presence of the Creator in His works: It will be much the greater satisfaction both to my reader and to myself if, as we proceed on our way, this obscurely dawning light rise upon us at length with the splendor of an unclouded sun."[30]

This light, though it pervades the entire "Ideas," shines in its fullest radiance in the "Conversations." Religion and history were never far separate for Herder, and it was therefore natural that in 1787, in the midst of his most comprehensive work

[28] The resemblance of Herder's and Darwin's views of man as a product of nature, and his development in relation to environment, climate, etc., has often been pointed out. Nevinson op. cit. p. 357 ff. cites many passages which are close in "tone and often words" to Darwin, and cannot refrain from regarding the work as "a brilliant attempt to bridge the chasm between Spinoza and Darwin." The similarity between the two is exaggerated even more by F. von Bärenbach, *Herder als Vorgänger Darwins und der modernen Naturphilosophie* (Berlin, 1877). Cf., however, H. Götz, "War Herder ein Vorgänger Darwins?" *Vierteljahrschrift für wissenschaftliche Philosophie und Soziologie* (Leipzig, 1902), p. 391 ff. for a more sober estimate.

[29] This doctrine of *"Humanität"* was a feature of the literature of the times, but Herder developed it more fully than any of his contemporaries.

[30] *Outlines Phil. Hist.* (Churchill trans.), Vol. I, pp. XIII, XIV.

on history,[31] he should also bring out his most mature religious doctrines, and make explicit the conception of God which was implicit in the "Ideas." In this sense it is an accurate description of the relation which the "Conversations" bears to Herder's work as a whole to say of it, as Kühnemann does, that:

"As Herder's life work is crowned by the 'Ideas,' so the 'Ideas' are crowned by *God, Some Conversations.*"[32]

THE CONTEMPORARY SCENE, AND ITS RELATION TO THE "CONVERSATIONS"

If the "Conversations" occupy this important place in Herder's religious and philosophical development, their position in the development of German thought as a whole is scarcely less significant. Histories of philosophy, however, do not usually give Herder more than a passing mention. The justification for this would doubtless be that Herder's contributions fall more naturally into the fields of theology and literature, and that in any case he is not a speculative genius of the first rank.   To admit this, however, still does not explain the small attention which has been given to Herder's speculation.[33]

The real reason for his neglect seems to lie in the tendency of most historians of eighteenth and nineteenth century German thought to treat it as a continuous and simple development from Kant through Fichte and Schelling to Hegel. Such treatment has, however, only its simplicity to recommend it, for there is reason to believe that the growth of the later idealism of Schelling and Hegel, and even that of Fichte, becomes fully intelligible only when one relinquishes the notion that Kant is

---

[31] The various parts of the "Ideas" occupied Herder from 1784 to 1792.

[32] E. Kühnemann, *Herders Leben* (München, 1895), p. 287.

[33] Even such an indefatigable champion of the importance of minor thinkers in the history of philosophy as A. O. Lovejoy, in a work specifically concerned with a theme on which Herder had much to say: *The Great Chain of Being* (Cambridge, 1936) makes only a few scattered references to Herder.

the source from whom all later philosophy flows.[34] A consideration of Herder's "Conversations" will show that there were
certain other important factors in the intellectual climate which
must be taken into account in explaining the growth of post-
Kantian Idealism.

The development of German thought during the last half of
the eighteenth century reveals a steadily growing opposition
to the more dogmatic religious and philosophical aspects of
the Aufklärung world-view. By the time the "Conversations"
were published, this opposition had taken various forms, among
which three distinct tendencies became most important: (1)
the movement towards faith and irrationalism, (2) the critical
philosophy, and finally, (3) the movement centering around
the revival of Spinoza. All three meet, and as it were, cross
swords in the "Conversations" which were themselves the
philosophical expression of this third tendency.

The first reaction to the Aufklärung which assumed the pro-
portions of a movement was that of the so-called faith-philoso-
phers under the leadership of Hamann, Lavater and Jacobi.
Of these, Friedrich Jacobi[35] was the most influential, and
though his thought differed in some respects from the others,
he may be taken as typical of the whole tendency. The essence
of his view is his sharp distinction between two kinds of knowledge, the immediate and intuitive which he terms belief, and
the indirect, logical knowledge of the intellect. The first of
these, which he later somewhat confusingly also called "Reason"
(*Vernunft*) as distinguished from "Understanding" (*Verstand*),

---

[34] Cf. for example, the "Note on German Idealism" by H. L. Friess in
Columbia Studies in the History of Ideas (New York, 1918), I, which shows
the influence of Hamann on Fichte.

[35] For a full account of Jacobi's life and work, see L. Lévy-Bruhl, *La Philosophie de Jacobi* (Paris, 1894). In English, two short appraisals of his philosophy are A. Crawford, *The Philosophy of F. H. Jacobi* (N. Y., 1905); and
N. Wilde, *F. H. Jacobi* (N. Y., 1894).

alone possesses a knowledge of facts. The understanding connects and elaborates these facts, but because it is partial and limited, it can never grasp or explain their existence. As it is purely formal, it can never give knowledge of reality. For Jacobi, as for Hamann, understanding occupies a middle position between sense and belief, and is the least important member of the trio. Because it must necessarily work with the material given to it in consciousness, it cannot conceive the external world except as conditioned, and must inevitably arrive at a mechanistic conception of it. For the same reason it can never arrive at a knowledge of the Unconditioned or God, for which faith alone gives immediate and supreme evidence. Thus, since only knowledge of the conditioned and finite is possible to it, a logical, demonstrative philosophy must necessarily end in atheism and fatalism. Jacobi therefore saw no other recourse except that which he called his *salto mortale:* he turned his back on all demonstration and resorted entirely to the immediacy of faith.

At the head of one of his later books, "On Things Divine and Their Revelation," (*Von den göttlichen Dingen und ihrer Offenbarung,* 1811) Jacobi placed the following quotation from Pascal, which represents his position very succinctly:

"Les vérités divines sont infiniment au-dessus de la nature; Dieu seul peut les mettre dans l'âme. Il a voulu qu'elles entrent du coeur dans l'esprit, et non pas de l'esprit dans le coeur. Par cette raison, s'il faut connaître les choses humaines pour les aimer, il faut aimer les choses divines pour pouvoir les connaître." [36]

[36] Because of his emphasis upon the subjective factor of experience, Herder has sometimes been included with the philosophers of belief. At the most this might be said to be true of his Bückeburg period, but even then Herder never made the sharp distinction between the mind and "heart" which characterizes the philosophers of belief. Cf. R. Wielandt, *Herders Theorie von der Religion* (Naumberg, 1903), for a good discussion of the relation of Herder to the philosophers of belief.

This anti-rational movement had its antithesis in a tradition which culminated in Kant's *Critique of Pure Reason*. This work was the greatest and most revolutionary expression of a critical tendency which had been developing since 1760, and which was aimed primarily at the Leibniz-Wolffian theory of knowledge. In that year, J. N. Tetens (1736–1807) published a work significantly entitled: "Why There Are Only a Few Certain Truths in Metaphysics," and in 1763, the Berlin Academy, reflecting the general interest in the problem, offered as its subject for a prize essay, the topic: "The Evidence of Which Metaphysics is Capable." In the following year J. H. Lambert, a mathematician and a correspondent of Kant's, to whom Herder refers enthusiastically in the third of the "Conversations," brought out his "New Organon." This work was mainly a treatise on scientific method, in which Lambert maintained that there are certain definite limits which science cannot transcend. Ultimate knowledge of the real, he asserted, could never be attained because of the necessary subjective factor in human cognition.[37]

The development of such a view led inevitably to a thorough-going revision of the Wolffian metaphysics which maintained the logical identity of thought and reality. Lambert, however, never embarked upon it, being more inclined to seek a reconciliation between rationalism and empiricism, than a reconstruction of the two. Nevertheless, his stressing of the limits of knowledge and the *a priori* elements in reason was an important anticipation of the epoch-making criticism along analogous lines which was contained in Kant's first *Critique*.

[37] Cf. H. Griffing, "Lambert: A study in the Development of the Critical Philosophy," *Philosophical Review*, Vol. 2, 1893. See also E. Cassirer's *Die Philosophie der Aufklärung* (Tübingen, 1932), p. 174 ff., for another view of Lambert's relation to Kant. Cassirer discourages an exaggerated estimate of Lambert as a precursor of Kant. A fuller discussion of Lambert is also to be found in Vol. II of *Das Erkenntnisproblem in der Philosophie u. Wissenschaft d. Neueren Zeit* (Berlin, 1907), by the same author.

In Kant's philosophy the Aufklärung may be said to have reached a self-critical height. Reason, of which the "enlightened" philosophers had made so much, was still affirmed as universal and necessary, though as a purely formal element. Real intuition was denied to the intellect, and knowledge of objects was confined strictly to phenomena.

These doctrines and the effect which they had upon their time are too familiar to need retelling here. It is important, however, to realize the predominantly epistemological and methodological character of this Kantian reaction to the Enlightenment. In the province of religion, his work played directly into the hands of the philosophers of belief, for the destructive doctrines of the "Transcendental Dialectic" were taken by them to be virtually a justification of faith:

". . . . most men welcomed Kant's philosophy as the open door to the freedom to believe almost anything they sincerely wanted to believe. . . . Almost any kind of faith had been made intellectually respectable." [38]

This reception, it is true, was based upon a misunderstanding of Kant's views, for he himself was concerned to keep the postulates of faith within the limits of reason. It is therefore somewhat ironical that among others, Jacobi should have used Kant's work extensively to justify his own philosophy of faith. [39] But, ironical or not, the immediate consequence of the *Critique of Pure Reason* was a strengthening of the forces of anti-rationalism in religion.

Such foundation as there was for this attitude lay primarily in Kant's failure to give satisfaction either to the orthodox or the new religious consciousness in their struggle with athe-

[38] J. H. Randall, Jr., *The Making of the Modern Mind* (New York, 1926), p. 409.
[39] In his *Über die Lehre des Spinoza* (Breslau, 1785).

ism. Under his attacks, the whole metaphysical edifice which
contained the traditional rationalistic proofs of the existence
of God, of freedom and immortality, crumbled. Valuable as
this work was in clearing the ground, it was of the essence
of his system that he could offer no positive substitutes, no definite answers to renewed questions as to the nature of God,
or of His relation to the world. According to Kant, God could
be regarded only as an ideal of the pure reason, a regulative
idea for the theoretic reason and a necessary postulate for the
practical reason. What is generally understood as religion became entirely subordinate to morality. In this tendency of his
doctrines toward the emphasis of the moral consciousness as
the core of religion, as well as in such a conception of the
Deity as the practical reason required, Kant remained entirely
within the Aufklärung tradition.

"It must be remembered," says one of his critics on this
point, "that in spite of the ample materials which Kant sup-
plies for the construction of a new theology, he never got fairly
outside the old-fashioned mechanical construction of Deism.
God is, according to this conception, a Being by himself, to
whom no necessary relations attach; but he is supposed by an
exercise of 'will' to have 'created' the world, and with it finite
intelligence. The manner or meaning of this creation is not
explained, and so its assertion becomes simply a word." [40]

It was precisely in this field of theology, in which both the
critical and the belief philosophies made no really new advances, that the third movement opposed to the Aufklärung
was most strong. It offered a very definite conception of God,
and of his relation to the world. It rested upon a basis which
both of the other tendencies refused to accept: namely, the
conviction that the nature of God and the real world could be

[40] Pringle-Pattison, A. Seth, *From Kant to Hegel* (London, 1882), p. 142.

adequately known by human reason, and that a scientific knowledge of the world leads to a greater comprehension of the Deity.

Strictly speaking, this last movement was not a philosophical movement at all. It grew up among three primarily literary men: Lessing, Herder, and Goethe. They had wide philosophical and religious interests, but scarcely anything which might with justice be called a "system" to offer the world. They were bound together by a strong dislike for the rationalistic dogma of the "school-philosophers" and a dissatisfaction with the contemporary answers to religious problems. They were, however, in no position to sweep past views aside and to start afresh with an entirely new philosophical outlook. Instead, their doctrines are characterized by an eclectic use of the materials which the times offered for a new conception of the universe.

Among the many and various influences which contributed to this new conception, the two most important were the doctrines of the new, as opposed to the Wolffian Leibniz, and the system of the much abused Spinoza. Because the interest in the latter's thought linked Lessing, Herder and Goethe together, and because it gave the view they held in common its distinctive character, the movement has been called Neo-Spinozism.[41]

This name will serve as well as any, providing that it be remembered that it does not refer to any unified and closed philosophical system, but to an extremely amorphous, half-philosophical and half-poetical view of the world. It has the

---

[41] By M. Kronenberg in his *Geschichte des deutschen Idealismus* (München, 1909). The work finds in Neo-Spinozism the "antithesis" to the Kant-Fichtean "thesis," with the thought of Schelling and Hegel forming the great "synthesis." Such a view, though often extraordinarily true to the large and general issues, is somewhat too facile, and often influences the judgment of those movements by forcing them into too distinctly defined compartments which are not only ill-suited, but entirely unnecessary for a correct understanding of their nature and scope.

advantage of calling attention to the pervasive theme which gave to that movement a particular significance: the revival of Spinoza.

It has already been seen how the publication of Leibniz's *Nouveaux essais* in 1765 led to an interest in the doctrines of that philosopher in their original form. The reasons for the revival of Spinoza are much less clear. In the "Conversations," however, which form the highest philosophical expression of this Neo-Spinozistic tendency,[42] there can be seen something of what Spinoza had to offer these men. Most of all, minds weary of a God who resembled a skilled mechanic, must have been intoxicated by the grandiose conception of Substance, the One and All. The conception of *Deus sive Natura* was also particularly appealing to Herder and Goethe,[43] with their interest in both religion and natural science. Spinoza's God was the intelligible aspect of the universe, and, in contrast to the Deistic notion, its immanent cause. Spinoza's world was not anthropocentric, nor teleological, and the Neo-Spinozists too had come to regard final causes as human fictions. Finally, there was the attraction of his solution of the problems of evil and of human freedom, both of which were the subject of widespread theological controversy at that time.

The predominant tone of these doctrines gives at least a partial[44] explanation of the paradox of why men who were

[42] The highest poetical expression is in Goethe, especially his later work. Besides *Faust,* such poems as *Gott und die Welt* (1816), *Eins und Alles* (1821) are the finest examples.

[43] "Goethe's philosophy derives from the study of the world, observed with a pre-occupation with absolute unity; it comes out of a contemplation of general laws, seen through a poetic Spinozism." E. Caro, *La Philosophie de Goethe* (Paris, 1866), p. 149.

[44] There were, of course, other reasons, such as, in Herder and Goethe, the reaction to the sentimentality of the *Sturm und Drang.* Furthermore, the aesthetic aspect of the unity of Spinoza's world-view had undoubtedly a great attraction. Goethe in Bk. XIV of *Dichtung und Wahrheit* gives also a number of important personal reasons for his interest.

tired of rationalism and dogmatism, should have been drawn to the greatest rationalist and dogmatist of them all. It was the religious implications of Spinoza's system which distinguished him most sharply from the thought of the early eighteenth century. Thus those who refused to be ruled by the majority who cried "atheist!", found in his doctrines significant answers to the most vital religious problems of the age. They saw his system as a doctrine of salvation.

It must not be supposed, however, that what was thus effected was a revival of Spinozism in its original form. The men chiefly responsible for the renaissance of that system were neither Spinoza scholars, nor critics schooled in technical philosophy. They caught mainly at the vague outlines of his system, and to a certain extent poetized it. Much in Spinoza seemed to them in need of change because of the development in the natural sciences since his day. What actually resulted, especially with Herder, was on the whole a loose synthesis of Leibniz and Spinoza, in which the doctrines of the one were used to augment and modify those of the other.

With the publication of the "Conversations," Neo-Spinozism came out into the open, and became in a large sense, the rival of both the Kantian and the faith philosophies. In addition to its strength in religion, it offered powerful opposition to both of these movements in its emphasis upon a dynamic philosophy of nature, and in its refusal to accept the limitation of human knowledge which was characteristic of the other tendencies. Although, as in Kant, the content of knowledge is considered to be derived from experience, the function of reason is seen as essentially the abstracting and refining of the experiential data until clear ideas are produced which give a true knowledge of objective reality. In such a view, there could be no division of phenomenon and noumenon, and rightly or wrongly, it thus offered an alternative to those unable or unwilling to accept the Kantian *Ding-an-sich* and the agnosticism connected therewith.

Of the three movements, the Kantian was by far the most exact, and it soon developed into a powerful school of thought with a well-formulated system of doctrines. Neo-Spinozism on the contrary, was never shaped into a system but remained a comparatively vague and indefinite philosophical outlook. Nevertheless, the large audience which the works of Herder and Goethe commanded gave it a widespread influence, and even during the years of the Kantian predominance it grew stronger. It was not a victory for the critical philosophy which ended the open rivalry, but the absorption of both tendencies into post-Kantian Idealism.

Even in the great system of absolute idealism the two strains are often only superficially reconciled. The deep-going disparateness of these views was later an important factor leading to an effort at philosophical purification by a "back to Kant" movement.

The manner in which this absorption took place will be dealt with in a later section.[45] The present discussion seeks only to delineate the features of the contemporary scene, and the place of the "Conversations" in it. All of the tendencies which have been discussed, the opposition to the Aufklärung, the rehabilitation of Spinoza, the re-interpretation of his system, and the opposition to Kant and Jacobi, are prominent subjects of that work. Insofar, the "Conversations" are a running commentary on the philosophic currents of their day, and they thus serve as an excellent introduction to a highly significant period in the intellectual history of Germany. These relationships with the contemporary scene are, in turn, all part of the theme

---

[45] See below, Introduction, p. 56 ff.

which pervades the entire work—the search for a more mean-
ingful conception of God and the world. In this quest, the "Conversations" express the demand of an age.

THE SPECIFIC FEATURES OF THE "CONVERSATIONS"

A. Relation to the Spinoza Controversy

In the exposition of his philosophy of religion as it is presented in the "Conversations," Herder chose the system of
Spinoza as his point of departure. As he says, the reason for
this choice "lay partly in the sequence of his thoughts, and
partly in the inducements which the times offered him."[46] The
first reason is clear from what has already been discussed, the
second, however, requires further explanation.

The "inducements" to which Herder here refers, were offered
by the famous "Spinoza Controversy"[47] between Jacobi and
Moses Mendelssohn which was made public in 1785, and which
immediately became the cause of a nation-wide interest in the
long-neglected philosophy of Spinoza.

The quarrel began in 1783 when Jacobi, hearing that Mendelssohn was planning a work in memory of Lessing (who had
died in 1781), wrote asking Mendelssohn if he were aware
that Lessing had been a Spinozist. This question evidently
shocked that good Aufklärung Deist, and he wrote asking for
more precise information concerning this infamous charge.
Jacobi thereupon sent him the account of a memorable conversation which he had had with Lessing in 1780 while they were
the guests of a mutual friend, Gleim. In it, Lessing had confessed himself to be completely in accord with the Spinozistic

---

[46] See p. 67, [**403**].
[47] All the relevant material has been collected by H. Scholz in *Hauptschriften zum Pantheismusstreit zwischen Jacobi und Mendelssohn* (Berlin,
1916). In English, an adequate summary is in F. Pollock's *Spinoza* (London,
1912).

ἐν καὶ πᾶν and had acknowledged his adherence to that system.[48] Jacobi had been somewhat upset by this admission, for, although he had studied Spinoza intensively and regarded his system as a perfect example of rational demonstration, that study had convinced him that such demonstration must inevitably end in atheism and fatalism, as indeed, in his judgment, it had for Spinoza.

The upshot of this account was that Mendelssohn decided to give up his first plan, and to write instead a work which should make clear Lessing's relation to Spinoza. Jacobi's narration had convinced him, not that Lessing was a Spinozist, but that he had at most taken Spinoza's doctrines and improved them in the direction of an enlightened pantheism. Jacobi, however, declared this to be an impossibility, for it was plain to him that Spinoza's atheistical system was itself the highest and most consistent development of pantheism. As such, it was final, and any improvement of it was unthinkable. He therefore decided to print his own thoughts on Lessing and Spinoza, in order to counteract Mendelssohn's book which he felt would lead to grave misunderstanding of both men.

The two books appeared almost simultaneously in 1785 and caused an immediate sensation. Of Jacobi's contemporaries, only Hamann championed him. Most of the others felt that Jacobi in linking Lessing and Spinoza had committed an unwarrantable breach of taste by indulging in the slander of a great man's reputation.

Herder and Goethe who had been stimulated by the controversy to a renewed study of Spinoza, sided more with Lessing and Spinoza than with either of the contestants. Both of them had been interested in the quarrel since its beginning. Jacobi, anxious to have corroboration of his views, had written to

---

[48] Many of Lessing's utterances have been reproduced by Herder in the Fourth Conversation, p. 136, [**495**] ff.

Herder asking his opinion and advice. In his reply,[49] which shocked Jacobi almost as much as Lessing's confession, Herder evinced himself as in complete agreement with the latter's ἐν καὶ πᾶν and said that ever since he had occupied himself with philosophy, he had repeatedly come upon the truth of Lessing's doctrine. Like Lessing, however, he was unwilling to call his system Spinozism, because it seemed to him that there was much that was obscure and undeveloped in Spinoza, especially where the latter stood "too close to the doctrines of Descartes."

Herder was thus unwilling to grant Jacobi's contention that Spinoza's system was in any sense final. The correspondence shows, however, that his disagreement with Jacobi went much deeper than this. "If there is no need to make a *salto mortale*," he asks, "then why make one?"[50] In other words, Herder saw no reason to despair of ever reaching knowledge of God through the exercise of rational power. He is inclined to believe that the source of Jacobi's apprehensions is a gross misunderstanding of Spinoza's conception of Substance or God:

"The *proton pseudos,* dear Jacobi, of your own and every anti-Spinozistic system, is that God, as the great *ens entium,* the eternally active cause of all phenomena, is taken to be a Naught, an abstract idea. . . . According to Spinoza, however, He is not that, but the most real and active One. . . ."[51]

Again:

"If you turn this highest . . . all-comprising conception into mere vacuity, then you are an atheist and not Spinoza."[52]

When Jacobi, despite these criticisms, persisted in his view and eventually published his work against Mendelssohn,

[49] Feb. 1784. *Aus Herders Nachlass* (ed. Düntzer und Herder. Frankfurt a. M., 1857), II, 261.

[50] Ibid., p. 254.   [51] Ibid., pp. 254–5.   [52] Dec. 1784. Ibid., p. 265.

Herder decided to take this opportunity to bring out his own doctrines in the form of a reinterpretation of Spinoza, and at the same time to vindicate that thinker in the face of both Jacobi's and Mendelssohn's criticisms. In the "Conversations," which were the result, his opposition to taking Spinoza's God to be a mere abstract and empty conception, reappears as one of the main arguments.

Quite apart from the desire to do justice to Spinoza, this attempt of Herder's to formulate a conception of the Deity whose reality is indubitable, whose evidence is on every hand in the very life of the universe, is the keystone of his philosophy of religion. The intensity of Herder's convictions on this point is well exhibited in the genuine indignation and exasperation aroused in him by the conception which Mendelssohn had put forward,[53] that Spinoza's God was merely a collective name for the various extensions and thoughts of the phenomenal world.[54] Such a view he rightly regards as typical of the misunderstandings of the Enlightenment Deism.

The "Conversations" as a whole make clear that Herder realized the true issue of the controversy to be what Spinoza was, rather than whether or not Lessing was his disciple. In the first part of the Fourth Conversation he points out that Lessing's utterances in his discussion with Jacobi, are highly ambiguous and full of irony which Jacobi took seriously. He concludes that they give but little indication of the manner in which Lessing understood Spinoza, and that their value consists almost solely in the great service rendered Spinoza by Lessing's avowal of his regard for the doctrines of that much-neglected thinker.

The recurring polemical theme of the work is therefore di-

---

[53] In his *Morgenstunden oder Vorlesungen über das Daseyn Gottes* (Berlin 1785), p. 186 ff. 195 ff.

[54] See p. 121, [476–7].

rected far more at Jacobi's interpretation of Spinoza as an atheist, pantheist and fatalist, than at his assertion of Lessing's Spinozism, which, after all, Herder was only too glad to acknowledge. It is clear also that Herder was unwilling to grant Jacobi's contention that Spinozism is the most perfect and final example of rationalism, for a main theme of the "Conversations" is precisely his conviction that Spinoza can be made more consistent with himself, and that the results of science and speculation since that philosopher's death have made it possible to enlarge the truth of his doctrines into a more significant and coherent world-view.

Herder's polemics in this section extend also to Jacobi's own conception of God and of the limits of philosophy. The view of God as supra- and extra-mundane, Herder condemns as contributing nothing to an understanding of the Deity, and as being in effect, mere anthropomorphism.[55] His discussion of Jacobi's principle of *Glaube* or "Faith," is especially interesting. Ten years earlier Herder would have been more in agreement with this anti-rationalism, but his study of Spinoza since then has made him more appreciative of the powers of reason. Thus he now finds Jacobi's principle "unusual" and "confusing," and is unwilling to make such a sharp distinction between belief and reason.[56] He ends rather weakly with an attempt to reconcile both Jacobi and Mendelssohn, saying that the truth behind Jacobi's confusing terminology is one to which every true philosopher would give assent: that all philosophizing must pre-suppose external existence and internal laws of thought. Its value he finds chiefly in its antagonism to metaphysical hairsplitting and verbalism. However, as Herder must have realized, Jacobi's doctrine was not at all aimed merely against abstract and verbal philosophy, but against all rational demonstration as such.

[55] See p. 145, [**511**].
[56] "Reason" is here used in the usual, not Jacobi's, sense of the word.

In fact, this "truth to which all true philosophers will give assent," is the essence of Herder's own theory of knowledge, insofar as he may be said to have had such a theory. The affirmation of the idea of Being or Existence as the basic notion for all thinking, which the latter can never transcend, is the foundation of both his philosophy of religion and his epistemology. According to him, this all-comprising conception, the beginning and end of all knowledge, is God Himself; and, as he affirms, without the conception of God, no knowledge whatever is possible.

As a contribution to the Spinoza Quarrel, the "Conversations," though fruitful, were by no means decisive. It was obvious that Herder was making a rather eclectic use of Spinoza for his own ends, despite his very sincere defense of that thinker. Thus, although Mendelssohn had died in 1786, Jacobi persisted in his attack by bringing out a second edition of his "Letters," in which he answered various criticisms, including those of Herder. The controversy wore on for many years, with Spinoza now as the main issue. In 1800, Herder brought out a new edition of the "Conversations" fortifying his own interpretation by more specific references to Spinoza, but, since a personal reconciliation between him and Jacobi had been effected, he expunged his criticism of the principle of belief. Schelling had by this time also entered the field, but it was not until 1812, nine years after Herder's death, that a violent exchange of polemics between Schelling and Jacobi brought the controversy to an end.[57]

This was, however, somewhat of an anti-climax insofar as

[57] Schelling, after several writings in which he evinced a high regard for Spinoza's system, finally openly opposed Jacobi in his *Philosophische Untersuchungen über das Wesen der menschlichen Freiheit* (1809). Jacobi replied in his *Von den göttlichen Dingen* (1811) accusing Schelling of atheism. The latter replied in his *Denkmal der Schrift von den göttlichen Dingen des Herrn Jacobi* (1812) and is generally credited with having finished Jacobi both as an interpreter of Spinoza and as an original philosopher.

the rehabilitation of Spinozism was concerned. After the "Conversations" which were the first extensive work in Germany to justify Spinoza's system and to acclaim him as a great thinker, the obnoxious charge of atheism which had been the most effective bar to his acceptance, could no longer be tolerated. A wave of enthusiasm for Spinoza followed, and although they cannot be credited with being the sole cause of this revival, the "Conversations" have a place of prime importance in the encouragement of the study and appreciation of Spinozism which played such a very significant role in post-Kantian Idealism.[58]

B.   Relation to Kant

The Spinoza controversy, though the most important, is not the only object of Herder's polemics in the "Conversations." Throughout the work there are various uniformly derogatory references to a "new philosophy,"[59] a "hypercriticism,"[60] a "transcendental philosopher"[61] and the like which, though Herder is reluctant to name their object, obviously refer to Kant.

The tone of these references to the author of the *Critique of Pure Reason*, is somewhat surprising when one remembers the intimate relationship which existed between the two men at an earlier time. But the philosopher whom the youth from Mohrungen had so esteemed, had altered greatly with the years, and the doctrines which had so impressed Herder had been radically transformed by Kant as he developed toward his "Copernican revolution" in philosophy. Herder's views too had developed since Königsberg, and they had developed along very different lines.

[58] Carl Siegel, in his Foreword to *Herder als Philosoph* (Stuttgart u. Berlin, 1907), says that his enquiries into the influence of Spinoza on German philosophy, led him not only to the German Classicists, but *particularly to Herder*. (Unfortunately he does not seem to have published the result of these enquiries.)
[59] See p. 81, [**419**].   [60] See p. 153, [**521**].   [61] See p. 149, [**516**].

All through the Bückeburg years, Herder and Kant had remained on friendly terms, although Kant showed scant approval of his younger friend's work. After that, relations grew cooler until the publication of the *Critique* made the breach obvious. Herder does not seem to have studied that work very carefully. He relied for the most part on the judgment of Hamann who wrote a "Metacritique on the Purism of Pure Reason," in which he characteristically inveighed against Kant's "empty formalism" and "verbiage."[62]

Herder, evidently out of respect for his former teacher, kept his counsel until 1785 when, most unexpectedly, a scathing review of the first two books of the "Ideas" appeared in an article written by Kant.[63] In it the latter bemoaned Herder's lack of logical precision, his indiscriminate synthesis of natural science and religion. He pointed out that the author of the "Ideas" had not at all fulfilled his promise to "put metaphysics aside," for the doctrine of organic forces and their unity, said Kant, was nothing less than highly dogmatic metaphysics.

This criticism was in many respects well founded, but it is nevertheless doubtful whether Kant appreciated the true significance of the work. Of the two men, Kant stood closer to the Aufklärung tradition of forcing history into artificial channels. Herder's method, even though he departed from it occasionally, was by far the more fruitful, and he felt justly proud of it. Kant's criticism therefore wounded and angered him, particularly because he regarded his opponent as an intruder in a field of which he had made himself master. "It is extraordinary," he wrote bitterly to Hamann, "that metaphysicians like your Kant want no history even in history. . . ."[64]

---

[62] *Metakritik über den Purismus der reinen Vernunft* (Hamann Schriften ed. Roth, VII). It was not published at the time. Hamann had sent it to Herder in manuscript.

[63] *Jenaische allgemeine Literaturzeitung* (Jena, 1785).

[64] To Hamann, February 28, 1785. *Herders Briefe an Hamann,* ed. by O. Hoffmann, p. 212.

Herder waited for someone to come to his defense, but finding that none of his contemporaries dared to oppose so powerful a foe, he himself answered most of Kant's criticism in the third book of the "Ideas." As Herder was also engaged in the writing of the "Conversations" at that time, he took advantage of the opportunity to oppose Kant on what seemed to him to be the outstanding faults of the *Critique of Pure Reason,* namely, the denial of a possibility of a proof of God, and the denial of the possibility of a true knowledge of Being.

In the First Conversation he refers in passing to Kant's position that in the absence of either proof or disproof of the existence of God, it is nevertheless rationally necessary to believe that He does exist.[65] When Herder observes that this is tantamount to saying that one may affirm anything one truly believes, he is guilty of the same misunderstanding which provoked such a flood of anti-rationalism in the years following the *Critique.* However, as he makes clear further on,[66] he is totally unwilling to admit the truth of Kant's statement in the first place. What he says amounts less to a criticism of Kant than to an affirmation of his own view in the face of the critical philosophy. It is clear that he has made no serious attempt to understand his opponent's method or outlook. Indeed, it is scarcely an exaggeration to say that the profound difference between their views on the whole made such an understanding impossible. Here, and everywhere in the "Conversations," Herder's naturalism, monism, and objectivism stand opposed to Kant's "criticism," dualism and transcendental subjectivism. It is the very depth of this opposition which impels Herder to describe Kant's philosophy as a "hypercriticism . . . in which one builds without materials, exists without existence, knows without experience and works without powers."[67]

[65] See p. 81, [**419**].   [66] See p. 149, [**516**] ff.   [67] See p. 153, [**521**].

To Kant's denial of any rational demonstration of God's existence, Herder answers that "without the conception of God there would be no reason, much less a demonstration."[68] The immediate proof of God's existence lies in the immutable laws of reason in which man can see most clearly the laws which are active everywhere in the universe. Thus the copula "is," the mere sign " = " is his proof of God. To deny God is to deny reason itself, and conversely, to vitiate reason is to close forever the door to the knowledge of the Deity. The proof which Herder here offers is a restatement of the argument from the structure of truth, seen in the light of divine immanence. It rests ultimately upon the order and harmony of the universe, but, instead of conceiving these as the arbitrary plan of an extra-mundane God, Herder conceives them as the inherently necessary activity of God himself in the universe.

It is clear from this discussion, that Herder refuses to accept the epistemological basis upon which Kant rests his distinction between the phenomenal world and the world of the "thing-in-itself." Whereas for Kant the examination of knowledge is the starting point of all philosophy, Herder, for whom there is no such "problem" in the Kantian sense, starts from the conception of Being or Existence as ultimate and fundamental. In all our philosophizing, he implies, we cannot rid ourselves of this conception. It is assumed in all knowledge. To him, Kant's dualism of experience and Being, must have seemed a gigantic and fatal delusion, for it relegated to a realm utterly beyond the reach of reason, what was for Herder most real and immediate to it. Although he is not explicit on the point, Herder's statements about Kant indicate that it was Kant's failure to realize the true starting-point of speculation which led him to a false *a priorism* and submitted philosophy to the tyranny of the "thing-in-itself." According to Herder there is only a difference of degree not of kind, between experience and reason.

[68] See p. 149, [**516**].

Reason has no content whatever save that given by experience. All ideas are derived through the senses, and the clearer these ideas are, the more they correspond to reality.

There are other references to Kant in the "Conversations," [69] such as the just objection to the latter's burlesque of Spinoza's conception of pure necessity, [70] but they are not extensive and are on the whole merely derogatory.

Herder's opposition, however, did not cease with the "Conversations" but continued to gather momentum until at the close of the century, it rose to a peak of bitterness rarely equalled in philosophical controversy. The reason for this continued struggle was not merely doctrinal disagreement, but was rooted in practical difficulties as well. As Superintendent of the Clergy, it was his duty to examine theological candidates, and, when the Kantian influence began to grow, its effect upon these young men became a serious problem to Herder:

"It is pathetic," says Heine on this matter, "to read in his posthumous letters how the poor man was embarrassed by the candidates of theology, who, after studying at Jena (i.e., under Fichte) came before him at Weimar to undergo examinations as Protestant preachers. About Christ the Son he no longer dared to put a single question; he was glad enough to have the mere acknowledgment of the existence of the Father." [71]

In 1799, Herder determined to go to the root of this evil, and wrote his "Metacritique to the Critique of Pure Reason." [72] In many ways, it was a poor book, full of mockery and violent outbursts, but as an example of his position it is nevertheless

---

[69] See pp. 146 [**513**] (ed. I and II); 192 [**572**]; 213 [**576**] (ed. II).

[70] See p. 167, [**538**].

[71] H. Heine, *Religion and Philosophy in Germany* (Snodgrass trans., London, 1882), p. 132.

[72] *Metakritik zur Kritik der reinen Vernunft,* Su. XXI. In the following year his *Kalligone,* a "metacritique" of Kant's *Critique of Judgment* appeared. Su. XXII.

interesting. At the very start he points out that it is impossible to criticize reason objectively as Kant pretends to do, for in that case reason must become at one and the same time the judge and the judged. He denies that there are any *a priori* synthetic judgments, and questions the possibility of deriving four classes of categories if, as Kant himself says, only the form of judgment is known. Herder regards all the categories not as subjective forms, but as general ideas derived from experience. He accuses Kant of having two reasons, and finds the kernel of his errors to be in the recurrent dualism of phenomena and noumena, sense and reason. His own outlook, in which the continuity of the universe is fundamental, could tolerate no such distinctions. Rational analysis of the reasoning process, as Herder saw it, treats as static what is really in continual motion, breaks the continuous flow of existence into artificial sections, and in consequence becomes involved in a host of false problems of epistemology. It is in this sense that he considers it a term of utmost reproof when he calls Kant the great "divider" in philosophy.

The book was much read, but it, and Herder's polemics as a whole, had little effect in stemming the overwhelming tide of Kantianism. The resistance which really had some effect came not so much from direct criticism as from the positive doctrines of the Neo-Spinozistic tendency as a whole. What these doctrines were can best be seen in the "Conversations," the work in which Herder set forth his philosophical creed in its fullest detail.

C. Doctrines

The two great themes of the "Conversations" are the interrelated conceptions of divine immanence and the dynamism of nature. God is found revealed in every point of nature. The universe is conceived as a unified complex of forces, arranged in a hierarchy, and operating according to immutable laws which are at one and the same time the evidence of the divine power, and the activity of God himself realized in the world-order. The whole is continuous; there are neither gaps nor leaps in nature. Quiescence is negation; death is merely apparent. As Goethe, who shared these conceptions with Herder, put it, it is nature's way of having many lives. Only change is real, and this change Herder conceives as progressive development, a grand teleology whose goal is the realization of all the potentialities of nature. In all the great variety and life of the universe there is a unity which is God, the One in All.

A recent student of the "Conversations"[73] has maintained that it contains not only one conception of God, but four which she enumerates as follows: (1) the logico-conceptualistic God conceived as Being or Existence; (2) the orthodox theistic conception; (3) the Deity conceived as the hypostatization of the laws of nature; and finally, (4) God as the active, immanent Life-force in Creation.

It cannot be denied that Herder often makes statements which would make such a judgment plausible. Indeed, the nature of the conversations is such as to make it inevitable if they are submitted to a rigorous logical analysis. Not only is their polemical tone very often conducive to the over-statement and distortion of his views, but, especially when he is engaged in discussing Spinoza, Herder's sympathy and power of entering into the spirit of his subject frequently cause him to express himself in much the same manner and even words as that philosopher. Where he is most himself, as in the last conversation, he is least exact in his expression, and more inclined to picturesque and emotional ways of stating his case. The difference in tone between this and the other parts of the work, is striking even to the casual reader. Consequently, when all

[73] Elisabeth Hoffart, *Herders "Gott"* (Halle. a. S. 1918), p. 8 ff.

of Herder's utterances are taken to be of equal value and are balanced against one another, it is only natural that discrepancies and inconsistencies should become evident in the thought.

However, if allowance is made for these shortcomings (and those who have the interests of systematic philosophy at heart will find much in Herder for which to make allowance) it would be truer to Herder's original meaning to regard these four conceptions of God not as distinct, but as aspects of the one God, whose unique nature Herder constantly stresses. Insofar as God is the ground of all existence and truth, He is Being or Existence,[74] without whom, as Spinoza put it, "nothing can either be, or be conceived."[75] He is "the idea from which all else follows."[76] Insofar as God is all-powerful, wise and good (and it will be seen how Herder finds it consistent so to conceive Him, though He is the necessary cause of the universe), He has these qualities in common with the God of orthodox theism.[77] Finally God, as the immanent and active cause of the world and as its sustaining power, is conceived now as the immutable and eternal laws which are active throughout nature, now as the life-force which courses through the veins of the great organism of the universe.

This last conception is the one upon which Herder places most emphasis in the "Conversations." The others are there, too, it is true, and often occupy an important place in the discussion, but on the whole, they are tributary to the view with which Herder is most concerned, and which may be called a dynamic panentheism.

The First Conversation serves as a prologue to the main body of the work. Herder portrays, in the character of Phil-

---

[74] p. 140, [**502**]. (All future references, unless otherwise specified will be to the "Conversations.")
[75] *Ethics,* Bk. I Appendix.   [76] p. 95, [**438**].   [77] p. 118, [**473**] ff.

olaus, the attitude of the typical cultured gentleman of his day toward Spinoza, and the gradual transformation of his opinions as he becomes better acquainted with that thinker. Its chief contribution aside from the criticism of Bayle as an authority on Spinoza, is the advice which Herder, in the person of Theophron, gives to his friend for reading and understanding Spinoza.[78] His attitude is not that of the reverent scholar, but that of a man who is primarily interested in extracting from past systems what is alive and pertinent to his own problems. The free use of modern philosophy which he advocates in the interpretation of Spinoza's system and the solution of its errors, is again evidence that his desire was not merely to interpret, but to revise and harmonize it with the thought of his own day.

This is especially clear in the Second and Third Conversations, where Herder is engaged in defending Spinoza against the charges of pantheism and fatalism. The accusation of atheism is dispensed with summarily, because it is obviously false to anyone having the least acquaintance with Spinoza's works. Spinoza, far from being a denier of God, Herder asserts, was a philosopher for whom the idea of God was the first, last, and only idea of all. In the second edition, Herder fortified his implication that the charge of atheism came from ignorance even more than from misunderstanding by quoting some very unambiguous passages from the *Ethics*.[79]

That he was no pantheist is equally clear to Herder as soon as the distinction between the truly infinite, that is, the self-contained and self-limited, and the merely indefinite or endless in time and space, is realized. Though God is the immanent cause of the universe, He cannot be conceived to be in crude identity with it; for the universe is neither eternal

[78] p. 90, [**431**]. Theophron throughout the conversations represents Herder.
[79] p. 95 [**438**].

nor is it truly infinite, because it is spatially and temporally conditioned, and it is completely dependent upon God—the unique, the self-dependent and the un-conditioned.[80]

This conception gives rise to a very important problem which Herder leaves unsolved throughout the work, namely, the question of how the infinite and self-contained God became, and still becomes, realized in spatio-temporal, finite terms. The how or why of it, Herder says, must remain forever an insoluble mystery.[81] He merely states it as a fact that the creation of the finite world followed necessarily from the eternal power of God, and that those powers could never be inactive.[82]

In this sense there exists as Miss Hoffart has pointed out, the dichotomy between God as existing before the world both logically and temporally as Absolute Being, and God as maintaining the physical world and revealing Himself in it. The problem of the reconciliation of these two aspects of the existence of God remained for later Idealism, and especially for Schelling and Hegel, both of whom advanced new solutions for it in their systems.

It should be noted how early in his consideration of Spinoza, Herder deviates from that thinker, for this concern with the problem of creation is thoroughly out of tune with Spinozism. For Spinoza, such a problem was completely meaningless, as God is not to be conceived in any sense as existing apart from, or before the world. Herder, though he concurs in this, nevertheless has the Christian theologian's concern with the question of a "beginning" of the finite world, and often, as in the passages referred to above, uses language which suggests that he confused logical and temporal priority. Thus, the Spinozistic distinction between God as free cause (*natura naturans*)

[80] p. 99–100, [444–5].   [81] p. 154, [523].   [82] p. 100, [446].

and that which follows from the nature of God (*natura naturata*), receives probably unconsciously, a theological connotation which is lacking in the original. Once the problem of creation has arisen, Herder finds himself at a loss to explain it, for it is clear that he is unwilling to accept the prevailing solutions in which God was represented as a transcendent being who plans, chooses, and creates by an act of volition.[83] Rather than capitulate to such superficial explanations, he prefers to leave the solution a mystery.

Up to this point Herder believes himself essentially in agreement with Spinozism, but the Second Conversation is not long under way before he finds it necessary to leave Spinoza, or as he puts it, "to show him to the light." The reason for this departure is essentially the same stumbling block which caused Spinoza's contemporaries so much trouble, namely, the doctrine of the attributes of God,[84] and specifically, the problem of why God, who according to Spinoza must possess an infinity of attributes, reveals Himself in the world in only two of them, thought and extension.

Herder sees in the conception of these two necessarily distinct attributes, a dualism which is the "weakest point of an otherwise well-reasoned system,"[85] and he regards it as particularly unfortunate because it is detrimental to the all-embracing monistic ideal of Spinoza. The root of the evil he conceives to have been Spinoza's inability to free himself from the Cartesian conception of matter, in which its essence is defined to be extension. Because he could not escape this conception, Herder maintains, Spinoza was forced to make extension an attribute of God.[86]

For Herder, however, space and time are only necessary

---

[83] p. 125, [**482**] ff.
[84] p. 100, [**446**] ff. Cf. Spinoza's Epist. LXV, LXX, LXVIII A.
[85] p. 102, [**449**].   [86] p. 101, [**447**].

conditions of the togetherness of things in the universe, the frames, as it were, of finite knowledge of the external world, and neither of them according to him, can in any sense be considered the essence of matter.[87] Spinoza had rightly discerned this to be true of time, but could not see his way toward treating extension similarly. What he lacked says Herder was the conception which Leibniz and natural science since Spinoza's day had come upon: substantial or organic forces.[88] This conception, Herder continues, defines the true essence of matter, and resolves the dualism of Spinoza into a true unity. Furthermore, the problem of the infinite attributes of God is immediately solved if once it is accepted, because instead of revealing Himself only in the two attributes of thought and extension, "God reveals Himself in an infinite number of forces, in an infinite number of ways."[89] Of these, thought is but one force (though it stands highest of all) among the countless forces which pervade the universe.

Conceived thus dynamically, Nature becomes in the truest sense unified with God. It springs to life, and that life is the activity of the one and eternal God Himself. "Everywhere organic forces alone can be active, and every one of them makes attributes of an infinite God known to us."[90] There is no longer any problem of how God worked upon dead matter, for matter is not dead extension, but alive. Nor, once the universe is conceived as composed of organic forces, is there any problem of a union or harmony of mind and matter, of body and soul, for those forces and the organs through which they function, are indissolubly united. One cannot exist without the other.[91] The universe as a whole is no longer to be

[87] pp. 101, 102, 104, [**448, 449, 452**].
[88] p. 103, [**451**]. [89] p. 103, [**451**].
[90] p. 104, [**452**]. [91] p. 104, [**453**].

conceived on the analogy of a mechanism, but as a great living organism.

This whole discussion is one of the most interesting parts of the work. It should be noted, however, that the basis of Herder's criticism is not an actual inconsistency in Spinoza's system, but an entirely different conception of extension. Herder cannot conceive extension to be an attribute of a Substance which is indivisible in itself. For Spinoza, this presents no difficulty, for according to him extension has no parts, but is divisible only through the medium of the imagination. Herder, on the contrary, regards it as simply and purely a representation of the imagination, a symbolical image of the "absolute infinity of the indivisible." [92]

As Herder indicates, the source of this doctrine is the Leibnizian criticism of the doctrine of extension held by Descartes and Malebranche. It is clear, however, that his use of Leibniz is as free as his interpretation of Spinoza. For instance, he does not conserve Leibniz's distinction between extension and space, but loosely identifies the two. [93] Moreover, Leibniz's denial of extension as the essence of matter had led him to a plurality of individual substances, as opposed to Spinoza's single Substance. Herder, however, finds it possible to conserve both the unity and the plurality by disregarding Leibniz's assertion of the necessary individuality of the monads. [94] Unlike Leibniz's, Herder's forces interact, and he conceives

---

[92] p. 107, [456]. A. C. McGiffert in "The God of Spinoza as Interpreted by Herder," *Hibbert Journal,* III (1904–5), 718, says that Herder's "freeing Spinoza's system from a serious inconsistency, made it possible at the same time to understand him as teaching divine immanence instead of pantheism, [and] is historically of great importance." Cf. however R. McKeon, *Philosophy of Spinoza* (New York, 1928), pp. 182–192, who sees no such inconsistency in Spinoza, and whose interpretation is here followed.

[93] For an exposition of Leibniz on this doctrine see B. Russell, *Philosophy of Leibniz* (Cambridge, 1900), p. 100 ff.

[94] Herder's conception of individuality is radically different from Leibniz's. See below, end of this section and text, p. 210, [573].

the infinite forces as manifestations of a single world-force, which is God, the force of all forces.

Herder's doctrine of God as immanent in the world, and manifesting Himself in a system of interacting organic forces is usually considered the result of a synthesis of the thought of Leibniz and Spinoza. The loose and imaginative manner in which Herder treats of the forces, as well as the differences between them and the Leibnizian monads, suggest, however, the possibility of another source. It links Herder with the tradition of the medieval *anima mundi* and More's and Shaftesbury's "Spirit of Nature."

In the "Moralists" there is a passage in which Shaftesbury describes in fashionable mythological language a conception which has much in common with Herder's:

"Besides the living genius of each place, the woods, too, which by your account are animated, have their hamadryads no doubt, and the springs and rivulets their nymphs in store belonging to 'em: And these too, by what I can apprehend, of immaterial and immortal substances.

"We injure 'em then, reply'd Theocles, to say 'they belong to these trees;' and not rather 'these trees to them.' But as for their immortality, let them look to it themselves. I only know that both theirs and all other natures must for their duration depend alone on that Nature on which the World depends: and that every genius else must be subordinate to that one good Genius, whom I would willingly persuade you to think belonging to this world, according to our present way of speaking." [95]

Whether or not it was this more poetic conception rather than the Leibnizian *Monadology* which inspired Herder, is perhaps impossible to determine. The fact that Herder appended a poetic translation of the "Moralists" to the second edition

[95] Shaftesbury, *Characteristics,* Vol. II, "The Moralists," Part 3, Section 1.

of the "Conversations" is highly significant, but it should also be noted that the language in which Herder speaks of the forces is that of Leibniz and the natural sciences of his day.

Herder's capacity for assimilation and synthesis was such that any clear-cut decision as to sources is extremely difficult. What emerges quite clearly from the consideration of Herder's doctrine of forces, however, is that this was no mere exposition of Spinoza's system, as Herder sometimes seems to claim, but a deliberate and radical transformation. Herder was here engaged in a task, which, in the light of subsequent philosophical developments, is of the greatest importance. It may be described in general terms as the attempt to imbue the abstract and logical system of Spinoza with life. To a man excited by the dynamic conception of nature, the Spinozistic conception of things as mere modes of Substance seemed completely inadequate. Herder took it upon himself to "harmonize" this dynamism with Spinoza's God. Not only did he believe this to be possible without doing injury to the truth of Spinoza's system, but he was convinced that it gave to that system a transcendent significance. Not only was God the One and All, the great totality of the universe, but He was its all-pervading life, the source and sustenance of its activity. Every law of nature discovered by the scientist was for Herder a revelation of the omnipresence of the Deity. "We are surrounded by omnipotence, we swim in an ocean of omnipotence," he exclaims, intoxicated by the sublimity of the conception.[96]

In connection with the Spinozistic conception of God there remained still another great problem for Herder, and this he attempts to solve in the Third Conversation. If the necessary and eternal laws of nature are the revelation of the Deity, are, in fact, the laws of God's essential activity, what guarantee is

[96] p. 107, [**456**].

there that God Himself is not determined, that His activity is not one of blind necessity?

That Spinoza's Substance was a free or self-determined cause of the universe, Herder would have had no difficulty in showing, but he was also interested in proving that highest wisdom and goodness are essential to God, and not as Spinoza said, mere *propria,* or human attributions which give no knowledge or explanation of God's essential nature. Herder therefore set out to prove that the necessary laws of nature must derive from a highest intelligence, and that they must be consequences of a highest wisdom and goodness inherent in God.

At the end of the first book of the *Ethics* Spinoza summarizes his conclusions as to the nature of God as follows:

"I have shown that He necessarily exists; that He is one God; that from the necessity alone of His own nature He is and acts; that He is, and in what way He is, the free cause of all things; that all things are in Him and so depend upon Him that without Him they can neither be nor be conceived; and finally, that all things have been pre-determined by Him, not indeed from freedom of the will, or from absolute good pleasure, but from His absolute nature or infinite power."[97]

There is nothing here with which Herder would not have agreed, but when he comes to the problem of God's intellect, he does not seem properly to understand the significance of Spinoza's statement that the intellect of God can no more resemble the human intellect, than the Dog-Star resembles the animal which we know. Herder regards this merely as Spinoza's tendency to state his case over-strongly rather than give an opportunity for a mean conception of the Deity in human terms.[98] For Herder, to be sure, there is a distinction between

[97] *Ethics* Bk. I. App. (Hale White trans.)
[98] p. 120, [**476**].

the divine and the human intellect, but it is a distinction of degree, and not, as in Spinoza, one of kind.

Hence, when Spinoza says, "The intellect of God, so far as it is conceived to constitute the divine essence, differs from our intellect both with regard to its essence and its existence, nor can it be coincided with our intellect in anything except the name"[99] Herder takes leave of him. Arguing from Prop. I, Bk. 2 of the *Ethics* "that thought is an attribute of God, or God is a thinking thing," he proceeds to show what Spinoza himself never pretended to demonstrate, namely that the thought of God must also be the highest wisdom.

The crux of the argument lies in the conception of the power of God, which, Herder maintains, Spinoza developed in order to bridge the Cartesian dualism between the attributes of thought and extension, for in it both of these attributes are subsumed. Had Spinoza but developed this conception further, says Herder, this divine power could never have been accused of being blind, for it would in turn have yielded the conception of forces, which includes both thought and power alike. "In that conception he would have regarded power and thought as forces, as identical in nature."[100] Since in the preceding Conversation, Herder has demonstrated that these forces are the infinite attributes of God, it therefore follows that the power of God must be essentially an intelligent power.

Herder has not yet shown that this attribute of thought, which is equivalent to the power of thought as it is revealed in the world, necessarily implies a highest wisdom. He has, however, prepared for this conclusion by showing that "since, according to Spinoza, reason and will are identical, a power which conceives the best, must also will the best, and, if it has the power, must also work the best."[101] Thus, since Spinoza

[99] *Ethics* Bk. I. App. (Hale White trans.)
[100] p. 123, [**480**].   [101] p. 122, [**478**].

had never denied infinite power to God, He is demonstrated to be the highest, wisest, efficient power.

It must however be observed that Spinoza had made plain that all assertions of God's reason and will were to be assigned to the *natura naturata* not to the *natura naturans,* and also that so far as Spinoza is concerned, there can be no talk of God's "conceiving the best." Here Herder is committing the very breach which Spinoza was most anxious to avoid, that of assuming an analogy between the human and divine intellects.

This doctrine of Herder's, in which Spinoza's pure necessity becomes also intelligent, was condemned by Jacobi, as a syncretism of Spinoza and orthodox theism. There is much truth in this criticism, for these doctrines again reveal Herder transforming the Spinozistic system to fit his own theological interests. There is no ground, however, for supposing this procedure to be merely the result of a desire to conciliate Spinozism and orthodoxy. The idea of God as the highest Power, Wisdom and Goodness, is, it is true, similar to orthodox theology, but it is also clear that Herder has not brought these conceptions ready-made and merely fitted them to the Spinozistic God. They are consequences of his own view, the development of which has led him to these doctrines. In the process of that development, however, the traditional conceptions have become imbued with new meaning. Throughout the work he is most emphatic in his opposition to the old-fashioned theistic conceptions of the Deity because of their tendency to debase the nature of God. He invariably deserts Leibniz for Spinoza on this matter, because he finds the former's views of God too much inclined to cater to the popular taste.[102] He is firm in his disapproval of final causes and an anthropocentric view of the universe, and often speaks against degrading the conception of God by means of anthropomorphic representa-

---

[102] p. 124, [481]. It should be noted that the criticism refers only to Leibniz's *Theodicy.*

tions. On these grounds, he condemns even the view of God as the World-Soul, which he himself had once held.[103] In the second edition, moreover, in reply to Jacobi's criticism, he is at pains to point out that his attribution of intelligence to the Supreme Being does not imply that he conceived God to be a personality.[104]

If the reconciliation which Herder is here effecting is regarded in the light of his development, it would be nearer the truth to say that rather than between Spinoza and orthodoxy, it is a reconciliation of Spinoza and Shaftesbury's optimism, which regarded the all-embracing harmony of the universe as the beautiful revelation of God's wisdom. It springs, not from a cautious desire to preserve traditional doctrines, but from the conclusions Herder had come to as a result of his feeling for, and study of, nature.

It is significant that the Third Conversation in which this conception of a wise necessity is developed, is introduced by a consideration of the natural sciences and the order and regularity which pervades the universe. There the doctrine of the wisdom of this order is already established when Herder makes the statement that "the more true physics advances, the more we depart from the realm of blind power and arbitrariness, and enter the realm of the wisest necessity, of a beauty and goodness steadfast in itself."[105] His view thus is in reality not derived primarily from a logical deduction or development of Spinoza's system, nor from any specific preoccupation with orthodox theology, though both these factors play a part, but rather from the appraisal of a scheme of interdependent and immutable laws which is apparent to him in the teeming multiplicity of things. Herder reasons that all this harmony could

[103] p. 156, [526].
[104] In Appendix A to this volume, which contains the variations between the first and second editions, p. 199, [497].   [105] p. 117, [471].

not come from an unintelligent cause, or, as he puts it: "An unorganized, lawless, blind power is never the highest. It can never be the prototype and summation of all the order, wisdom and regularity which we, although finite beings, perceive in creation as eternal laws, if it does not itself know these laws and exercise them according to its eternal intrinsic nature. A blind power must necessarily have been surpassed by an ordered one, and thus could not be God."[106]

Once Herder has established the conception of God as the One and All, the immanent and necessary cause of the world, he becomes almost exclusively concerned with the activity and revelation of the Deity in the universe. The stimulus for this search lies in the suggestion which Herder makes in the Second Conversation, that things should be considered as "modified appearances of divine powers" rather than as modes of Substance.[107] The finest knowledge of God comes, therefore, from natural science, which explores the universe and reveals its inmost life and unity in the form of the laws of nature. In this sense, as Herder says, science becomes the prolegomena to metaphysics, which is, literally, an "after physics."[108] Goethe, who shared this view of nature with Herder, expressed the same idea in a letter to Jacobi, when he wrote: "Before I write one syllable, $M\epsilon\tau\alpha$ $\tau\alpha$ $\phi\nu\sigma\iota\kappa\alpha$, I must have clearly settled my $\phi\nu\sigma\iota\kappa\alpha$."[109]

The intimate relationship between Herder and Goethe at Weimar has already been mentioned. It was during the time of their friendship and mutual studies there that Goethe made his great discovery of the intermaxillary bone, which fortified

[106] p. 123, [479]. Note the presupposition, which underlies this contrast between a "blind" and an "ordered" power, that regularity necessarily implies intelligence, and that this regularity is real.

[107] p. 97, [441].   [108] p. 111, [464].

[109] To Jacobi, June 9, 1785.

both men in their conviction of the unity and of the continuity of nature. This common interest of theirs is echoed in the "Conversations," and particularly so in the last section, in which Herder deals with a philosophy of nature in idealistic terms.

With the dynamic conception of nature uppermost in their minds, these men sought everywhere for "the symbols expressive of God in the universe,"[110] and everywhere they found the same laws in operation, bringing the multiplicity of nature into a coherent unity. Herder could find the identical laws active in the drop of water in the calyx of a rose, and in the formation of planetary systems.[111] Goethe, in examining a piece of granite could say: "You will find there the most ancient laws of nature . . . you will find in it an element which seeks out another, penetrates it, and by this combination, creates a third. There at bottom is the résumé of all the operations of nature."[112]

Most of the other doctrines which Herder advances depend in one way or another upon this dynamic panentheistic worldview. For example, his conception of knowledge as a natural process, rests directly upon the unity of forces in nature. It has already been seen how this doctrine, together with his fundamental conviction as to the rationality of the universe, led him to oppose the concern with *Erkenntnistheorie* which Kant made so important in philosophy.

In connection with this theory, mention must be made of Herder's conception of *Genuss* ("enjoyment"), to which he frequently refers in the final section of the work. Both he and Goethe often use the word in an unusual sense, meaning thereby no mere sensuous enjoyment but rather the absorption of the individual with all his sense and reason, in the whole of reality. In this identification is achieved the most intimate pos-

---

[110] pp. 159, 162, [**529, 532**].   [111] p. 179, [**554**].
[112] Quoted in E. Caro, *La Philosophie de Goethe,* p. 165.

sible knowledge of the great totality of things. Although, in a way, there is a disappearance of the individual in the whole, there is, at the same time, a finding of the self in that submergence. In Herder and Goethe, this conception corresponds functionally to the *amor Dei intellectualis* of Spinoza or the *fruitio Dei* of the Scholastics.

From his dynamic panentheism Herder also derives his conception of immortality, which he merely hints at in the Fifth Conversation. The soul, as a substantial force, must be deathless like all other forces. If the body dies, the soul "can never lack a new organ in a creation in which there is no gap, no leap, no island."[113] It is interesting to note that Herder seems to have taken Kant's criticism of the same doctrine in the "Ideas" to heart,[114] for in the "Conversations" he does not venture on to a proof of personal immortality from this conception.

It has already been seen how Herder softened the Spinozistic doctrine of divine necessity. On the question of the moral determinism of man, however, he reveals himself to be in complete agreement with Spinoza. Like him, Herder conceives freedom as action in accordance with one's nature. Moral necessity is thus not irreconcilable with freedom if the latter is truly understood. Herder agrees further with Spinoza in the conception of the unreality of evil. What men call evil is merely limit or privation. So too for Herder, error and falsity are merely negative, but insofar as they form a contrast to the truth, they help man to the attainment of the latter.

In conclusion, some mention must be made of Herder's three fundamental laws of nature, and of his interesting conception of individuality. He finds everywhere in the universe, three

[113] p. 174, [548].
[114] In the review mentioned above, p. 35, Kant pointed out that even if Herder's hypothesis of organic development is accepted, it does not prove the possibility of a continued personal development but only the possibility of organisms higher than man developing eventually.

principles operating: the tendency of things to persist in their own essence, the attraction of likes and the repulsion of opposites, and the principle of self-assimilation and reproduction. In themselves, these are not new,[115] but they are important insofar as they show Herder approaching an interpretation of the universe in terms of the self, a doctrine which later Romantic Idealism was to make famous. In it the barriers between subject and object fall away completely, and the truths of the individual self are seen as identical with those which hold of nature as a whole.

The same view is in evidence in Herder's conception of individuality.[116] In the ascending scale of nature, "the more life and reality, that is, the more rational, powerful and perfect energy a being has for the maintenance of a whole which it feels belongs to itself, to which it imparts itself inwardly and entirely, the more it is an individual, a self." Ultimately therefore, there is but one true self: God. "He alone, in whom all is, who holds and sustains all, can say: 'I am the Self, outside me there is no one.' "[117] For all the looseness and the poetry of Herder's exposition of it, there are some striking similarities between this view and the tendency in philosophy which was eventually to culminate in the Idealism of Schelling and Hegel.

The Relation of the "Conversations" to Post-Kantian Thought

It is difficult to ascertain the precise extent of the effect which the "Conversations" had upon their time. That they were widely read, because of their connection with the Spinoza

---

[115] Lambert, Leibniz and the natural science of his day might have supplied Herder with these doctrines. He himself refers to a work called *Betrachtungen über das Universum* (Erfurt, 1777), written by a friend of his, Karl von Dalberg. See note, p. 184, [562].

[116] Appendix A. p. 210, [573] ff.   [117] Ibid. p. 213, [575].

controversy, is not to be doubted. It is also known that the work was not well received by many of Herder's more notable contemporaries. All of the belief philosophers condemned it. Hamann wrote that the book was an "owl" (*Shu-hu*) "which had better creep away and hide itself in the dark."[118] Lavater saw "many significant and true things in the work, . . . but I miss the biblical God in it."[119] Jacobi, as has been mentioned, wrote against it in the second edition of his "Letters on the Doctrine of Spinoza" defending his own interpretation of Spinoza, and accusing Herder of anthropomorphising Spinoza's conception of God and imbuing it with theistic notions. Kant complimented Jacobi on his refutation of Herder, although Kant seems to have had a very poor opinion of Jacobi's book as well.[120]

Only Goethe, writing from Italy, declared himself completely in agreement with it, calling it the mark from which they could henceforth count off their miles. "It encouraged me," he wrote, "to push further on in natural things," and he tells how he was rewarded by finding an ἐν καὶ πᾶν in botany, his *Urpflanze*.[121]

Its effect upon later thought, however, is a matter for speculation. It is tempting to see in it, as A. C. McGiffert does, "a work which I am inclined to think did more than any other to bring Spinoza into favor with the thinkers of the time and to prepare the way for the tremendous influence which he exerted in Germany in the first half of the nineteenth century."[122] It should be remembered, however, that, although Herder was the first to defend Spinoza publicly, the subsequent rehabilitation would never have been so complete and overwhelming if the times had not been ripe for such a revival. A quick-

[118] Quoted by Nevinson, *Herder and His Times*, p. 350.
[119] To Jacobi, June 23, 1787.
[120] Kant to Jacobi, Oct. 1789; to Herz, 1786.
[121] To Herder, September 6, 1787.   [122] A. C. McGiffert, op. cit., p. 710.

ening of interest in the doctrines of Spinoza was therefore far more important than any "defense" of him, and that interest had already been stimulated by the Spinoza Quarrel itself. To transfer the credit to that controversy as a whole, however, in no way detracts from the importance of the "Conversations" as a monument in the history of Spinozism, for this essay was, in many respects, the most fruitful contribution to that famous quarrel.

The renaissance which followed straight upon the heels of the Spinoza Controversy was both rapid and extensive. In 1794 Fichte could write:

"There are only two completely consistent systems, the Critical . . . and the Spinozistic."[123]

In 1795 appeared Schelling's "Of the Ego as a Principle of Philosophy," followed by the "Letters on Dogmatism and Criticism," (1796). Both revealed unmistakable Spinozistic tendencies. Then, at the turn of the century, Schleiermacher wrote in his "Speeches on Religion."

"Offer up a lock of hair in honor of the spirit of the holy outcast. The sublime world-spirit penetrated him. The infinite was his beginning and end, the universe his only and eternal love."[124]

In Hegel, the restoration reached its culmination when he wrote: "Spinoza is the high-point of modern philosophy; either Spinozism or no philosophy."[125]

The encouragement which the "Conversations," and Neo-Spinozism on the whole gave to this revival of Spinoza, was perhaps a more important contribution to nineteenth century German thought than any special doctrine. Nevertheless, the

---

[123] *"Wissenschaftslehre"* (1794), *Werke,* I, 101.
[124] *Reden über die Religion,* 2nd ed. p. 68.
[125] Hegel, *Geschichte der Philosophie* (1805–6), p. 374. Besides the men here mentioned, many others, including Tieck, Novalis, and Heinrich Steffens participated in the revival.

doctrines which developed out of the Spinoza renaissance have a greater significance in the formation of later thought than is usually attributed to them, for, during the closing years of the eighteenth century, certain tendencies began to appear in German Idealism which can be better explained as the effect of Neo-Spinozistic influence than as simply a development of the Kantian doctrines.

It has been seen that among the most distinctive themes in the "Conversations" were the monistic world-view, the dynamic conception of nature, and the tendency to conceive the universe as manifesting the Divine Life or Spirit. In the post-Kantian philosophy, as well as in the general Romantic literature, all of these views received further emphasis and development. There was on the whole, a reaction to the Kantian dualism, a reaction which took the form of a reconciliation of the subjective and objective worlds. The emphasis upon external nature which was so important in Neo-Spinozism, brought about a dissatisfaction with the subordinate place and mechanistic construction of that aspect of the universe in the systems of Kant and Fichte. During this period the problem of the relation between nature and self became of transcendent importance. In the Romanticists it received poetic expression in the transformation of the whole of nature into a great Self, the divine life of the universe being conceived in essentially personal terms. In the liberal theology of Schleiermacher, the conception of divine immanence is basic. The core of religion is defined as the feeling of dependence of the self on the great totality of Being which is God. Finally, in Schelling and Hegel, the problem of subject and object culminated in the *Identität* system on the one hand, and the philosophy of Absolute Spirit on the other. In them, the conception of the universe as the expression of God, the Absolute, received its fullest rational expression.

It is further significant that the method which was used in the interpretation of Spinozism by these philosophers, and the manner in which that thought was employed by them, was in general very like that which Herder had used in the "Conversations." Especially in Schelling and Hegel, it was characterized by a tendency to add to Spinoza, to revise and develop his ideas so that they might harmonize with modern thought. In Schelling's "Letters on Dogmatism and Criticism" for example, there is an explicit attempt to bring together the truth of the critical philosophy, as exemplified by Fichte, and the dogmatism of Spinoza. Both Fichte and Spinoza, he maintains, fulfill the work of philosophy in the highest degree. Both start from the Absolute and return to it. They are both monistic, as all philosophy must be, and both are complete in themselves. Neither of them can be contradicted. They both offer genuine solutions of the problem of the relation of the conditioned to the unconditioned.

Schelling, however, was not entirely satisfied with the details of these two systems. He found much to be in need of improvement, especially in the conception of nature. Fichte's Egoism he saw as devoting too little attention to the objective world. The latter must not be subsumed under the Ego, for this merely explains it away without making it comprehensible. The real solution lay in what he calls his *Durchbruch zur Realität,* in the working out of the intelligible system of nature, and the demonstration of its unity with the Absolute Ego.

In Spinoza, on the other hand, Schelling condemned the "abstract conception of nature" and he found it necessary to correct it by means of the more elevated view of the universe as dynamic:

"If the doctrine that all things are conceived in God is the basis of the entire system (of Spinoza) it must at least first be vitalized and severed from abstractness before it can become the principle of a system of reason. How general and vague is the expression that the eternal beings are modes or consequences of God; what a chasm there is here, needing to be filled in; what questions remain to be answered!"[126]

Pringle-Pattison, in his consideration of Schelling's principle of dynamic nature on the analogy of the life of organic beings,[127] is inclined to see the *Critique of Judgment* as the starting point of this new line of thought. However, as must be apparent from the discussion of Herder's views, Kant was not the only source of such a doctrine. It had already been developed by Herder and Goethe as part of the philosophy of Neo-Spinozism, and had by Schelling's time become a part of the intellectual outlook of his generation. This view which in Kant, as far as it is treated at all, is not admitted as belonging to the science of nature but only to a further reflective consideration of it, was conceived in Neo-Spinozism to be a necessary alteration of the Spinozistic conception of Substance. The conception, moreover, had already been extensively applied in Herder's work on history and religion, and in Goethe's natural research, with very tangible results.

With this changed conception of nature, there came also a change in the Spinozistic conception of God. The Deity as independent self-sufficient Being, immanent in the universe, had to be conceived as actualized in the objective world in the process of Becoming. As has been seen, something of this problem was already realized in the "Conversations," although Herder made no attempt to bridge the gulf between these two conceptions.

A solution was formulated by Hegel.[128] Starting with the conception of the Absolute as the identity of nature and mind,

[126] Schelling, *Of Human Freedom* (Gutmann trans. Chicago, 1936), p. 350.
[127] Op. cit., p. 54.
[128] There is in these few pages no attempt to present either the philosophy of Hegel or that of Schelling with any degree of adequacy. The discussion is limited to those themes which they have in common with Herder.

he maintained that the emergence of nature and mind from such an Absolute was not proved as necessary, but merely postulated. He therefore set out to transform this view of the Absolute, and he too refers to Spinoza's solution of the problem.

"The Absolute Substance of Spinoza" he says "is the true one, but it is not yet the wholly true one; it must be conceived as in itself active, living, and it must therefore 'determine itself' (*sich bestimmen*) as 'Spirit' (*Geist*). The Spinozistic Substance is the general and therefore abstract *Bestimmung;* one can say that it is the foundation of Mind, but not as the absolute, firmly established ground but rather as the abstract oneness, which Spirit is in itself. Thus if one remains with this Substance, no spirituality, no activity is arrived at. His philosophy is merely stark Substance, not yet Spirit . . ."[129]

The Hegelian solution, thus, was the philosophy of Mind, of Spirit, as the culmination of the Absolute Process. The latter is conceived as revealing itself in both the subjective and objective worlds, not only because it underlies both as their Substance, but also because these worlds are stages in its own progressive self-realization. The Absolute is living spirit, and as such is constantly developing and growing. In this sense both subject and object are truly real. They are not, however, real in themselves, but only in the great all-embracing reality which is the Absolute. The latter is not a fixed and constant life, or being, or thought, but "a life, a being, a thought which exists only as it opposes itself within itself, sets itself apart from itself, and projects its meaning and relation upwards and outwards, and yet retains and carries out the power of reuniting itself."[130] Such is the great dialectic of Spirit as it manifests

---

[129] *Geschichte der Philosophie* (1805–6), p. 377.
[130] W. Wallace, *Prolegomena to the Study of Hegel's Philosophy* (2nd ed.; Oxford, 1894), p. 193.

itself in the eternal process of nature and history. Reason is the ground, law, and object of all Becoming.

This is a far cry from the philosophy of the "Conversations" and yet Hegel's doctrines have with some justice been called the philosophy of the Goethesque world-view,[131] which, as was seen above, had much in common with Herder. The truth which this comparison may be said to contain, lies in the development which Hegel, and Schelling before him, gave to the outstanding features of the Neo-Spinozistic views of the universe and God: monism, divine immanence, the all-embracing unity of the Deity, the dynamic and evolutionary conception of the universe, and the progress of history. These elements were part of the cultural environment in which Schelling and Hegel matured, and they offered a significant supplement to the views of Kant and Fichte. In Schelling and Hegel, however greatly they differ in other respects, there is a development away from the Kantian dualism and its stumbling block of the *Ding-an-sich* on the one hand, and from the Fichtean Ego doctrine on the other, toward monism of God and the world, and of subject and object. Both of these philosophers went to the newly revived Spinozism, but it was the Spinozism of Herder and Goethe rather than that of Spinoza to which they turned.

Although both Schelling and Hegel show traces of the influence of Herder and Goethe, especially in their early development,[132] it is more probable that their inspiration was drawn rather from the general cultural atmosphere than from these two men directly. However, the part which both Herder and Goethe had in creating that atmosphere, especially in their

[131] R. Steiner, *Goethes Weltanschauung* (Berlin, 1918), p. 169. H. Falkenheim in his *Goethe u. Hegel* (Tübingen, 1934), also stresses the similarity between the two.
[132] R. Haym, *Die romantische Schule* (Berlin, 1928), p. 616. M. Kronenberg, *Geschichte des deutschen Idealismus* (München, 1909), p. 667.

influential years at Weimar, cannot be overlooked in any full appreciation of the development of German Idealism. Their thought, unsystematic and quasi-literary though it was, had its own coherence and emphasis which would justify its being called the philosophy of Weimar, in contrast to that of Jena. It is in both of these world-views, rather than in the latter alone, that the roots of Schelling and Hegel are to be sought. If this is so, then the "Conversations," as the most extensive expression of the Weimar philosophy, deserve serious consideration as a monument of an important transitional stage of German thought.

GOD

SOME CONVERSATIONS

PREFACE TO THE FIRST EDITION

FOR SOME ten or twelve years, I have had in mind a little essay which was to be called, "Spinoza-Shaftesbury-[403] Leibniz." It was complete in my thoughts, and I set out several times to execute it. However I was always interrupted and had to leave it for another hour.

Imperceptibly new circumstances led me to write the following conversations. Their purpose would be greatly misunderstood, if they were held to be merely a vindication of Spinoza. Spinoza has no need of this vindication, and so far as my purpose is concerned, he here becomes merely the handle of a sacrificial vase out of which I would pour a few drops upon the altar of my youth. My reason for taking him as my starting point lay partly in the sequence of my thoughts, and partly in the inducements which the times themselves offered me. (B1)

Let no one interpret my work, however, as if I wished to anticipate, interfere with, or supersede in some way any current philosophy, to arouse factions, or to become a self-appointed arbiter between factions. These are discussions between persons who express their opinions with that same right which anyone else has to present his doctrines. (B2) Discussions are not final judgments, still less are they designed to arouse contentiousness. For I shall never quarrel about God.

But I ardently wish that what could only be suggested here in discussion, may some day achieve a form more suited to [404] our philosophy. I desire but one quiet and peaceful summer for my "Adrastea," or "Of the Laws of Nature, insofar as they rest upon Wisdom, Power and Goodness, as upon an Inner Necessity." (B1) But since in my own life I too am constrained to follow necessity and not caprice, may Eternal Truth, if my work is agreeable to her, also grant me the leisure for it. I should be satisfied if this little preparatory study charmed some unprejudiced lovers of philosophy, pleased connoisseurs, and here and there showed the way to one astray.

HERDER

WEIMAR
   APRIL 23RD, 1787

Preface to the Second Edition

THIS EDITION could have appeared several years ago, but for various reasons I have delayed it.

To be more specific, since 1787 (the year in which these [405] conversations were first published), a great deal has changed on the philosophical horizon in Germany. (B1) Spinoza's name, which before that time was usually mentioned with horror and loathing, thereafter rose so high in the estimation of some, that they could not speak of him save at the expense of Leibniz and of other excellent spirits. Indeed, his system was so misused that, forgetting all the limits of human knowledge which Spinoza recognized so well, some turned things upside down and made bold to spin out the contents of the entire universe from a confined and imaginary Ego. This senseless dream was called "Transcendental Spinozism," and the old Spinoza was derided because he had not gone so far. (B2) On the other hand, some continued to maintain that "Spinoza had divided God up, and robbed Him of thought. His God was only a collective name." (B3) They also went on to maintain that "for Spinoza under this collective name, everything is caught up in the chains of blind necessity. Spinoza's God was a despotic and savage Polyphemus, whose eye he had put out." In such arrogant and contrary times, unassuming conversations about Spinoza's system could scarcely expect a friendly reception from the world.

Since, however, their purpose was not to defend Spinoza's system in its every expression, nor to apotheosize it, but rather [406] to make it understandable, and by removing some of the verbal barriers, to show where Spinoza wanted to go, I

could not, and cannot now, feel ashamed of this plain debt of
humanity paid to an estimable thinker. The shade of Archytas
in Horace seemed to call to me; (B1)

> Nor thou, my friend, refuse with impious hand
> A little portion of this wandering sand
> To these my poor remains . . . .
> . . . .
> Whate'er my haste, oh! let my prayer prevail
> Thrice strow the sand, then hoist the flying sail.

Why should I not show him such love as this? The dominion
of truth is one and indivisible throughout the centuries. He who
removes or lessens the misunderstandings of the past, thereby
enlightens the understanding of times to come.

Spinoza, reared in another manner of speech and thought,
was to a certain extent a stranger to the idiom in which he
wrote. Do not reason and fairness demand, then, that one
should help to make his expressions clear and not merely gnaw
away at the stones, that is to say, restrict oneself exclusively
to his most difficult language? It is a debt of honesty to every
honest man, to explain an author in his own totality.

In any case, to judge and comprehend a system in which all
is directed towards the freedom and joy of the soul, towards
true knowledge and active blessedness, an unprejudiced, liberal temper is above all essential. For how could true knowledge, a cheerful disposition and active love be constrained?
"Blessedness," says Spinoza, "is not the reward of virtue, but
is virtue itself; nor do we delight in blessedness because we
restrain our lusts, but on the contrary, because we delight in
it, therefore are we able to restrain them." (B2) So too is it
with the knowledge of truth. Because we know truth, we con-
[407]quer prejudice. What seems to be the hard yoke of truth
to those benighted in their knowledge, becomes, in contrast,
the active, regal law of freedom to the truly knowing. "In Him

we live and move and have our being," said the Apostle. An earlier poet whom the Apostle quotes approvingly had said: "We are His offspring." (B1) With the same freedom with which Paul quotes a poet whose words are the essence of this system I was able to explain it.

For the present, let Shaftesbury's "Hymn to Nature" (B2) take the place of the promised "Adrastea." I could not give the Hymn a further elaboration than that permitted by the context of those amiable dialogues, the "Moralists." I trust that the content will make amends for whatever is lacking in lyrical perfection.

> Not merely perfect He, nor true nor good
> Nor beautiful! But Truth and Goodness is,
> Perfection's self! Makes friends of foes, and Night
> To Light transforms! The loved of God loves too,
> Is blessed, and loved of all.

TABLE OF CONTENTS OF THE SECOND EDITION

the relation between cause and effect. Whether or not crea-
[410] tion is emanation. Whether or not Spinoza derived his
system from the Cabbala. Whether or not the expression
"World-Soul" befits the Deity. "God," a sura from Gleim's
"Halladat."

FIFTH CONVERSATION. Introduction. There are in Creation
expressive symbols of reality, i.e. of power, wisdom and goodness. Existence as an object of our knowledge. The conception
of necessity is not oppressive, but rather gladdening. Reality
is the ground of all conceptions and all truth; Nothingness is
nothing. Reality is an indivisible conception, the ground of all
forces. The first proposition: Existence cannot reveal itself
except as existing. The highest Existence gave His creatures
what was highest: reality, existence. The truest Existence cannot reveal Himself otherwise than as inherently true; hence
everyone of His representations is an expression of essential
power, goodness and wisdom. Second proposition: All organizations are expressions of these attributes as living forces.
The conception of matter. Spinoza's conception of the body as
an essential form of the soul. The harmony which reveals itself in every organized being. Simple laws of organized beings:
persistence, union or dissolution, self-assimilation and reproduction. The law of persistence, by means of the separation of
the opposed, by poles. Assimilation of beings through mutual
participation. Imperceptible activity of Being according to
grades, and the most eminent Being. Self-assimilation brings
apparent destruction into Creation. It is necessary law; Death
a continual life. Whether or not this continuity is also a progressive life. Doctrines derived from this. The advantages of a
philosophical conversation. Whether or not Spinoza, with his
single substance, destroyed particular forms of existence, that
is, individuals. What are individuation and self? The grades
of self-awareness or self.

First Conversation

PHILOLAUS: My friend, observe the refreshing hour which has followed the frightful thunderstorm. Sulphurous clouds were [412] piled up which hid the sun from our view, and made it difficult to breathe on earth. Now they are dispersed, and once again everything breathes easily and happily. Such, I imagine, was the state of wisdom when Spinoza and his like sought to rob the world of the sight of God with their heavy mists. These too piled themselves up to heaven and overcast the skies. But a sounder philosophy overthrew them like the giants of old, and the reflective mind once more beholds the radiant sun.

THEOPHRON: Have you read Spinoza, dear friend?

PHILOLAUS: No, I have not read him. And who would want to read every obscure book a madman might write? But I have heard from many who have read him, that he was an atheist and pantheist, a teacher of blind necessity, an enemy of revelation, a mocker of religion, and withal, a destroyer of the state and of all civil society. In short, he was an enemy of the human race, and as such he died. He therefore deserves the hatred and aversion of all friends of humanity and of true philosophers.

THEOPHRON: The thundercloud with which you have just compared him, does not however suit him, for it too belongs [413] to the order of nature, and is salutary and good. But to dispense with comparisons, my friend, have you read nothing more specific and definite about Spinoza which we might discuss?

PHILOLAUS: A good deal. For instance, the article about him in Bayle. (B1)

THEOPHRON: In this instance Bayle is not your best authority. He, to whom all systems were alike indifferent because fundamentally he had no system himself, did not remain impartial towards Spinoza. He zealously took sides against him, encouraged undoubtedly by the circumstances of his time and place. Perhaps he lived too close to the dead Spinoza. The doctrine, even the very name of Spinoza was at that time a term of invective, just as for the most part, they still are. Everything preposterous and godless was, and to a certain extent is still, called Spinozistic. Then, too, it was not the forte of Bayle, the keen dialectician, to get to the bottom of a system as such, or to consider it with the deepest feeling for truth. He skimmed over all systems, and keenly noted their discrepancies insofar as they served his skepticism. Now one view was important to him, now another. But of what can be called inner philosophical conviction, his superficial mind had scarcely any conception, as his "Dictionary" almost incontestably shows.

PHILOLAUS: Very true! I have often wondered how so keen [414] a mind could have been so unstable, so loose in its views. Now this absurdity, now that, is equally important to him; for example, now an erroneously cited date of Moreri's then the question, "Is there a God?" and, "How many of the latter are there?" or "Whence springs the evil of the world?" and similar questions, all occupy him with equal interest. (B1)

THEOPHRON: You should rather say with equally little interest, yet with all the more skill in the keenest play of wit. That is precisely Bayle's rare quality. Can you name me another author whose mind embraced, or treated with the lightest touch, so great a variety of things with equal grace and discernment? He was the philosophico-historical Voltaire of his day, whose fancy ranged from the highest matter down to the smallest detail of an historical event, an anecdote, the title of a book, or even a smutty story.

Spinoza's system was not at all for a mind of this kind. That retired and grave thinker had a very contemptuous conception of all opinion, and with mathematical exactness went after pure and plain truth, wherever he thought to find it. He forgot all else, and had not a thousandth part of Bayle's erudition, wit or keenness. Two minds of such caliber will scarcely do justice to each other. Yet I am convinced that Spinoza would sooner have shown it to the author of the "Dictionary," than [415] that sprightly busybody Bayle could to Spinoza. Even during his lifetime Bayle was reproached for not having rightly grasped Spinoza's system, and had to defend himself against this accusation in one of his letters.*

PHILOLAUS: That was unfortunate for Spinoza. For after all, the conception which is now held of him was established for the mass of the people by Bayle. (B1) How few read the obscure works of Spinoza, while all the world reads the manifoldly useful, varied and pleasant Bayle!

THEOPHRON: Just so, my friend! Bayle has fixed the conception of Spinoza for the light troop of readers, while for the heavy phalanx, it has been done mainly by militant philosophers and theologians. (B2) And with them it befell him even worse. He fared as in the Gospel: his closest relations, the Cartesians, immediately became his bitterest enemies. They wanted and were obliged to separate their philosophy, from which he proceeded and whose language he spoke, from his, so that they too would not come under the suspicion of Spinozism. Naturally this philosophical caution spread from the Cartesian school to every following one. Then the theologians of almost all confessions set upon him even more bitterly, for he had not only expressed very free opinions on Judaism and the books of the Old Testament, but, what must have seemed much worse to them, he had in the first instance lifted

* *Oeuvr. de Bayle* T. IV. pp. 169, 170.

his pen against them particularly. (B3) To their quarrelsome nature and continual wrangling, he attributed in great part the [416] decline of Christianity, and the inefficacy of its finest teachings. And, though he did all this without any bitterness, you can easily imagine how his book was received.

PHILOLAUS: I can imagine it very vividly. A peacemaker without authority has but to step between two heated factions, and he has both against him.

THEOPHRON: Spinoza had no other authority than that which he believed he had received from the hand of justice and truth. To be sure, he did not make use of it in a worldly-wise manner. He made known his religious politics in a work whose theology inevitably aroused both Jews and Christians.* And his political doctrines were so severe and stringent, that they certainly could not have been acceptable in those times. He granted the state full power to regulate public worship. Yet, at the same time, he retained unlimited freedom in the exercise of reason. This seemed to most people as excessive as if he had wanted to mix fire and water. Thus his theory was an inevitable failure, for in a good many respects it is even now too severe for us, and as it were, too Hobbesian, even though we have advanced a great deal in tolerance and statecraft. Locke, Bayle, Shaftesbury and others proceeded more gently.

PHILOLAUS: And yet they too had to suffer enough before [417] their most reasonable propositions were generally accepted. In such precarious matters a disputatious dialectician like Bayle, or a creator of poetic forms like Voltaire, has indeed a great advantage over the serious philosopher who states his propositions directly. The former are always safer, because they can always say: "I was merely disputing, merely

* *Tractatus theologico-politicus continens dissertationes aliquot, quibus ostenditur, libertatem philosophandi non tantum salva pietate et reipublicae pace posse concedi, sed eamdem nisi cum pace reipublicae ipsaque pietate tolli non posse.* Hamburg (Amstelod.) (1670.) [n. 2nd ed.]

speaking figuratively." And yet in this pleasant and varied guise they have all the more widespread influence. Bayle certainly had a greater influence upon his age than Spinoza and Leibniz, and Voltaire a greater than Rousseau and a hundred even more formal philosophers.

THEOPHRON: That depends, Philolaus. There is an outer and an inner influence. The former spreads itself far and wide; the latter takes root all the more firmly. I wish that some philosophical and critical man who is no novice would bring out in our day an annotated edition of Spinoza's theologico-political essay.* It would be a useful venture to see what time may have confirmed or refuted in him. In the criticism of the Old Testament writings much, which already stood more soundly in Spinoza, has since been advanced as new discovery, yet less adequately stated. In the matter of tolerance, our [418] states have been disposed to take almost no other direction than that which Spinoza in his day anticipated to the hatred of all. To be sure, everything in this work, as in all his other writings, is put in a severe manner, and much is extreme. He had, for example, only a metaphysical sense of the poetry of the Prophets; and in the whole composition of his works, he is a solitary thinker, to whom the graces of the social world and an ingratiating manner are entirely unknown.

PHILOLAUS: I marvel, Theophron, that you attribute it solely to that. On what subject could a person without healthy principles, an atheist, a pantheist and the like, write so that it would find a reception among reasonable people? He is even said to have attempted a proof of atheism and pantheism! What could be more preposterous?

THEOPHRON: So it was atheism and pantheism, then? But how are both possible in one and the same system? After all,

---

* It has since appeared in translation (Gera 1787) but without the notes which are here wished for. His *Ethics* is annotated. [n. 2nd ed.]

the pantheist has always a God, although he is mistaken about His nature. On the other hand, the atheist, who absolutely denies God, can be neither a pantheist nor a polytheist, unless one trifles with the names. And, moreover, my friend, how can one demonstrate atheism, which is a negation?

PHILOLAUS: Why not, if one found, or thought one had found, a self-contradiction in the nature of God?

THEOPHRON: A self-contradiction in a simple idea, the high-[419] est possible to humanity? I must confess, I do not understand that.

PHILOLAUS: That is exactly why he was a fool, who sought to demonstrate what could not be demonstrated. For our new philosophy says distinctly: "Neither that a God exists, nor that he does not, can be proved. One must believe the former." (B1)

THEOPHRON: Wherefore, I, at least, should think it follows that one or the other must be believed, that we are free to be atheists, deists, or theists according to our belief. But let us not touch on this point just yet.

Spinoza is supposed to have been an atheist, pantheist, or a monstrous hybrid of the two. It grieves me to hear these appellations, which you give to one unknown to you. In philosophy we have passed the times of the honorifics with which Spinoza was still being dubbed by Korthold, Brucker and others. (B2) The first thought himself witty when he perverted the *Benedictus* into a *Maledictus,* and the word "Spinoza" into "spiny thornbush." With others, the usual epithets by means of which they conjure him up out of the realm of spirits are, "insolent, godless, preposterous, shameless, blasphemous, pestilential, execrable." One of the elect has even found the mark of eternal banishment on his face, [420] and others have heard him whine for mercy on his deathbed. I am no Spinozist, and shall never become one, but

I confess, friend Philolaus, that it is intolerable to me that
people in our time still wish to repeat against this departed
and silent sage, the judgments of the past century, that century of most deplorable controversy. Here you have a booklet
of but eight sheets,* in which, moreover, the most part is a
miscellany of comments which you may skip entirely. It is
nothing but the life of Spinoza, very prosaically told, but with
historical accuracy. For one can see that the author was careful about every detail. It is written by an impartial man who
was no Spinozist, but a Lutheran pastor who "takes God to
witness that he has found nothing well grounded in Spinoza's
Tractatus theologico-politicus, nor anything which was in
the least capable of disturbing him in the confession of faith,
wherein he followed the Gospel word, because instead of well-
grounded proofs, one finds therein nothing but pre-determined
conclusions, and what in the Schools are called *petitiones prin-
cipii."* You can surely trust yourself to such a cautious guide,
if you wish to know the man better.**

My affairs call me away now, but we shall soon see each
other again. In case you should like to look into them, I am
also leaving you some of the works of the atheist himself. Unfortunately there are only two small volumes.

PHILOLAUS: I don't understand Theophron. Taking up the
[421] cause of a demonstrator of that sort! And what light
can his biography, written and published by a Lutheran pastor, possibly shed on the matter?

A most unusual man, this Spinoza! Whatever the source of
his ideas, and whatever their nature, there is something con-

* *Life of Spinoza* by Joh. Colerus. Frkf. 1733. [n. 2nd ed.]
** In Heydenreich's *Nature and God* (Leipzig, 1789), Vol. I, there is translated the first part of an essay "La vie et l'esprit de Mr. Benoit de Spinoza."
Although its style is enthusiastic, this *elogium* of one of his friends and ac-
quaintances is yet in accord with Colerus' biography, and is worthy of mention.
[n. 2nd ed.]

sistent about his whole life. (B1) He devotes himself to Jewish philosophy, and then forsakes it in order to get a thorough
knowledge of natural science. The works of Descartes come
into his hands. He reads them with extraordinary avidity, and
later acknowledges that he has drawn from them whatever
philosophical learning he has. So he quietly gives up Judaism
because he believes himself convinced that he can follow its
teachings no further. He is offered an annual stipend of 1000
guilders, if only he will further attend the synagogue. He refuses it, and withdraws quietly into retirement. He is put
under the ban of the synagogue. He answers it, and in his re-
treat learns a craft in order to provide for himself. How different is this conduct from that of unhappy Acosta,* who in
similar circumstances could find no peace until he finally shot
himself. (B2) I wish one could get Spinoza's answer to the
ban from the Portuguese synagogue at Amsterdam. I imagine it
would give us the grounds for his decision very gently and
calmly, for a gentle and calm spirit reigns in this man's life.
[**422**] He makes optical lenses and teaches himself to draw.
The author had a collection of his drawings in his possession,
among which many were of persons who had merely visited
him, and whom he apparently drew from memory. Among
these sketches there was also one of Masaniello in his familiar
fisherman's garb, and Spinoza's landlord testified that this
portrait looked very like Spinoza himself. (B1) An extraordinary notion that, to draw himself as Masaniello! I wish the
picture could be found.

He grinds lenses, then. His friends sell them, and he lives
frugally. Often he sees no one for two or three days at a time.
Many people offer their purses and their help, but he modestly refuses them all and lives on very meager fare. He settles
his accounts quarterly so that he may not spend more than he

---

* See "Uriel. Acostae exemplar humanae vitae" at the back of Limborch's
amica collatio cum Judaeo (Basil, 1740).

has. He is, as he tells the household, a snake which makes a
circle with its tail in its mouth, to signify that nothing remains
over from his annual income. I have seen the symbol under his
portrait and foolishly connected it with his pantheism. (B2)
What a truer philosopher, even than Rousseau, he is in all
this! He wishes to save no more than is necessary to be de-
cently buried. But he also wishes to be a burden to no one, and
to live by his own efforts. His conduct is calm and peaceful.
He is master of his passions, and he is never to be seen either
very sad, or very gay.

In conversation he comforts the sufferers of his house and
[423] counsels them to endure their misfortunes patiently as
the lot God has sent them. He exhorts the children to attend
church diligently, and instructs them to be obedient to their
parents. He asks the household what benefit they have derived
from the sermon they have heard, and sets great store by the
good and edifying clergyman mentioned here.* "Your religion
is good;" says the tranquil sage, "you have no need to seek
another, nor to doubt that you will attain blessedness through
it if only you devote yourselves to godliness, and at the same
time lead a peaceful and calm life."

His best friend offers him a present of two thousand guilders
so that he may live in somewhat greater comfort. He refuses it
courteously. Another wishes to make him his heir, but he does
not accept the benefit. He reduces by almost half the pension
which still another, out of friendship, presses upon him in his
last years. In such wise he lives, and dies in his forty-fifth year
as gently and peaceably as he had lived. Just a few hours before, he had held a long conversation with his household on the
sermon they had heard, and before they left church that after-
noon, he expired in the presence of his physician. After the
sale, his entire estate amounted to 390 guilders and fourteen
stivers.   His relatives wrangled even over that sum.

* A predecessor of the Colerus who wrote his biography.

A benign, philanthropic radiance illumines his whole life. For one sees how his friends love him and how all who know him prize him, how this never makes him unduly proud, and yet he never ungraciously rebuffs anyone. When the Elector Palatine offered him a teaching post at his university, with the [424] freedom to expound his principles in whatever form would best serve his purpose, he circumspectly and modestly answered that he did not know how this freedom should be circumscribed, so that it might not seem as if he wanted to disturb the established religion; so he did not accept the offer. (B1)

I do not yet know what to think of Spinoza's writings and opinions. But even the erroneous passages quoted here, which are probably his worst, paradoxically bear the stamp of the convictions of him who held them. He wishes to force them on no one. He wishes to found no sect, not from fear of men, but from aversion to disturbing the views of other people even after his death. During his life he published nothing but a small tractate with which he thought to make peace. When this effort failed, he lived alone with his philosophy. A few days before his death he burnt a translation of the Old Testament which he had begun, so that it too might not cause strife after his death. I wish that he had not burnt it. For had it possessed no value on its own merits, time would have effaced it in any case.

I shall look at his writings themselves. They appeared after his death, and it would seem that he wrote them for himself, for they are mostly fragments.*

"On the Improvement of the Understanding and the Manner [425] in which a True Knowledge of Things Can Best Be Attained."** (B1)

* B. d. S. *opera posthuma* (Hagae Com.), 1677. [n. 2nd ed.]
** *Tractatus de intellectus emendatione in opp. posth. Spinozae*, p. 356.

After experience had taught me that all the usual surroundings of social life are vain and futile; seeing that none of the objects of my fears contained in themselves anything either good or bad, except in so far as the mind is affected by them, I finally resolved to inquire whether there might be some real good, having power to communicate itself, which would affect the mind singly to the exclusion of all else; whether, in fact, there might be anything of which the discovery and attainment would enable me to enjoy continuous, supreme, and unending happiness. I say "I *finally* resolved," for at first sight it seemed unwise willingly to lose hold of what was sure for the sake of something then uncertain. I could see the benefits which are acquired through fame and riches, and that I should be obliged to abandon the quest of such objects, if I seriously devoted myself to the search for something different and new. I perceived that if true happiness chanced to be placed in the former I should necessarily miss it; while if, on the other hand, it were not so placed, and I gave them my whole attention, I should equally fail.

I therefore debated whether it would not be possible to arrive at the new principle, or at any rate at a certainty concerning its existence, without changing the conduct and usual plan of my life; with this end in view I made many efforts, but in vain. For the ordinary [426] surroundings of life which are esteemed by men (as their actions testify) to be the highest good, may be classed under the three heads—Riches, Fame, and the Pleasures of Sense: with these three the mind is so absorbed that it has little power to reflect on any different good. By sensual pleasure the mind is enthralled to the extent of quiescence, as if the supreme good were actually attained, so that it is quite incapable of thinking of any other object; when such pleasure has been gratified it is followed by extreme melancholy, whereby the mind, though not enthralled, is disturbed and dulled.

The pursuit of honors and riches is likewise very absorbing, especially if such objects be sought simply for their own sake, inasmuch as they are then supposed to constitute the highest good. In the case of fame the mind is still more absorbed, for fame is conceived as always good for its own sake, and as the ultimate end to which all actions are directed. Further, the attainment of riches and fame is not followed as in the case of sensual pleasures by repentance, but, the more we acquire, the greater is our delight, and, consequently, the more are we incited to increase both the one and the other; on the other hand, if our hopes happen to be frustrated we are plunged into the deepest sadness. Fame has the further drawback that it compels its votaries to order their lives according to the opinions of their fellow-men, shunning what they usually shun, and seeking what they usually seek.

When I saw that all these ordinary objects of desire would be obstacles in the way of a search for something different and new— nay, that they were so opposed thereto, that either they or it would have to be abandoned, I was forced to inquire which would prove the most useful to me: for, as I say, I seemed to be willingly losing hold of a sure good for the sake of something uncertain. However, after [**427**] I had reflected on the matter, I came in the first place to the conclusion that by abandoning the ordinary objects of pursuit, and betaking myself to a new quest, I should be leaving a good, uncertain by reason of its own nature, as may be gathered from what has been said, for the sake of a good not uncertain in its nature (for I sought for a fixed good), but only in the possibility of its attainment.

Further reflection convinced me, that if I could really get to the root of the matter, I should be leaving certain evils for a certain good. I thus perceived that I was in a state of great peril, and I compelled myself to seek with all my strength for a remedy, however uncertain it might be; as a sick man struggling with a deadly disease, when he sees that death will surely be upon him unless a remedy be found, is compelled to seek such a remedy with all his strength, inasmuch as his whole hope lies therein. All the objects pursued by the multitude, not only bring no remedy that tends to preserve our being, but even act as hindrances, causing the death not seldom of those who possess them, and always of those who are possessed by them. There are many examples of men who have suffered persecution even to death for the sake of their riches, and of men who in pursuit of wealth have exposed themselves to so many dangers, that they have paid away their life as a penalty for their folly. Examples are no less numerous of men, who have endured the utmost wretchedness for the sake of gaining or preserving their reputation. Lastly, there are innumerable cases of men, who have hastened their death through over-indulgence in sensual pleasure.

All these evils seem to have arisen from the fact that happiness or unhappiness is made wholly to depend on the quality of the object which we love. When a thing is not loved, no quarrels will arise [428] concerning it—no sadness will be felt if it perishes—no envy if it is possessed by another—no fear, no hatred, in short no disturbances of the mind. All these arise from the love of what is perishable, such as the objects already mentioned. But love toward a thing eternal and infinite feeds the mind wholly with joy, and is itself unmingled with any sadness, wherefore it is greatly to be desired and sought for with all our strength. Yet it was not at random that I used the words, "If I could go to the root of the matter," for, though what I have urged was perfectly clear to my mind, I could not forthwith lay aside all love of riches, sensual enjoyment, and fame. One thing was evident, namely, that while my mind was employed with these thoughts it turned away from its former objects of desire, and seriously considered the search for a new principle; this state of things was a great comfort to me, for I perceived that the evils were not such as to resist all remedies. Although these intervals were at first rare, and of very short duration, yet afterwards, as the true good became more and more discernible to me, they became more frequent and more lasting; especially after I had recognized that the acquisition of wealth, sensual pleasure, or fame, is only a hindrance, so long as they are sought as ends not as means; if they be sought as means they will be under restraint, and, far from being hindrances, will further not a little the end for which they are sought, as I will show in due time.

I will here only briefly state what I mean by true good, and also what is the nature of the highest good. In order that this may be rightly understood, we must bear in mind that the terms good and evil are only applied relatively, so that the same thing may be called both good and bad, according to the relations in view, in the same way as it may be called perfect or imperfect. Nothing regarded in [429] its own nature can be called perfect or imperfect; especially when we are aware that all things which come to pass, come to pass according to the eternal order and fixed laws of nature. However, human weakness cannot attain to this order in its own thoughts, but meanwhile man conceives a human character much more stable than his own, and sees that there is no reason why he should not himself acquire such a character. Thus he is led to seek for means which will bring him to this pitch of perfection, and calls everything which will serve as such means a true good. The chief good is that he should arrive, together with other individuals if possible, at the possession of the aforesaid character. What that character is we shall show in due time, namely, that it is the knowledge of the union existing between the mind and the whole of nature. This, then, is the end for which I strive, to attain to such a character myself, and to endeavour that many should attain to it with me. In other words, it is part of my happiness to lend a helping hand that many others may understand even as I do, so that their understanding and desire may entirely agree with my own. In order to bring this about, it is necessary to understand as much of nature as will enable us to attain to the aforesaid character, and also to form a social order such as is most conducive to the attainment of this character by the greatest number with the least difficulty and danger. We must seek the assistance of Moral Philosophy and the Theory of Education; further, as health is no insignificant means for attaining our end, we must also include the whole science of Medicine, and, as many difficult things are by contrivance rendered easy, and we can in this way gain much time and convenience, the science of Mechanics must in no way be despised. But, before all things, a means must be de- [430] vised for improving the understanding and purifying it, as far as may be at the outset, so that it may apprehend things without error, and in the best possible way.

Thus it is apparent to every one that I wish to direct all sciences to one end and aim, so that we may attain to the supreme human perfection which we have named; and, therefore, whatsoever in the sciences does not serve to promote our object will have to be rejected as useless. To sum up the matter in a word, all our actions and thoughts must be directed to this one end. Yet, as it is necessary that while we are endeavoring to attain our purpose and bring the understanding into the right path, we should carry on our life, we are compelled first of all to lay down certain rules of life as provisionally good, to wit, the following:

I. To speak in a manner intelligible to the multitude, and to comply with every general custom that does not hinder the attainment of our purpose. For we can gain from the multitude no small advantages, provided that we strive to accommodate ourselves to its understanding as far as possible: moreover, we shall in this way gain a friendly audience for the reception of the truth.

II. To indulge ourselves with pleasures only in so far as they are necessary for preserving health.

III. Lastly, to endeavor to obtain only sufficient money or other commodities to enable us to preserve our life and health, and to follow such general customs as are consistent with our purpose.

Am I dreaming, or have I really been reading? I thought that I should find an insolent atheist, and here I discover virtually a metaphysical and moral enthusiast. What an ideal of humanity, of science, and of the knowledge of nature, there is in his soul! And he approaches it with such a considered, deliberate pace and style as few have who enter the cloister to transform their lives. This essay plainly belongs to the [431] man's younger years, when he left Judaism and chose his philosophical way of life.* He followed this way until the end of his days. What did he achieve in it? But look, here comes Theophron.

THEOPHRON: Still busy? Philolaus, you did not foretell the weather entirely correctly. Your Spinozistic rain clouds have rained themselves out and caused a spell of cold, which one should not have expected from your analogy.

PHILOLAUS: Forget my analogy, and give me this volume to take with me. I see that I have been mistaken about Spinoza. What do you think I should read first?

THEOPHRON: First and almost exclusively his *Ethics*. What remains is fragmentary, and the *Tractatus theologico-politicus* was merely a tract for the times. But take a few rules with you on your journey.

I. Before you read Spinoza, you must necessarily read Des-

* The editor's Foreword mentions this and asks pardon, "if much in the essay seems obscure and crude; the essay is not finished." [n. 2nd ed.]

cartes, if only as a dictionary. (B1) In the latter, you will see the source of Spinoza's words and thoughts, and also the [432] source of his extraordinary, difficult expressions. For this purpose, use either of the main works of Descartes or an exposition by any of his disciples.* Among the latter Clauberg especially renders the Cartesian doctrines very clearly and methodically. (B1) You will find them together here in a single volume. Then go on to the "Principles of Descartes' Philosophy" by Spinoza himself, which he drew up for one of his students.** In it you will find the transition to his own system. One should learn about a tree from its beginning, not only in its parts, but also in the conditions of its origin and growth, even though it is known to be a poisonous Upas tree. (B2) For if you read this philosopher of the last century in the language of contemporary philosophy, then he must needs appear a monster to you.

II. Pay very careful attention to his geometrical method. Do not allow yourself to be misled by it, but notice also where it misleads him. He took it from Descartes, only he made the [433] bolder attempt of applying this form to everything, even to the most involved moral matters, and just this attempt should have warned his followers in the geometrical method of metaphysics.

III. Never confine yourself to him, but rather at every one of his paradoxical statements call modern philosophy to your aid, so that you ask yourself how the latter cleared up this or a similar statement, or expressed it more easily, more hap-

* Des-Cartes opp. Philosoph. Amstelod. 1685. Regii philos. natural. Amst. 1654. Raaei clav. philos. nat. Lugd. 1654. Clauberg's Phys. Metaphys. etc. [n. 1st ed.] [1]

[1] "In Cartesio displicet," says Leibniz, "audacia et fastus nimius coniunctus cum styli obscuritate, confusione, maledicentia. Longe magis mihi probatur Claubergius, discipulus eius, planus, perspicuus, brevis, methodicus." Leibniz. Otium Hannoveran. ed. Fellerus. p. 181. [n. 2nd ed.]

** Amstel. 1663. [n. 1st ed.] [1]

[1] "Quem ego cuidam iuveni, quem meas opiniones aperte docere nolebam, antehac dictaveram" says Spinoza in his ninth [olim] letter. p. 423. [n. 2nd. ed.]

pily and less objectionably. It will immediately strike you
why their author could not have expressed them equally felici-
tously, and you will perceive both the source of his error, and
the progressive advance of the truth. For this purpose use
his few letters* side by side with his *Ethics*. In many places
they are very illuminating. In the margin of my copy you will
find references to the *Ethics* written by an old hand, and in
the *Ethics* references back to them. If these letters served
no other purpose, they would show how very much in earnest
Spinoza was about his philosophy, how completely he was
convinced by it, and how happy he felt himself in it.

When you have finished this task, and if you are so inclined,
we shall discuss your doubts or his errors further. I hope you
will not regret the trouble, for a demonstrator of atheism, as
you and others consider this author, is at any rate worth the
effort of an analysis.

PHILOLAUS: I shall follow your advice, although it asks
[**434**] much of me.

THEOPHRON: An ode has just come into my hands, which I
want to share with you. It is addressed to God and it too is
written by an atheist.

PHILOLAUS: By Spinoza?

THEOPHRON: No, for he was no poet, but by an atheist who
was actually burnt for his atheism. (B1)

PHILOLAUS: And wrote an ode to God? I shall read it.

Deo**

Dei supremo percita flamine
mentem voluntas exstimulat meam;
hinc per negatum tentat alta
Daedaliis iter ire ceris;

* Opp. posth. p. 395. seq.
** Inasmuch as this ode has since been euphoniously translated in Kosegarten's
Poesien, Vol. 1, p. 35) this translation is here set down. [n. 2nd ed. the
German text appeared as a footnote in that edition.]

Audetque coeli non memorabile
metare Numen principio carens
et fine, diffinire Musae
    exiguae breviore gyro.

[435]   Origo rerum et terminus omnium,
origo, fons et principium sui
suique finis terminusque
    principio sine terminoque.

Ubique Totus, tempore in omnibus
omni quiescens ipse Deus locis,
partes in omnes distributus
    integer usque, manens ubique.

Nec comprehensum ullis regionibus
ullisve clausum limitibus loca
tenent, sed omnis liber omne
    diditus in spatium vagatur.

Illius alta est velle potentia,
opus voluntas invariabilis;
et magnus absque est quantitate
    atque bonus sine qualitate.

Quod dicit, uno tempore perficit;
mirere, fiat vox vel opus prius?
cum dixit, en cum voce cuncta
    universa simul creata.

[436]   Cuncta intuetur, perspicit omnia
atque in sua unus, solus est omnia,
quae sunt, fuerunt et futura
    praevidet ipse perennitate.

Atque ipse plenus cuncta replet sui
et semper idem sustinet omnia
et fert movetque amplectiturque
    atque supercilio gubernat.

Te Te oro, tandem respice me bonus,
Tibique nodo iunge adamantino:
id namque solum unumque et omne
    reddere quod potis est beatos.

Quicunque iunxit Te sibi et altius
Uni adhaerescit, continet omnia
Teque omnibus circumfluentem
    divitiis nihilique egentem.

Tu, cum necesse est, nullibi deficis
ultroque praebes omnibus omnia
ipsumque Te qui sis futurus;
    omnibus omnia subministras.

[437]   Laboriosis Tu vigor inclitus,
Tu portus alto navifragantibus,
Tu fons perennis perstrepentes
    qui latices salientis ardent.

Tu summa nostris pectoribus quies,
tranquillitasque et pax placidissima,
Tu mensus es rerum modusque,
    Tu species et amata forma.

Tu meta, pondus, Tu numerus, decor
Tuque ordo, Tu par atque honor atque amor
cunctis, salusque et vita et aucta
    nectare et ambrosia voluptas.

Tu verus altae fons sapientiae,
Tu vera lux, Tu lex venerabilis,
Tu certa spes, Tuque aeviterna
    et ratio et via veritasque;

Decus iubarque et lumen amabile
et lumen almum atque inviolabile;
Tu summa summarum, quid ultra?
    Maximus, optimus, unus, idem.

SECOND CONVERSATION

PHILOLAUS: Here I am with my Spinoza, but almost more [438] in the dark than I was before. It is plain on every page that he is no atheist. For him the idea of God is the first and last, yes, I might even say the only idea of all, for on it he bases knowledge of the world and of nature, consciousness of self and of all things around him, his ethics and his politics. Without the idea of God, his mind has no power, not even to conceive of itself. For him it is well nigh inconceivable, how men can, as it were, turn God into a mere consequence of other truths, or even of sensuous perceptions, since all truth, like all existence, follows only from eternal truth, from the eternal, infinite existence of God.* This conception became so present, [439] so immediate and intimate to him, that I certainly would rather have taken him to be an enthusiast concerning the existence of God, than a doubter or denier of it. He places all mankind's perfection, virtue and blessedness in the knowledge and love of God. And that this is not some sort of mask

---

* v. *Ethic* p. 49. schol. et epist. 21, 39, 40, 49, etc.[1]

[1] "Everyone must admit that without God nothing can be nor can be conceived; for everyone admits that God is the sole cause both of the essence and of the existence of all things. . . But many people say that that pertains to the essence of a thing without which a thing can neither be nor can be conceived, and they therefore believe either that the nature of God belongs to the essence of created things, or that created things can be or can be conceived without God; or which is more probable, there is no consistency in their thought. I believe that the cause of this confusion is that they have not observed a proper order of philosophic study. For although the divine nature ought to be studied first because it is first in the order of knowledge and in the order of things, they think it last; while, on the other hand, those things which are called (the) objects of the senses are believed to stand before everything else. Hence it has come to pass that there was nothing of which men thought less than the divine nature while they have been studying natural objects, and when they afterwards applied themselves to think about God, there was nothing of which they could think less than those prior fictions upon which they had built their knowledge of natural things, for these fictions could in no way help to the knowledge of the divine nature." [Eth. Bk. II Prop X. Schol: Hale White trans:] [n. 2nd ed.]

which he has assumed, but rather his deepest feeling, is shown by his letters, yes, I might even say, by every part of his philosophical system, by every line of his writings. Spinoza may have erred in a thousand ways about the idea of God, but how readers of his works could ever say that he denied the idea of God and proved atheism, is incomprehensible to me.

THEOPHRON: I am glad my friend, that you have found the same thing that I found. For I too scarcely trusted myself when I read this author and compared my impression with what others had said of him. This feeling was the more intense for me, since I did not read him as a novice in philosophy, nor with some subsidiary interest in mind, but entirely dispassionately, and if anything, with hostile prejudice, after I had not only read but studied the works of Baumgarten (B1), Leibniz, Shaftesbury, and Berkeley, in addition to the ancient philosophers. However, let us not linger in this astonishment which will clear up of itself when we examine his system. What criticisms have you to make of it?

PHILOLAUS: Where shall I begin? Where end? The whole system is a paradox to me. "There is but one Substance, and that is God. All things are but modifications of it."

THEOPHRON: Do not be mistaken about the word "Sub-[440] stance." Spinoza took it in its purest meaning, and had to take it in that way if he wanted to proceed geometrically and set down a primitive notion as a basis. What is Substance but a thing which is self-dependent, which has the cause of its existence in itself? I wish that this pure meaning of the word could have been introduced into our philosophy. In the strictest sense, nothing in the world is a Substance, because everything depends on everything else, and finally on God, who therefore is the highest and only Substance. This geometrical conception could not have become generally adopted in a philosophy which must preserve its popular character, for we, in all our dependence yet consider ourselves independent, and in a certain sense, as we shall soon see, we may so consider ourselves.

PHILOLAUS: But we are not mere modifications, are we?

THEOPHRON: The word offends us and will therefore never [441] win a place in our philosophy. However, if the Leibnizian school dared to call matter an "appearance of substances," why should not Spinoza be allowed his more drastic expression? The substances of the world are all maintained by divine power, just as they derived their existence from it alone. Therefore they constitute, if you will, appearances of divine powers, each modified according to the place, the time, and the organs in, and with which, they appear. In his single Substance, Spinoza thus employed a short formula which certainly gives his system much coherence, but which sounds strange to our ears. Nevertheless, it was better than the "occasional causes" of the Cartesians, from whom Spinoza started, and according to whom God is supposed to effect all things, but only on occasion. A far more awkward expression, yet how long it was current! Even the Leibnizian philosophy could only do away with it by means of another hypothesis, which indeed sounds more pleasant, but which also has its difficulties. It is the "pre-established harmony of all things," which we shall soon discuss.

You see, my friend, there is no heresy in any of these expressions. One is merely more awkward than another, and at bot- [442] tom we understand equally little by any of them. We do not know what power is, or how power works. Still less do we know how the Divine Power has produced anything, and how it imparts itself to everything according to its nature. (A1) However, that all things must depend upon one self-dependent nature, in their existence, their relationships, as well as in every expression of their powers, no consistent mind can doubt. What are you smiling at, Philolaus?

PHILOLAUS: I see so many pathetic declamations against

Spinoza, which quarrelled with nothing but his names "single Substance" and "modifications," suddenly dwindling to nothing. They were all fighting merely with a fog of troublesome words. You know, Theophron, what a host of ridiculous contradictions and blasphemies were imputed to him, as for example that, according to his system, God had to do all the evil as well as the good in the world; that He had to commit all follies, think all errors, to fight against Himself, and in the person of Spinoza, to blaspheme and deny Himself, and so on. What is true of Spinoza's "modifications," is true of Descarte's "occasional causes," of Leibniz's "pre-established harmony," yes, and no less true of the *influxus physicus*. If [**443**] these things happen in God's world, they happen through the use and misuse of His powers, that is to say, the powers which He created in dependent beings and which He maintains in them. His providence or His concurrent activity may be conceived in one way or another. In general I have found that if one sets forth the meaning of a man too absurdly and preposterously, one usually does an injustice, or pronounces some absurdity oneself. Such formulas, indeed, give one an easy victory over the most difficult matters. It is, however, only the semblance of a victory.

THEOPHRON: Then you will also find it no blasphemy, when Spinoza calls the Independent Being the immanent and not the transitive cause of all things?*

PHILOLAUS: How could I find it so, when, on the contrary, it is impossible to think of God as a transitive cause of things?

---

* Prop. 18 compared with Ep. 21. "Like Paul, and perhaps also like all ancient philosophers, though in another way, I assert that all things live and move in God; and I would dare to say that I agree also with all the ancient Hebrews as far as it is possible to surmise from their traditions, even if these have become corrupt in many ways. However, those who think that the *Tractatus theologico-politicus* rests on this, namely, that God and nature (by which they mean a certain Mass or corporal matter) are one and the same, are entirely mistaken." *Opp. posth.* p. 499 [Epist. LXXIII. Wolf trans.].

How and when and to what is He transitive? A creature without His support is nothing, and how can He be transitive who
has no place, leaves no place, in whom there can be no change
nor alteration?

THEOPHRON: But what if God dwells out of the world?

PHILOLAUS: Where is there a place out of the world? The
[**444**] world itself, and space and time therein, the sole means
by which we measure and count things, all exist only through
Him, the Infinite One.

THEOPHRON: Excellent, Philolaus. For then neither will you
wander in that labyrinth of questions, asking:

> How lonely God erst spent Eternity in thought?
> Why Now a world He made and not Before?

Or:

> . . . . How the vast round
> Of Birthless Time was checked upon its course?
> How came that Timeless changed to Time,
> That once again must lose its tide in Timeless Sea?

PHILOLAUS: Nor shall I add:

> That this is not for me to comprehend, nor ask,
> Such speculations may my foes alone disturb.   (B1)

For I would not wish even upon my enemy such a phantom
of the imagination as a fathomless object of knowledge. God
spent no "Eternity" in solitary thought. There was no "now"
and no "before" before there was a world. God's eternity is
not a "birthless time" and there is no "course" in it. The
eternal can as little become time, as time become eternity, or
the finite become the infinite.

THEOPHRON: You have not learned that for the first time
from Spinoza, have you?

PHILOLAUS: On the contrary, it pleased me that he passed
straight over the usual wholly unphilosophical confusions on
this matter, and rightly distinguished between time and eter-

[**445**] nity, between the indefinitely unending and the infinite-in-itself. (A1)* The eternity of God (A2) cannot be defined in terms of any duration or time, even though one assumes the latter to be without limit (*indefinite*). Duration is an indefinite prolongation of existence, but at every point it carries with it a measure of transitoriness. Thus it can in no way be ascribed to the intransitive and completely changeless.

THEOPHRON: Then it follows also that the world is not eternal like God?

PHILOLAUS: It cannot be because it is a world, that is, a system of things ordered in, and according to time, and to none of which absolute existence or immutable eternity without measure and duration of time ever accrues.

THEOPHRON: Then it does not cause you any confusion in [**446**] ideas, that the eternal power of God created, and yet, none of His creatures acquired His eternity, not even in their totality as a system?

PHILOLAUS: The eternal power of God created necessarily (B1) because it could never be inactive. But no created thing is eternal like God. For its existence depends upon a sequence, and like everything of its kind, has a temporal measure of change in it. Thus, too, a continuous creation of the world, though it be prolonged forever, will never become eternal through that prolongation. Its measure is endless, but in our minds it is nevertheless a measure.

I understand all that easily, but I have another question on my mind, which I could wish answered. It concerns the attri-

---

* v. *Epist.* 29.[1]

[1] ". . . . Measure, Time and Number are nothing but modes of thought or rather of imagination. Therefore it is not to be wondered at that all who have tried to understand the course of Nature by such Notions, and these moreover, ill understood, should have so marvelously entangled themselves . . . . For since there are many things which we cannot grasp with the imagination, but only with the intellect, such as Substance, Eternity and others—if anyone tries to explain such things by Notions of this kind, which are merely aids to the imagination, he does nothing more than take pains to rave with his imagination." *Opp. posth.* p. 468. [n. 2nd ed. Hale White trans.]

butes of this infinite eternal God of Spinoza. How can he who
so rightly distinguished between time and eternity, be on the
other hand so loose as to make "extension an attribute of God?"
He cannot often and strongly enough say: "God is an extensum." Yet what applies to time applies equally to space, and
if time be entirely incomparable with the idea of eternity,
then space is equally incommensurable with the idea of a
"simple Substance," which Spinoza however insists upon with
rock-like firmness.*

THEOPHRON: What you say is very true. But if you note
[**447**] where Spinoza propounds this error, the reason for it
will be immediately obvious.

PHILOLAUS: He propounds it when he distinguishes spirit
from matter, that is, thought from extension.**

THEOPHRON: Are matter and extension then the same?
There you see the Cartesian error from which the philosopher
could not free himself, and which makes half of his system
obscure. Descartes defined matter in terms of extension. It
could just as well be defined in terms of time, for both the one
and the other are external conditions of its existence in spatial
and temporal relations. Thus both become also the necessary
conditions of measurement for all thinking minds, which are
themselves limited by place and time, but they never become
the essence of matter. (A1) (B1)

Spinoza struggled for a long time against this Cartesian
explanation, probably because he felt that something about
[**448**] it was not clear. He was not satisfied with his teacher's
sharp distinction between matter and spirit, but, since he
lacked a unifying intermediate conception, what could he do?
Unfortunately then, in his *Ethics* he still took matter for

* No attribute of substance can be truly conceived from which it follows
that substance can be divided. Bk. 1. Prop. XII. Substance absolutely infinite
is indivisible. Bk. 1. Prop. XIII. [n. 2nd ed.]
** *Ethic* P. II. In the second part of the *Ethics, de mente.* [n. 2nd ed.]

extension, that is space, and set it up beside thought, an entirely different kind of thing. Now he was indeed on the way to a very intricate confusion. For tell me, my friend, what have thought and extension to do with each other? And how can just these two, out of an infinity of other attributes whose totality is supposed to express a supreme reality, be the only two attributes through which the Infinite has revealed Himself? What sort of reality is there in extension even if you take it to be endless, that is to say, indefinitely continued like an everlasting duration? Without essence, without active forces, extension is empty. It is only the condition of a world, of a co-existence of various creatures. It does not appertain to the absolutely Infinite, to the Creator, any more than it expresses any of the inner essential perfection of His existence which occupies no space, not even an endless space, and which endures in no time, not even an endless time.

PHILOLAUS: (A1) There, my dear Theophron, you take a [449] weight from my heart, for this infinitely extended God of Spinoza was wholly unthinkable to me, besides seeming unworthy of a geometrical philosopher. I saw very well how he wished to escape the divisibility of this infinitely extended and yet simple being by means of the notion of mathematical space, since one cannot get physical bodies out of mathematical lines and surfaces. But since mathematical space is only an abstraction of the imagination, that is to say a condition of the truths which cannot be thought of save in space, it still gives no solution when regarded as an attribute of God through which physical bodies should be explained. I wish Spinoza had escaped this error which now seems to me to be the weakest point in his otherwise well-reasoned system.

THEOPHRON: Do not blame him for that. Truth quietly [450] marches on. Spinoza's times were the childhood of natural science, without which metaphysics only builds castles in the air or gropes about in the dark. The more corporeal matter was physically investigated, the more active or interactive forces were discovered in it, and the empty concept of extension was abandoned. Leibniz, in whose mind were assembled fruitful ideas from every province of nature and the sciences, even in his time insisted that in the conception of bodies too, it was necessary in the end to come to simple substances, about which he had so much to say under the name of monads. Since this man's active mind so readily conceived everything in a hypothetical manner and expressed it half-poetically, his monads, which Wolff himself does not seem to have understood rightly, were soon regarded as a clever fiction. Yet I am convinced that of the three significant hypotheses with which he enriched metaphysics (B1), this is the soundest, and will certainly be duly recognized sometime. Boscowich, (B2) though from an entirely different angle, arrived at exactly the same indivisible active elements without which the [451] nature of matter cannot be explained even physically.* Do you now know what the intermediate conception between spirit and matter is, which, in order to escape the Cartesian dualism, Spinoza sought in vain? (A1)

PHILOLAUS: Substantial forces. (A2) Nothing is plainer than this, and nothing gives the Spinozistic system itself a more beautiful unity. If his Deity comprises within Himself infinite attributes each of which expresses an eternal and an infinite essence, then we no longer have to assert two attributes of thought and extension which have nothing in common. We dispense with that offensive and inappropriate word "attribute" entirely and replace it with the doctrine: *"That the Deity reveals Himself in an infinite number of forces in an infinite number of ways."*

* Boscowich, *Philosophiae natur. theoria redacta ad unicam legem virium in natura exsistentium.* Vienna, 1760.

Immediately that difficult barrier to his system is also lifted, namely the question, "In what attributes other than thought and extension, does the Deity of other universes reveal Himself?" For according to our philosopher, God is supposed to possess an infinity of similar attributes which express His essence, and of which he could only name us these two. In all universes He reveals Himself through forces. Furthermore [452] this infinity of forces in God which expresses His essence, has no limits whatever, although it reveals the same God everywhere. Thus, we must not enviously inquire of any other universe how the Deity has revealed Himself in it. Everywhere it is the same as here. Everywhere organic forces alone can be active, and every one of them makes attributes of an infinite God known to us. (A1)

You see, my friend, what a fine inference as to the inner unity of the world follows from this. The world is not held together by space and time alone as if by external conditions, but much more intimately by its very essence, by the principle of its own existence, since everywhere only organic forces may be at work in it. In the world which we know, the power of thought stands highest, but it is followed by millions of other [453] powers of feeling and activity, and He, the Self-dependent, is Power in the highest and only sense of the word, that is, the primal Force of all forces, the Soul of all souls. Without Him none of them came into being, without Him none are active, and all in their innermost connection express in every limitation, form, and appearance, His self-dependent nature, through which they all exist and work.

THEOPHRON: It makes me happy, Philolaus, that you understand this idea so clearly and make such rich use of it. You have thereby already almost molded our philosopher's system into a faultless unity which it lacked before. But do you not perceive still other consequences following from this conception intermediate between mind and body, namely the conception of substantial organic forces?

PHILOLAUS: A whole set of others. For example, there is an end to all the objectionable expressions of how God, according to this or that system, may work on and through dead matter. It is not dead, but lives. For in it and conforming to its outer and inner organs, a thousand living, manifold forces are at work. The more we learn about matter, the more forces we discover in it, so that the empty conception of a dead extension completely disappears. Just in recent times, what numerous and different forces have been discovered in the atmosphere! [454] How many different forces of attraction, union, dissolution and repulsion, has not modern chemistry already found in all bodies? Before the magnetic, and the electrical forces were discovered, who would have suspected their existence in bodies, and what countless others may still lie dormant and undetected in them? It is a pity that such a thinker as Spinoza had to leave our stage so soon. He could not live to see the enormous progress of science which would also have improved his system.

THEOPHRON: We too must depart my friend, and shall not live to see what is reserved for questing posterity. It is enough if we now, so long as we are here, apprehend the presence and activity of the Deity where and however He reveals Himself to us. Spinoza says that every attribute, or as we called it every force of God revealed in creation, expresses an infinite. What do you make of that, since every part of the world has its limits, not only in time and place, but also by reason of its inherent natural or divine energies?

PHILOLAUS: Are not space and time infinite? What an uncountable multitude of divine forces and forms can thus reveal itself in them! And since no two phenomena can be alike in time and place, what an infinity springs from this ever-new and ever-renewed source of divine beauty! Look out into the

[**455**] heavens at those galaxies of suns and worlds. Even now the Columbus of our nation is perhaps discovering with his telescope new hosts of them in one tiny cloud of mist invisible to our eyes. (B1) In what remarkable times we live, when hitherto unheard-of, unbelieved revelations of God come down to us from heaven, every one of them expressing anew the majestic glory of the Primal Being who created and sustains all these worlds.

> The One and the Eternal Infinite
> In Infinity resides, in Being
> And in Act, Sustaining and Creating,
> Ever One and Same and Infinite.
> Like timeless columns stand the laws He thought,
> Fixed as the thought. Change issues from their plan,
> Omnipotence within them rests. . . . . . *

THEOPHRON: Excellent, my good Philolaus, and in that last passage you have also suggested the infinity that lies intrinsically in every force of nature, even without regard to its connections in an endless time and space. Think of the inner abundance of force which shows itself in every living thing, how it came into existence through an enormous activity implanted in it, and how it could not maintain and reproduce itself otherwise than through such a force. Consider the forces which work so secretly in the structure of an animal! With what strength its parts hang together! What a mechanism of wheels and springs it needs to move, to prepare its vital secretions, to perform all the functions for which it is determined, and finally to bring forth and generate its own kind, living [**456**] and active images of itself issuing from its own nature through its own power and condition. In generation itself there lies the marvel of an implanted, indwelling power of the Deity who, if I may speak so boldly, has limited Himself, as it were, in

* From August Henning's *Philosophische Versuche* (Copenhagen, 1780).

the natural constitution of every organism, and in this nature, works according to eternal laws, constant and immutable as Deity alone can work. In what we call dead matter there converge at every point, no fewer and no lesser divine forces. We are surrounded by omnipotence. We swim in an ocean of omnipotence, so that the old metaphor still remains true: "God is a circle whose center is everywhere, whose circumference is nowhere," because neither in space nor in time, as in mere figures of the imagination, does the imagination find an end anywhere. Thus it seems to me that Spinoza's expression that: "Time is only a symbolical image of eternity" is a very happy one. I wish with you, that he had considered space similarly as against the absolute infinity of the indivisible. The essence of the eternal is not immeasurable for us alone. By its very nature it is impossible to measure. In every point of its activity which is a point only for us, it carries all its infinity in itself.

PHILOLAUS: I am afraid, my friend, that few will understand this distinction between the infinite-in-itself and the endless [457] conceived in the imagination in terms of time and space, a distinction which is yet true and necessary. (A1) As limited beings we swim in space and time. We count and measure everything by them, and rise with difficulty from figures of the imagination to the pure idea which excludes all spatial and temporal measure. If this distinction had been understood, there would certainly not have been so much said of the mundane and extra-mundane God. Still less would Spinoza have ever been accused of enclosing his God within the world and identifying Him with it. His infinite and most real Being is no more the world itself than the infinite of reason is the same as the endless of the imagination. And thus, no part of the world can also be a part of God, because the simple highest Essence has no parts whatsoever. I now see clearly that our philosopher has been as unjustly accused of pantheism as of atheism. (B1)

All things, he says, are modifications, or as we would put it less objectionably, expressions of divine force, products of an immanent eternal activity of God in the world. But they are not separable parts of an entirely indivisible, single Being.

THEOPHRON: However we do not wish to deny, Philolaus, that many of Spinoza's difficult expressions afforded an opportunity for misunderstandings of that sort to his opponents who confined themselves to only a few of his words, and had [458] no desire to explain these by others of his clearest principles. He had conceived his system too loftily, and in addition based it on an unusual meaning of the word "Substance." Then since he could not lift himself above the Cartesian fog that matter is only extension, he had to elect abstruse expressions in almost half of his system. However one should not have charged him with the error of having confused the nature of God and the world. Many of his theorems are so awkward for the very reason that he continually wants to distinguish God from the world, and he cannot often enough repeat the expression: "God regarded under such a mode, under such an attribute." (A1) If he had chosen the conception of force and activity, then everything would have been easier for him, and his system would have been much more clear and unified. But this easier unity of philosophical truths was only developed gradually, and Leibniz, that Proteus of science, a mind more apt in synthesis than a million others, has the honor of having contributed much to this easier unity, after so many awkward ways of representing it in Descartes, Spinoza, Hobbes and others.

A happy facility in forming manifold combinations it seems to me, was Leibniz's shining talent. In his most insignificant [459] passages he often sowed seeds which were by no means all cultivated, much less brought to a full harvest, by his follower Wolff who resembled him so little. He himself lacked the time to exhaust his own riches because he spread his genius over too many things, and death at last overtook him.

PHILOLAUS: With this observation, dear Theophron, you anticipate a similar one which I wanted to make earlier when you referred me to the intermediate conception between spirit and matter, that of substantial forces. After the crude expressions of Descartes, Spinoza, Hobbes and others who attributed to matter either everything or nothing, that is to say mere extension, you ascribed to our German philosopher the honor of being the first to introduce into metaphysics the ground of its appearances, immaterial substances. Then what of his very ingenious but, it seems to me, very strained hypothesis of the pre-established harmony between thought and matter, which work like two clocks in agreement, though entirely independent of one another? Was it necessary after the introduction of the former hypothesis? (B1) For there too, matter was animated by immaterial forces, and every higher [460] kind of immaterial force could work in it. Thus his own system confirmed the so-called *influxus physicus* which nature shows us everywhere and against which no arbitrary hypothesis is effective. The whole of God's world becomes a realm of immaterial forces in which none is unrelated to others, because it is only by reason of the relationship and reciprocal activity between them all that the appearances and changes of the world come about. And with what little sacrifice could Leibniz have taken this step! For his pre-established harmony was in fact already in Cartesianism (as one of its errors), and Spinoza, Geulinx (B1) and others founded their whole division of spirits and bodies on it. Thus he was not truly the discoverer of this hypothesis at all, or at most, it was such an easy discovery for him that he could well have sacrificed it for his own more beautiful truth.

THEOPHRON: And it was just this proximity to Cartesianism, my friend, that hindered him in using his better explanation, for it is the fate of even the most fruitful human mind, that it is encompassed by place and time and so to speak, is reared in certain ideas, from which it can free itself only with difficulty.

Spiritually Leibniz lived the most flourishing years of his philosophical life in France more than in Germany. It was there that he had so many connections, and from there that the light of his keen mind first shone over Europe. Because in France Descartes and Malebranche were most famous, whether [461] they were being defended or attacked, it was to this field of honor that his attention was primarily drawn. He thus framed his hypothesis of pre-established harmony with such ingenuity that it seemed new and capable of making the occasional causes of Descartes as well as Malebranche's direct influence of God entirely superfluous, although it was itself built upon the defective doctrine of the former philosopher. Leibniz liked to adapt himself to the comprehension of others, and it was in this way that he invented his most ingenious hypotheses.* When later, through the doctrine of the "Monadology" he pointed out an entirely different direction in the metaphysics of matter, he let stand the older hypothesis which had become well-known and had contributed much to his fame, because to a certain extent it could still be defended in conjunction with this new hypothesis. Though there no longer remained any pre-established harmony between spirit and body but rather a harmony between forces and forces, there was nevertheless still a harmony. For who could, and who indeed can now, explain how force works upon force?

---

* In schedis gallicis de systemate harmoniae praestabilitae agentibus, animam tantum, ut substantiam, non ut simul corporis Entelechiam consideravi, quia hoc ad rem, quam tunc agebam, ad explicandum nimirum consensum inter corpus et mentem non pertinebat; neque aliud a Cartesianis desiderabatur. Opp. Leibniz. T. II. P. 1, p. 269. [n. 2nd ed.]

PHILOLAUS: You rescue your honored philosopher very nicely! Permit me to say, however, that in all of Spinoza, in [462] whom there is enough difficulty in any case, I find nothing so strained as this very pre-established harmony, which he too used as a starting point. (A1) (B1)

THEOPHRON: Are you not aware, Philolaus, that there is much art in attaining an easy victory over difficult matters, [463] that is, in the rare gift of giving a facile exposition to highly involved matters and exercising a pleasant deception with it? So Columbus stood his egg on end, so Leibniz formed this hypothesis, and so many another hypothesis is formed.

PHILOLAUS: These are arts the like of which I do not want in philosophy even though they come from the most ingenious mind. The course of nature should be followed honestly.

THEOPHRON: Honestly, but also warily, for nature is as rich as it is simple. What Leibniz could not do (for he wrote no metaphysical system), others will do, and many attempts have already been made. Philosophy never stands still, as some wrongly believe, and even though it does rest for a time, then this apparent halt is certainly to its advantage. Physics and natural history are meanwhile progressing with mighty steps and, since speculative philosophy is only metaphysics, that is, [464] an after-physics, it will always be rewarding to the human mind if philosophy does not press on ahead of it as it has done for centuries and, unfortunately, was forced to . . . . .

PHILOLAUS: But since Descartes' time, it has sought to follow the purest and most exact science, mathematics.

THEOPHRON: It did follow mathematics, and has learned from its guidance all that the latter could teach it; definiteness in ideas and exactness in proof and organization. But if ideas are once arbitrarily assumed or defectively abstracted, then no mathematically pure exposition of them in the best methodical order is of avail. The proofs become sophistry, and the strict formalism itself can become a hindrance to the truth. We saw this happen in Spinoza. The one arbitrarily assumed conception of matter necessitated a host of other arbitrary definitions of attributes, modes, space, body and so on, which the mathematical method could not remedy. (A1) In criticism there is a test which says that what is nonsense in prose must also be nonsense in poetry. So, too, crude expressions which give [465] offense in free prose, cannot be vindicated through geometrical form alone. Instead it is vexing to see such doctrines proved, and one has to take one's bearings. . . .

PHILOLAUS: A deceitful kind of philosophy that, in which one has to take one's bearings! For philosophy itself, in its very method, should orientate us. It is sufficient however that Spinoza is neither an atheist nor a pantheist. There still remains a third hard knot in him for me.

THEOPHRON: I can easily see what it is. But what if we found the most precious coin enclosed in this hard knot?

PHILOLAUS: It would make me very happy, and I should welcome all the trouble of undoing it. But who, my friend is the author of the scholastic ode which you recently gave me?

THEOPHRON: An atheist who was burnt at the stake, Vanini. When he was even at the place of execution, he took up a straw and said that if he were so unfortunate as to have no other proof of the existence of God than this straw, then it would be enough for him.

PHILOLAUS: And he was burnt nevertheless? Perhaps it was for some other heresy?

THEOPHRON: He was a vain young man of many abilities and with a great passion for glory. He wanted to become a [466] Julius Caesar in philosophy, (B1) and became its tragic victim. How do you like his ode?

PHILOLAUS: For Vanini's times it pleases me very well. The expression is in the Latin of that day, and the theory of the Highest Being is scholastic. But the second part of the poem is very sincere and from the heart. The poet is so absorbed in his theme that he summons up all the wealth of his language in order to represent to us the One without whom we are nothing, but through whom we are all that we are, and can, and do.

THEOPHRON: Then perhaps this page of Oriental maxims on the Highest Being will not displease you either. They are thought and expressed in the spirit of the Oriental languages, and cannot be read except in that spirit. Tomorrow we shall continue our discussion of Spinoza.

GOD

SOME SAYINGS OF THE ORIENTALS

In Him we live and move and have our being. We are His offspring
                    Paul (B1)

_____

All comes from Him, all lives in Him, all ends in Him.
Glory be to Him in all Eternity.
                    Paul (B2)

_____

Though we speak many words, still we shall not exhaust it.
[467] He is the essence of all thoughts, the All.
                    Sirach (B3)

_____

He alone has a right to say "I." He, whose realm is eternal and whose wish is sufficient unto itself. Whoe'er besides Him says "I" is a devil.

_____

The qualities of creatures are all two-fold, for as they on the one hand have power, so on the other have they weakness. If superabundance be found in a thing, then want shall be found there also. Knowledge and ignorance are bound together, power and weakness, life and death. Only the Maker's power is without limits, only His possessions without lack, His knowledge without obscurity, His life without death. All things are created with two-fold natures, God alone is One and eternal.

Mortals, O God, survey Thee not with that measure with which Thou oughtest to be surveyed. By Thy essence alone can Thy essence be conceived. For what relation can there be between Him who is eternal and him who was fashioned in time; between a little water and earth and the lord of all things?

Those who attend permanently at the temple of His glory confess the imperfection of their worship and say:— We have not worshipped Thee according to the requirements of Thy worship; and those who describe the splendour of His beauty are rapt in amazement, (saying):— We have not known Thee as Thou oughtest to [468] be known.   ·

> If someone asks me for His description,
> What shall I despairing say of One who has no form?
> The lovers have been slain by the beloved,
> No voice can come from the slain.

One of the devout who had deeply plunged his head into the cowl of meditation, and had been immersed in the ocean of visions, was asked, when he had come out of that state, by one of his companions, who had desired to cheer him up:— "What beautiful gift hast thou brought us from the garden in which thou hast been?" He replied: "I intended to fill the skirts of my robe with roses, when I reached the rose-tree, as presents for my friends, but the perfume of the flowers intoxicated me so much that I let go the hold of my skirts."

O bird of the morning! Learn love from the moth,
Because it burnt, lost its life, and found no voice.
These prattlers about God are ignorantly in search of Him,
Because he who obtained knowledge has not returned.
O Thou who art above all imaginations, conjectures, opinions and
    ideas,
Above anything people have said, or we have heard or read,
The assembly is finished, and life has reached its term,
And we are as at first, at the beginning in describing Thee.

    Sadi (B1).

THIRD CONVERSATION

PHILOLAUS: What lovely goddess have you there before you? Beautiful as Aphrodite and pensive as Athena, she looks down on her veiled bosom, and holds her left hand as if she [469] were measuring something on it. The measured hand holds a branch. There is something calm about her pose, and a stately grace in her whole bearing.

THEOPHRON: It is the Greek Nemesis, a personified idea which I like very much. She is pensive and fair, for she is a daughter of Justice who cannot be otherwise than wisely gracious. That is why she measures the conduct and the fortune of mortals with her right hand, whilst her impartial gaze is fixed upon her breast. But for him who comes up to the measure, she holds out the branch of reward. Usually she has a wheel under her feet as well, a sign that with the lightest touch she can in a moment overthrow and ruin the happiness of the over-exultant. The artist omitted this symbol from the statue, and gave her instead only the calm pose, the gentle and fine bearing which you noticed. Nor should our Nemesis, my friend, need the awesome and destructive wheel. The good and earnest aspect of the goddess herself, her wise measure, and the branch of fortune which she holds in her hand, are symbols enough to remind us of that steadfast truth of nature: "That all persistence, all well-being, yes, the very existence of things, are built upon measure, proportion and order, and are maintained through these alone." (B1)

PHILOLAUS: There, Theophron, you hit upon the doctrine of one of my most esteemed philosophers, whom I should like to call the Leibniz of our time, Lambert. (B2) In his *Architec-*

115

[**470**] *tonic* as well as in his *Organon,* he cannot return often enough to the truth: "That the persistence, and hence the being of every finite thing, rests everywhere upon a principle wherein opposite laws suspend or limit one another; hence the permanence of things and their inner truth, along with the proportion, order, beauty and goodness which accompany them, are founded on a kind of inherent necessity." In this way he expresses your Nemesis with her measuring arm and the branch in her hand, as a mathematico-physical and metaphysical formula.

THEOPHRON: I like her in that form also, and if dissimilar things could be compared, then I almost prefer her thus to the form in which the artist portrayed her. He had to be content with fusing various symbols. The abstract truth gives them to me as necessary determinations of the conception itself, and therewith the measure and the branch of reward take on a much more essential form. But where, in your mathematical formula, is the wheel of change which belongs to Nemesis?

PHILOLAUS: The philosopher did not forget it. He remarked "that if things or systems of things are disturbed in their state of persistence, they strive to return to it, or to approximate it again, in one way or another," and he specifies these ways.

THEOPHRON: Excellent! You see, Philolaus, the advantage of such scientific formulas. They clarify and turn into general laws, and indeed wherever possible into quantitative terms, what the ordinary understanding dimly but intuitively apprehends in everyday experience. Thereby judgments attain a [**471**] definite surety and a universal application which subsequently can be readily followed in every particular instance. In all probability your Lambert did that also.

PHILOLAUS: Abundantly! He gives many examples in which he applies his principle of persistence to the most varied cases and finds it in all finite and composite systems of forces. Thus in one of his treatises he calculated the movements of the human body, and discovered a series of its principles. He likewise attempted a theory of order, and also began to apply his principle of persistence to matters of beauty, morality and utility. He often expressed the wish that this formula might be tested and applied to all systems of composite, finite forces as, for example, to the cosmic system. He would surely have followed this favorite doctrine of his still further, had not an untimely death torn him away to the loss of several sciences to which he contributed.

THEOPHRON: His death is to be regretted. But other minds will build on what he left unfinished. In mathematical physics there have been found many such laws and compensations of the highest wisdom, which exclude all arbitrariness and give the thinking mind, to its inexpressible joy, the lofty conception of an "inner perfection, goodness, and beauty in the existence and the persistence of each thing." At first, no doubt, one sought to conclude too much from many of these observations, but that does not detract from the beauty of their discovery. Error wears away, but the truth remains. The more true physics advances, the more we depart from the realm of blind [472] power and arbitrariness and enter the realm of the wisest necessity, of a goodness and beauty steadfast in themselves. All senseless fear vanishes when on every hand there is discovered the joyous, clear security of a creation in whose smallest point, God with His wisdom and goodness is present in His totality, working according to the nature of each creature with His undivided and indivisible divine power. What remains for instance, of the empty fear that a comet may overtake the earth, now that we know the course of these celestial bodies more exactly, and have not only calculated more than seventy of them, but also the very cases in which such an accident is to be feared according to natural laws. The possibility of this accident becomes through computation so extraordinarily small, that it almost vanishes into nothing in virtue of the inherent nature of the forces by which the universe is maintained. What has not been falsely imagined about the irregularities and their evil consequences, which would entail the heavenly bodies' falling in time because of their reciprocal attraction! When it was found that these irregularities compensated one another according to immutable laws of nature, the clearer view of the matter sufficed to drive away the empty fear. How beneficent and beautiful is the necessity under whose all embracing sway we live! She is the child of highest [**473**] wisdom, the twin sister to eternal might, the mother of all goodness, happiness, security and order.* If I knew a more beautiful image for it in antiquity, then Nemesis would have to yield her place immediately to this higher Adrastea. (B1)

PHILOLAUS: So that was the gold piece that you promised me would be in the knot which Spinoza tied for us with his inner necessity of the nature of God. (A1) But, Theophron, the knot is not yet unravelled. How drastically he speaks against all God's purposes in creation! How definitely he denies reason and will to God, and derives everything that exists simply and solely from His infinite power which he not only sets above reason and purposes, but also completely separates from them.** You know, my friend, how those doctrines brought our philosopher the bitterest opponents.*** Even

---

* The astronomical essays of la Grange and la Place which are relevant to this matter are in the records of the Berlin and Paris Academies. The *Exposition du Système du Monde* of Pierre Simon la Place, the Newton of our time, which has been published (1796) is a celestial chart of these wise eternal laws of the universe. [n. 2nd ed.]

** "The actual intellect whether it be finite or infinite together with the will, love, desire, etc., must be referred to *natura naturata* and not to the *natura naturans*." (Prop: XXXI: Bk. 1.) "There is no predetermined purpose in nature. All final causes are inventions of man." (Prop. XXXVI App. and ff.) [n. 2nd ed. Hale White trans.]

*** See Letters 24, 25, etc. [n. 2nd ed.]

Leibniz, who esteemed Spinoza highly, declared himself most definitely against them in his *Theodicy*.* If you can recon-[474] cile these offensive doctrines with sound reason, or with Spinoza's very fine system, I could wish myself to be the Nemesis who hands you the branch.

THEOPHRON: I wish it from the hand of truth alone. For I can clearly prove on the one hand, that Spinoza did not fully understand himself in these doctrines because they are consequences of the pernicious Cartesian explanations which he took, and in those times was compelled to take into his system. (B1) On the other hand, I can show that misunderstandings of him have been much greater than were warranted even by his own obscurities of expression. (A1) Once we clear away these Cartesian errors (A2) and explain the doctrines of Spinoza solely in the light of the fundamental idea on which he built his own system, then they become luminous, the mists clear away, and Spinoza, it seems to me, gains a move even on Leibniz who followed him cautiously but perhaps too cautiously, on this point.

PHILOLAUS: I am very curious.

THEOPHRON: First, I completely deny that Spinoza turned God into an unthinking being. There could scarcely be an error more contrary to his system than this. For him, the nature of God is reality through and through, and Spinoza was too much of a thinker himself not to feel and esteem profoundly the reality of perfection in thought, the highest that we know. Thus his highest Being which possesses all perfection in the most perfect manner, cannot lack thought, the most excellent of these perfections; for how else (A3) could [475] there be thoughts and perceptions in finite thinking creatures which are all, according to Spinoza's system, only representations and real consequences of that most real Being,

---

* See in Register of his Opera, the name "Spinoza." [n. 2nd ed.]

who, as he explains, alone deserves the name self-dependent? As he plainly says,* among infinite attributes in God there is also the perfection of infinite thought which Spinoza only distinguishes from the reason and imagination of finite beings in order to designate the former as unique in its kind, and entirely incomparable with the latter. You must have noticed [**476**] his comparison, that the thought of God could no more resemble human thought than the star in the heavens called the Dog Star, could resemble a dog on earth.

PHILOLAUS: The comparison was more impressive than instructive to me.

THEOPHRON: Nor should it instruct you! And we shall

---

* As he often and clearly says:[1]

[1] "The more reality or being a thing possesses, the more attributes belong to it." (Prop. 9 Bk. I)
"God, or substance [Herder: the self-dependent Being] consisting of infinite attributes, each one of which expresses [H: His] eternal and infinite essence, necessarily exists." (Prop. 11) "From the necessity of the divine nature infinite numbers of things in infinite ways, i.e. all things which can be conceived by the [H: an] infinite intellect (quae sub intellectum infinitum cadere possunt) must follow." (Prop. 16) "God's intellect is the (sole) cause of things, both of their essence and of their existence . . . . it must necessarily differ from them with regard to both its essence and existence." (Prop. 18 Schol.) [In Hale White it is Prop. 17 Schol.]
"The existence of God and His essence are one and the same thing." (Prop. 20)
". . . things could have been produced by God in no other manner or order, this being a truth which follows from His absolute perfection [H: hence in the greatest perfection because this follows necessarily from the most perfect nature]. There is no sound reasoning which can persuade us to believe that God was unwilling to create all things which are in His intellect with the same perfection as that in which they exist in His intellect." (Prop. 33, Schol 2). "Thought is an attribute of God, . . . one of the infinite attributes of God which expresses His eternal and infinite essence." (Prop. I Bk. II.)
"In God there necessarily exists the idea of His essence, and of all things which necessarily follow from His essence. The common people understand by God's power His free will . . . . but we have shown that God does everything with that necessity with which he understands Himself (*seipsum intelligit*), i.e. as it follows from the necessity of the divine nature that God understands Himself . . . so by the same necessity it follows that God does an infinitude of things in infinite ways." (Prop. 3 Schol.)
"The idea of God from which infinite number of things follow in infinite ways, can be one only: [H: for] . . . . the infinite intellect comprehends nothing but the attributes of God and His affections." (Prop. 4).
"The order and connection of [H: His] ideas is the same as the order and connection of things." (Prop. 7).
"Everything which can be perceived by the infinite intellect as constituting the essence of substance pertains entirely to the one sole substance alone." And so on. (Prop. 7 Schol.) [n. 2nd ed.].

soon see that it really lacks the resemblance necessary to a comparison. However, it shows this much, that Spinoza here again preferred the sharper attack and expressed himself too drastically rather than suffer that he, who strove zealously for the worthiest and highest conception of God, should allow it to be degraded by any weak comparison with individual things in creation. But that all pure, true, complete knowledge in our soul is nothing but an expression of the divine knowledge, no one, I dare say, has maintained more strongly than Spinoza, who placed the divine essence in man solely in this pure, living knowledge of God, of His attributes and effects.

PHILOLAUS: Precisely so, my friend! And, therefore, is not his infinite thinking Being simply a collective name for all the powers of understanding and thought which are real and active solely in individual creatures? (B1)

THEOPHRON: So God is a collective name, the most real Being a nonentity, a shadow of the images of individual people, or rather a mere word, the echo of a name? That [477] which is most vital then, is dead? That which is universally efficient is the latest feeblest activity of human powers? Philolaus, if you ascribe this to Spinoza from your own convictions, and can thus make his system into its complete opposite, then I am sorry that I gave you his book and ever exchanged a single word with you about him. Forgive my frankness, for I cannot imagine how this could apply to you, since it is not possible that, page after page, and from beginning to end, you could have so misunderstood this philosopher who even in his errors is at least consistent. You probably voiced the opinions of one of his opponents of the past century, although you should not even have done that.

PHILOLAUS: Don't fly into a passion! In a discussion one sometimes introduces an alien opinion if it helps the matter on, and makes it clear by means of contrasts. As for myself, since reading his *Ethics* I was not at all doubtful of Spinoza's meaning in this matter. How he inveighs against those who want to make God into an abstract, lifeless deduction from the world, when, according to him, this unique nature is the cause of all being, hence also of our reason, of every truth and every relation between truths! How highly he esteems a complete and perfect idea!* For him it is knowledge of the eternal, divine Being, knowledge which also is divine [478] in that it conceives things not as contingent but as necessary under the aspect of eternity, and just because of this inner necessity is as sure of itself as only God can be.

No mortal has exalted more highly than Spinoza the essence of the human soul, which in virtue of its nature recognizes truth, and loves it as truth. And he is supposed to have portrayed his God, the source, object and essence of all knowledge, to be as blind as a Polyphemus? I become almost ashamed before the spirit of this man for bringing against him this charge which is as remote as the Antipodes.

THEOPHRON: Well then! An infinite, original power of thought, the source of all thoughts, is, according to Spinoza, of the essence of God. And in this system we cannot doubt His infinitely efficient power.

PHILOLAUS: No, because in Spinoza, reason and will are one and the same thing. That is, in our more moderate language, a reason which conceives the best, must also will the best, and if it has the power, it must effect the best. But there is no doubt as to the infinite power of his God, since he subordinates everything to this power, and derives everything from it.

THEOPHRON: Then what did he lack, that he did not unite the infinite powers of thought and action, and in their union, [479] did not express more clearly what he must necessarily

* The proof of this is Spinoza's entire *Ethics*. [n. 2nd ed.]

have found in them, namely that the highest Power must necessarily also be the wisest, that is to say an infinite goodness ordered according to inherent, eternal laws? For an unorganized lawless, blind power is never the highest. It can never be the prototype and summation of all the order, wisdom and regularity which we, although finite beings, perceive in creation as eternal laws, if it does not itself know these laws, and exercise them according to its eternal intrinsic nature. A blind power must necessarily have been surpassed by an ordered one, and thus could not be God. Why did Spinoza remain in such darkness at this point, and not recognize the integral strength of his own system? (A1)

PHILOLAUS: I understand now, Theophron, and I thank you for helping me on the way. It is still that false Cartesian explanation, which again shut off his own light from him. Thought and extension for him stand opposed as two isolated things. (A2) Thought cannot be delimited by extension, nor extension by thought. Now, since he adopted both as attributes of God, an indivisible Being, and could not explain one through the other, he had to adopt a third in which both were included, and this he called power. (A3) Had he developed the conception of power as he did that of matter, then [480] he would necessarily, and as a consequence of his own system, have come to the conception of forces which are active in matter, as well as in organs of thought. Then, in that conception, he would furthermore have regarded power and thought as forces, that is, as identical in nature. Thought is also a power, and indeed the most perfect, absolutely infinite power, just because it is and has everything which pertains to the infinite self-established power. (A1) Thus the knot is loosed, and the gold it contained lies before us. The eternal, primal power, the force of all forces, is but one, and in every attribute, however our frail reason may divide it up, it is still infinite and the same. According to the eternal laws of His nature, God thinks, acts, and is the most perfect, in every way conceivable to Him, that is to say, in the most perfect way. His thoughts are not wise, but wisdom. His acts are not good alone, but goodness. And all this is not through compulsion or arbitrariness, as if the opposite were possible, but rather through His eternal, essential inner nature, through the most perfect primal goodness and truth.

Now I see also, my friend, why Spinoza is so much opposed to purposes, and ostensibly speaks severely against them. For him, they are the wishes and arbitrary choices which the artist makes yet need not have made. What God effected, He [481] could not first deliberate and choose. The effect flowed out of the nature of the most perfect Being. It is unique, and nothing else was possible.

Now, too, I remember the many anthropomorphisms even in Leibniz's excellent *Theodicy*, which never really appealed to me, although at that time I knew nothing better to put in their place, for I shrank from blind necessity. I see now that my fear was in vain, and that no blind necessity is needed in order to recognize that luminous intelligent necessity which exists and works through its essential being. Have you the *Theodicy* at hand, Theophron?

THEOPHRON: In more than one language. But I want to give you a shorter "Theodicy" by one of our best-loved poets. (B1) Read these lines:*

PHILOLAUS:

> As God created and the gaping gulf
> Surveyed, realm upon realm potential rose
> From primal night. A thousand tempting schemes,
> His nod might substance make. Yet twilight
> And cold shadows fall on worlds which charmed me,
> But not the maker's choice. He wills our world
> The dwelling-place of monstrous. . . . . . .

* Uz: *Lyrical poems:* "Theodicy." [n. 2nd ed.]

Let me read no further. I know where it is all leading. It is Leibniz's faithful *Theodicy* in beautiful verse, but it [482] seems to me to be without the philosophical, pure truth worthy of God. God "surveyed" no "gaping gulfs." He did not sit like a brooding artist, who wracked his brains, planned, compared, rejected and chose. No realm of possibility exists without God and external to Him. For if He did not want to create it, or could not create it, then it was not possible. No world, much less a thousand worlds of "tempting schemes" which needed only a nod to exist, yet which God did not choose, could ever become a thought of God. He did not play with worlds as children play with soap bubbles, until one pleased Him and He selected it. If a thousand others besides this one were possible, then a greater God could create them, and the weaker, laboriously-meditating God would be no God. (A1)

THEOPHRON: Read on!

PHILOLAUS:

> E'er morning stars sang praise
> And deeps of chaos moved to His creating word,
> The wisest chose the finished plan.

These beautiful lines merely say the same thing. The Most [483] Wise did not choose, for no choice was necessary where no antecedent, hesitating deliberation was needed. All this sequence of thought, these plans, and these varying designs are incompatible with the most perfect nature of the eternal, immutable Spirit. They belong to that deaf and dumb eternity which the inactive God,

> - - - erst spent in lonely thought
> Til now a world He made, and not before. (B1)

on which we are already agreed. I am astonished that that great and exact thinker, Leibniz, could give way to anthropomorphisms of that sort.

THEOPHRON: Let that cause you no astonishment! He gave way to them in a popular work, his *Theodicy,* and you know how a popular mode of presentation often leads astray. Bayle's many and plausible objections forced him to make his counter-arguments also dazzling and many-faceted. The result was the anthropomorphisms, yes, often virtually a continuous anthropomorphizing which I, speaking for myself, wish were out of this beautiful book, but which was perhaps still necessary for Leibniz's times. But it is a pity that his followers did not always distinguish what was supposed to be mere ornament and popular expression in his work, from that which belongs strictly to his system. Thus, for example, it was long sought to refute Spinoza by means of a distinction between the world "out of God and in God." "The world," it was said, "existed in God eternally as idea," that is, as a soap bubble with which He played in imagination. He was delighted with [**484**] it, and through long, long eternities, He brooded over the unhatched egg. Then came the time (imagine to yourself this long, long time in the eternity of the inactive God!) when He resolved to create. Suddenly from God there issued the world which was so long in Him, and is now forever outside Him, and He outside the world. He has His little nook in the great nothingness of primeval, inactive eternity, where He contemplates Himself and everlastingly meditates. I confess that the gods of Epicurus are more tolerable to me than this inactive, melancholy Being through whom it was believed that Spinoza could be readily and easily refuted. Leibniz is not to blame for this nonsense, except insofar as his poetic mind never, even for the most rigorous truths, disdained ornament, that is, images, similes, allegories, anthropomorphisms, and so on.

PHILOLAUS: So much the worse for his followers! For a part of this verbiage is now sanctified by many as strict philosophy.

THEOPHRON: By many, but certainly not by all! The mediocre mind remains mediocre whether it follows Leibniz or Spinoza. The better mind thinks on everything for itself, and makes use of the best in every one of its predecessors. So Leibniz did with Descartes, with the ancients, and with Spinoza himself. He read and used him too.

PHILOLAUS: Yet he strongly affirmed his opposition to Spinoza's Necessity! (A1)

THEOPHRON: He had to do so in a popular "Theodicy," because here his purpose was not gently to set Spinoza right, [485] as he did with Locke in another excellent work,* but rather to distinguish his own system sharply from Spinoza's. (B1)

PHILOLAUS: And this system of his was. . . .?

THEOPHRON: The system of moral necessity in God, by which He chose the best possible according to the principle of fitness.

PHILOLAUS: And how is moral necessity different from our necessity, which I shall call the essential, inner and divine necessity? God must completely envision and effect the best, not through a weak caprice, but in accordance with His nature, and without tedious comparison with the less good which without Him is nothing. In Spinoza's system, too, there is no question of a physical necessity insofar as this means a blind, external compulsion. Spinoza opposes such a conception with all his might.** But as for moral laws external to Himself, God knows them not.

---

* *Oeuvres philosophiques de Leibniz* (Amst. Raspe, 1765) almost the most instructive of Leibniz's writings, in which, moreover, every line is instructive.
** For in no way do I subject God to fate, but I conceive that everything follows with inevitable necessity from the nature of God just as all conceive that it follows from the nature of God Himself that He should understand Himself. Certainly no one denies that this follows necessarily from the divine nature, and yet no one conceives that God is compelled by any fate to understand Himself, but that He does so absolutely free, although necessarily. Epist. 23. *Opp. posth.* p. 453. [n. 2nd ed. Epist. LXXV. Wolf trans.]

THEOPHRON: Nor was Leibniz thinking of such when he chose the term "moral necessity." He merely set this in [486] opposition to the physical, that is to say, blind power or external compulsion, and with reference to the former, he took offense at the extreme expressions of Spinoza. Those who ascribe blind fatalism to Leibniz do him injustice, in my opinion. He explained himself at length on this point against Clarke, (B1) and (A1) even softened as much as he could, his own doctrine of moral necessity in God, by means of such anthropomorphisms as "plan," "choice," "fitness," and so on.

PHILOLAUS: It seems to me, dear Theophron, that the punishment for this moderation followed close upon the heels of the mistake. (A2) Leibniz was forced in his doctrine of divine choice according to which God chooses the best possible, to refer often, to "divine purposes," which God alone knew, but which we assume to be good just because God chose them, otherwise He would not have chosen them, and so on.

THEOPHRON: That he was forced to do indeed!

PHILOLAUS: And what mortal would not be, as soon as he directs his attention away from the inner necessity which is goodness through its own nature, and seeks to conjecture about particular, external purposes possible to God? Unwittingly he sinks in a sea of fictitious, final causes which he marvels or guesses at, but through which he easily relinquishes the ground of concrete phenomena, and the investigation of the inner nature of the matter itself. What a host of Theodicies, Teleologies, and Physico-Theologies followed upon Leibniz's fine book, which through this idea of "fitness" not only frequently ascribed very limited, trivial and weak purposes [487] to the highest Being, but most often also ended in attributing everything to God's arbitrariness—thus tearing asunder the chain of nature, and isolating a few of its parts, so that here and there an electric spark of arbitrary divine

purpose might appear. I confess that that is not my philosophy.

THEOPHRON: And what is yours, Philolaus?

PHILOLAUS: It is to concern oneself with the inner nature
of things as they exist. The existence of the world is contingent; no one doubts that. For an effect exists only by reason
of its cause, not by itself. Now the world after all exists,
however it may have come into existence. And it shows traces
of wisdom and goodness, not only here and there, as is com-
monly said, but in every point, in the nature of everything and
its attributes, it reveals, if I may say so, God complete, that
is, as He could become visible and active in this guise, in this
point of space and time. What childishness therefore it would
be, solely and always to ask why and for what secret purposes
He may have thus revealed Himself, instead of making the
more necessary and beautiful enquiry, "What is it actually
that reveals itself, and in what form?" That is, "What forces
of nature work in this or that organ and according to what
laws?"

THEOPHRON: Go on Philolaus!

PHILOLAUS: We call the world "contingent" because it is an
effect and is full of effects. The expression is unsuitable and
[488] even incompatible with our very speech. The activity of
the highest reason which works according to necessary, inner
laws of its nature, and hence effects the most perfect goodness and wisdom, is as little "contingent" as the reason of God
itself is contingently wise or contingently good. He created
what was possible, and to an infinite reason joined with infinite
power, everything possible is possible. This is all, as we say,
united by space and time, that is, by order. Every created
thing is defined with a most perfect individuality, and circumscribed by it. Thus neither in the world as a whole, nor in its
smallest part, is there contingency. Beyond what the omnipo-

tently active Spirit found possible, every possibility is a mere dream, just as there is no space beyond space, no time beyond time. All these are empty phantoms of the imagination, words fabricated in a dream whose visions are only believed in a dream.

The Creator therefore, did not rest for a moment, for there are no moments in God's eternity, and the essentially active One never was at rest. But the world is not eternal like God because of that, for it is only a combination of temporal things. Hence every moment of the sequence of time, yes, the whole time-sequence itself, is not comparable with the absolute eternity of God. All things in the time-sequence are conditioned, are dependent on one another and on the cause which brought them into being. None of them can thus be compared [489] with the existence of God. What time is to sequence, space is to co-existence. God is not commensurable in spatial terms, because He co-exists with nothing like unto Himself. But the eternal, infinite root of all things is so exalted beyond our power of imagination, that all space and time vanishes in Him. We finite beings, encompassed by space and time so that we conceive all things only in their terms, can but say of the highest cause, "It is. It is active." But with these words we say all. With infinite power and goodness, it is effective in every point of space, in every moment of fleeting time. But for us, space and time are merely a more or less obscure image of the unity of things, according to that firmly established, eternal order which is the attribute and the effect of the infinite Reality itself, and which thus rests upon nothing less than this indivisible, eternal infinity. Hence our mind knows no nobler task than to contemplate the order which the Eternal conceived. Every one of His laws is itself the essence of things, and hence is not arbitrarily attached to them, but is one with them. Their nature is based on His law, His law on

their nature and on the connection of all natures. How child-
ish it would be then, if when I admire the beauty of the circle
and its manifold relations, I made a profound attempt to
fathom the secret and particular reasons why God created
such a circle, why He made the exact and beautiful relations
in it of the essence of space and of our measuring reason.
[**490**] Space would not be space, if in all its possible con-
structions the circle should not occur, and our reason would
not be reason if it could not perceive the beautiful relations
in every one of its parts.

THEOPHRON: I shall help you with other illustrations, Philolaus. If men had forever stood still in admiration because:—

> - - - Countless stars with constant pace
> And ever radiant beam move in their spheres,
> Mingling by hidden law, yet not confused,
> And never off their course . . . . . ,

then their admiration would, it is true, have been a kind of
prayer to the God, of whom it is said:

> - - - His will their force
> Apportions every quality, their rest,
> Their measured motion with a purpose. . .

and thereby many purposes, false and true, worthy and unworthy could have been thought out. But that natural philosopher who first looked away from these purposes and sought
for the "hidden law" by which the stars:—

> . . . move in their spheres
> Mingling . . . ., yet not confused
> And never off their course. . .   (B1)

assuredly did more than the greatest inventor of purposes
among men could do. He reflected upon the thought of God
and found it, not in a dream of arbitrary "fitness," but in the
nature of things themselves, whose relations he measured,

weighed, and counted. Now we know the great law of this
cosmic system, and our admiration is rational, whereas otherwise it would have been forever and ever a devout but empty
wonder.

PHILOLAUS: Add to that as well, a very deceptive wonder!
For if we bring *a priori,* particular purposes of God into
[491] creation, and desire to have heard in the eternal council
chamber why Saturn has a ring, our earth a moon, but Mars
and Venus none,—upon what a highway of deceptive hypotheses which are generally overthrown on the morrow, do
we venture! So much was said and believed to accord with
the register of divine purposes about the ring of Saturn and
the moon of the earth and of Venus, which had to be taken
back in shame when it was found that Venus had no moon,
and that with regard to the illumination of the inhabitants
of Saturn by its rings of diamond and even with our own
moon itself, conditions were very different from what they
seemed at first. All these deceptions in which God's name is
misused, are avoided by the sober natural scientist who, indeed, does not inform us about particular decisions from the
chamber of divine council, but instead, examines the condition
of things themselves and notes the essential laws implanted
in them. While seeming to forget the divine purposes, he seeks
and finds in every object and point of creation, God complete.
That is to say, he finds in everything an intrinsic truth, harmony and beauty, without which it would not be and could
not be, and upon which its existence depends with an inner,
though conditional necessity, but which in its way is just as
essential as the necessity upon which the existence of God
unconditionally rests. The very dependence of things on God,
[492] makes their essential natures into necessary images of
his goodness and beauty, as these can be revealed in such and
no other manifestations.

I wish that Spinoza had been born a century later, so that he might have philosophized far from the hypotheses of Descartes, in the freer and purer light of mathematical, natural science and of a truer natural history. What a different form even his abstract philosophy would have attained!

THEOPHRON: And I hope that others will courageously follow on the road which Spinoza opened up in the twilight of those days, namely to develop exact, pure natural laws without becoming concerned in so doing with the particular purposes of God. He who could show me the natural laws by which the phenomena of our so-called dead and living creation, such as salts, plants, animals, and men arose according to inner necessity and union of active forces in such and no other organs, would have encouraged the most wonderful admiration, love and worship of God, far more than he who preaches to me from the chamber of divine council that we have feet in order to walk, the eye in order to see and so on, which secret discoveries no one ever doubted.

PHILOLAUS: It seems to me also, that the usual physico-theologies are about dying out.

THEOPHRON: They were very useful in their time and, as a matter of fact, were nothing more than childishly-pretty, [493] popular applications of a new and more steadfast natural science. Their basis will thus always remain. Yes, the truth in them will become incomparably more glorious when people no longer snatch after particular small purposes in every single little circumstance, but rather attain more and more a view of the whole which, down to its smallest relations, is but a single system, wherein the wisest goodness reveals itself in accord with immutable, inner laws. An edifice in praise of God that metaphysically towers above the endlessness of space and time, as well as resting immovably firm in physics upon the nature of things themselves! Every true natural law which was found, would thus be a discovered law of the eternal divine intelligence, which can see only truth, and produce only reality.

PHILOLAUS: How it grieves me that Spinoza's philosophy which points in that direction, should be interwoven with so many forbidding difficulties! For in its present form it can be only for a few.

THEOPHRON: That is precisely its merit. The great mass must not read this philosophy. It must never found a sect.

PHILOLAUS: Its author has already seen to that with his own style.* However, I do not deny that I could wish a wider circulation and a deeper influence than most people can and will derive from his book, on account of the beautiful truths which he expresses about God, the world, the nature and essence of humanity, it weakness and strength, and the condition [**494**] of its slavery and freedom. As I was once prejudiced against him, so am I now convinced of this man's intrinsic love of truth, and of the excellence of his moral as well as his philosophical principles. I wish that more could learn to know him thus.

THEOPHRON: Time and truth will certainly accomplish that. Read this book and see what Lessing said about him.** Have you read nothing of the rumor which has arisen over that scholar's grave to the effect that he was a Spinozist?

PHILOLAUS: I did not want to hear it, because as you know, I was so badly informed about Spinoza, and I did not like to see Lessing's name sullied. Now I shall read with all the greater avidity what is said about it, although I can no more

---

* ". . . he who desires to assist other people, either by advice or by deed, in order that they may together enjoy the highest good, will strive, above all things, to win their love, and not to draw them into admiration, so that a doctrine may be named after him. . . ." (Eth. P. IV Appendix: XXV.) [n. 2nd ed.]

** *On the Doctrine of Spinoza* (Breslau, 1786). New enlarged edition Breslau 1789. [n. 2nd ed.]

imagine Lessing to be a Spinozist than we ourselves are. He was not made to be an "ist," whatever letters may be prefixed to that ending, and his scholarly acumen must surely have discerned the errors of the Cartesian residue in Spinoza's discourse.

THEOPHRON: Do not judge, but read. Then we shall continue our discussion.

Fourth Conversation

PHILOLAUS: Here is your little book* again, thank you. One hears Lessing speak in it even though he utters only a [495] few syllables. (B1) Yet I cannot deny that I should have liked to hear him at greater length upon our subject.

THEOPHRON: I also. Nevertheless, how do you like the little that he does say?

PHILOLAUS: It is too little to judge, and again, it is expressed too disjointedly, and perhaps too drastically here and there, as, indeed, was Lessing's way. If you have no objection I shall quote his words, and without any presumption whatever, give my opinion of them.

THEOPHRON: Do so. You thereby become but the commentator on an author who can no longer explain himself to us.

PHILOLAUS: "The orthodox conceptions of the Deity are no longer for me. I can take no pleasure in them." Nor I, now that the stumbling blocks have been removed from Spinoza for me. The inactive Being who sits outside the world and contemplates Himself, even as He contemplated Himself throughout eternities before He finished the plan of the world, is not for me. Nor for you either, Theophron.

THEOPHRON: But Philolaus, I do not know why Lessing [496] calls the phantom of this dreary, idle God, "orthodox conceptions." It has neither the consistency of a conception, nor has it ever been the view of orthodox philosophers, that

---

* *On the Doctrine of Spinoza*, p. 12.[1]

[1] The citations, which refer to the 1st Edition, have been retained, and are easily found in the 2nd ed [n. 2nd ed.]

is to say, of such philosophers as were capable of clear conceptions. Such a God is indeed orthodox to the Hindus whose god, Jagranat, has sat for many millenniums with his arms hanging folded on his belly, quite contented thus. Another of their gods has been lying asleep for aeons. His head rests in the lap of one of his wives who scratches his crown; his feet in the lap of another who strokes his soles. Incessantly the stream of milk and honey flows in him. He is content therewith, and rests in dreamy self-contemplation. These are veritably orthodox gods of the Hindus! But I do not see why our God must be a Jagranat or a Vishnu.

PHILOLAUS: However, you have admitted yourself, Theophron, that some of our popular philosophers encouraged such Hindu conceptions, or at least, did not earnestly enough oppose them. I read on in Lessing: "ἐν καὶ πᾶν! One and All! I know nothing else."* Nor do I! Only I should like to hear from Lessing's own soul, how he understood the union of these two most comprehensive words, the most comprehensive of which our language is capable. The world too is a One; Deity too is an All. Lessing himself felt that therewith he had as yet said nothing definite. He returned to explain himself more fully, but even his fuller explanation is not as extensive as I could wish it. I perceive Lessing's great respect for Spinoza's philosophy. But he, like us, was interested solely in the spirit of Spinozism. "I mean," he says,** "that spirit which pervaded Spinoza himself." And since he says,*** "My [497] credo stands in no book," and would only call himself a follower of anyone on one condition which actually destroys itself,**** then these and other hints, and indeed, Lessing's

* p. 12.   ** p. 14.   *** p. 17.
**** p. 12.[1]

[1] "If I must call myself after anyone, then I know no other." p. 12. (If! must! I know!) "Certainly! and yet! Do you know anything better?" (than Spinoza's system). [n. 2nd ed.]

whole manner of thinking, are guarantees enough that he did
not take as his system, a crude All-Oneness, which is not
Spinoza's system either. It was just here that my desire was
aroused to know how Lessing conjured up "the spirit which
pervaded Spinoza himself," and made it his own. And just
here, I must admit, my desire was in vain. Lessing hears of
an intelligent, personal cause of the world and is overjoyed
in his way, that he will now hear something entirely new.*
Lessing's reason could never doubt of God's reason. His curi-
osity was thus directed to the personal cause of the world,
and about that, naturally, he could learn nothing new. The
expression "person" even when used by theologians who do not
not set it in contrast with the world, but only take it to be a
distinction in the nature of God, is, as you yourself say, merely
anthropomorphic. Thus, philosophically nothing could be
settled on this point. (A1)

Lessing goes on to speak about the freedom of the will.
[498] "I desire," he says, "no freedom of the will. I remain
an honest Lutheran, and retain that more brutish than human
[499] blasphemy into which Spinoza's clear, pure mind also
[500] found its way, 'that there is no free will.' "** (B1) Thus
he jests with the words of the decision of the Imperial
Diet at Augsburg, and by referring to Spinoza's clear, pure
mind, he himself explains how he wished the unfree will of
man to be understood. I know no philosopher who has ex-
pounded the bondage of the human will more thoroughly, and
who has defined its freedom more excellently, than Spinoza.***
Man has been appointed no less a goal for his freedom than
the freedom of God Himself. By means of a kind of inner
necessity, that is, by means of perfect conceptions which only
the knowledge and love of God can reveal to us, we become

---

* p. 17.   ** p. 19.
*** Spinoza. *Ethic.* L. IV. V. [n. 2nd ed.]

lords of our passions, yes, even over fate itself. Spinoza thoroughly proves that if one takes freedom to be senseless, blind caprice, man as little as God Himself, deserves the high and noble name of freedom. Rather does it befit the perfection of God's nature that He should not be free in this manner, that He should know no blind caprice, even as it also befits the perfection of His works that such senseless caprice be banned from all creation. It would be (again using the words of the Diet of Augsburg) a "blasphemous defect in creation, and in every creature who possessed it, a blighting evil." It is fortunate therefore that it is a self-contradiction, and hence a clear absurdity. You agree do you not, Theophron?

THEOPHRON: Absolutely! But what does Lessing say of the thought of God? It seems to me that I found something new there.

PHILOLAUS: Here is the passage.* "It is a human prejudice to regard thought as first and highest, and to seek to derive [501] everything from it. For after all, everything, including ideas, depends upon higher principles. Extension, motion and thought are obviously grounded in a higher power which they by no means exhaust. It must be infinitely more excellent than any particular activity, and so it can also have a kind of enjoyment which not only surpasses all conception, but also lies completely outside conception. The fact that we cannot conceive of it, does not destroy its possibility." What do you think of this passage, Theophron?

THEOPHRON: I wished to know what you think of it?

PHILOLAUS: Then I must admit that I vainly struggle to make anything definite out of it. I readily agree that it is a human prejudice to regard thought as first and highest, and to seek to derive everything from it. We know nothing higher of its kind, than thought. Lessing himself could name nothing

* p. 19, 20.

higher. It has so far been a vain attempt to derive everything from it, for the manner in which gravity, motion and every other of the thousand active forces of the universe are related to thought is still a riddle. We know that thought acts upon many other forces subordinate to it, although we do not understand the manner of the activity. But who is to tell us in what higher force are grounded thought, motion and all the forces of nature, among which, as we have seen, extension [502] is by no means to be included? Lessing himself only says that such a power could exist, but he also confesses that we are not in a position to conceive it in any way.

THEOPHRON: It seems to me that there Lessing said too much. (A1) (B1) What if I name you, not indeed a higher force, but the real conception in which all these forces are not only grounded, but which all of them together do not exhaust? (A2) It has all the attributes that Lessing demands for his unknown force. "It is infinitely more excellent than each single activity of any single force, and really affords a kind of enjoyment which not only surpasses all conceptions, but also is above and prior to every conception although not outside of it," because every conception assumes it and rests upon it.

PHILOLAUS: And that conception is . . . .?

THEOPHRON: Existence. You see, Lessing went only halfway with Spinoza, else he would surely have developed this conception which our philosopher adequately presents as the ground and essence of all forces. Existence (A3) is more excellent than any of its effects. It affords an enjoyment which not only exceeds individual conceptions, but which is not at all commensurable with them; for the power of conception which many other forces obey is only one of its forces. So it is with men, and with all limited beings it must be the same. And how with God?

PHILOLAUS: In God's existence, everything that Lessing [503] surmised about this higher force which must surpass all thought, is proved pre-eminently true. His existence is the primal ground of all reality, the totality of all forces, an enjoyment which goes beyond all conceptions . . . .

THEOPHRON:—But which also lies outside all conception? Again and again you see that Lessing had not completely unravelled the knot of Spinozistic ideas. (A1) The highest power must know itself, otherwise it is a blind force which would surely be overthrown by a thinking power and hence not be Deity. (A2)

PHILOLAUS: "But Spinoza was far from considering our miserable method of acting according to purposes as the highest, and from putting thought above all else."*

THEOPHRON: After Existence as the basis of all forces, thought stands highest with him as well. Only he is far from attributing limited ways of conception, *a posteriori* knowledge, fallible deliberations, and arbitrary purposes to the Infinite, and that is precisely what gives his system its excellence.

PHILOLAUS: Lessing asks further**: "According to what conceptions does his friend assume a personal extra-mundane [504] God? Is it somewhat like the conceptions of Leibniz?" He fears that the latter was himself a Spinozist at heart.***

THEOPHRON: What Leibniz was at heart I do not know. His *Theodicy*, however, shows that he did not want to be so

---

* p. 20.   ** p. 21.

*** In case this fear of Lessing's as to the idle gossip about a letter of Leibniz to Pfaff concerning his *Theodicy* should be disturbing, then read Dieten's preface to the first part of Leibniz's *Works* on this point, and one will surely agree with Bulfinger's view that Leibniz answered Pfaff in Pfaff's manner. [n. 1st ed.]

"That Lessing did not venture to profess that Leibniz was in his understanding a Spinozist, or that he had recognized himself to be such, the rest of the conversation shows. An inner essential similarity, an identity of system was all that Lessing actually had in mind." On the Doctrine of Spinoza (2nd ed. 1789), p. 414. [n. 2nd ed. replacing n. to 1st ed.]

before the world. (A1) On the contrary, he favored such anthropomorphisms as a divine choice following upon delibera-
tion, and a selection of the better from much that was worse in accord with the principle of fitness. All this was only to escape the Spinozistic necessity, in opposition to which he chose the more prudent expression "moral necessity."

PHILOLAUS: I am astonished that that astute man could be content with such a solution.

THEOPHRON: It was a fine solution, Philolaus. It was the middle way by which Leibniz thought he would slip through between Bayle's skepticism and Spinoza's harsh system. And so indeed he did with great skill. But Bayle and Spinoza were no longer alive and neither of the two would have thought himself entirely vanquished. (A2)

PHILOLAUS: "Leibniz's conceptions of the truth," Lessing goes on to say,* "were of such a nature that he could not bear [505] it if too strict a construction were set upon them. Many of his statements were the result of this way of thinking, and it is often very difficult, even with the greatest astuteness, to discover his real meaning. That is exactly why I esteem him, I mean because of this grand manner of thought, and not because of this or that particular opinion which he only appeared to have or perhaps really did have."

THEOPHRON: Excellent! Excellent! It is only a small mind that sets up shop with a dozen prettily figured verbal band-boxes, not for retail trade alone, but as a monopoly, and is entirely unable to understand that other tradesmen carry other band-boxes. For the containers have very little importance for the true philosopher. He looks to see what is in them, and what serves him. Don't you think so too, Philolaus? Could you very well differ with someone about his metaphysical formula, and argue about it with him?

* p. 22.

PHILOLAUS: Not I! Spinoza taught me that the more complete our conceptions are, the more our emotions are silent, and the more readily do all human minds unite in clearly apprehended truth. For there is but one reason, but one truth. As for Leibniz, however, I cannot conceal that he often seems to me too pliable, too rich in hypotheses. It is his way to be complaisant with everything, so that he may use all for his own purpose.

THEOPHRON: Don't say that, my friend. He knew his own mind very well, and even clung much more firmly to many of his embellishments and hypotheses than was necessary. Either he unexpectedly comes out with them and remains true to [506] them, as in his correspondence with Clarke, Hartsoeker and others, or else he is polite and adjusts his opponent's view to his own. (A1)

PHILOLAUS: Who knows then to what Cabbalist he wanted to accommodate himself when, as Lessing points out, he said of God: "That He is in a state of perpetual expansion and contraction, and that this is the creation and state of the world." I am astonished that Lessing found that terrible materialization to his taste.

THEOPHRON: This passage in Leibniz is not yet known to me. But as to Lessing's being delighted with it, with what things, my friend, is not one often delighted in discussion, if not primarily and most frequently with the grotesque? I should be sorry if Lessing confused this mode of presentation with Spinoza's system. But at least it would be another sign that he had not yet got rid of that confusion of ideas, wherein extension is one of God's attributes and so on, and hence that [507] he was not entirely clear about the philosophy of Spinoza. (A1) I too would like, as Lessing says,* "naturally to have questioned to the end," the method of explanation of him

* p. 34.

who can explain the creation and condition of things through a perpetual expansion and contraction of God. For I now see nothing in it but a gross materialization of God in the manner of the Cabbalists, of which I can make nothing.

PHILOLAUS: And yet Spinoza drew his own system largely from the Jewish Cabbala.

THEOPHRON: For the Cabbala's sake! my friend. Let us put this aside for the time being, and finish Lessing's conversation.

PHILOLAUS: It is finished. We have learned little from Lessing this time.

THEOPHRON: And yet I am not sorry that his friend wrote down and made known this conversation in such a frank manner. Whatever the feeble sectarian may consider him to be can do no harm to the dead Lessing. And for us, it is pleasant to see that Spinoza did not remain unnoticed by so distinguished a thinker as Lessing,* and, as well, to see what he might have made of him, if he had had the time and leisure to [508] test and examine him more closely. In his friend's book you will surely have found much that was true and beautiful said with virile grace!

PHILOLAUS: Surely! Only I must admit just as frankly, Theophron, that I get on as little as Lessing with his "personal, supra- and extra-mundane Deity." God is not the world, and the world is not God, so much is certain. But it seems to me that with the "extra" and the "supra," not much good is done. When one speaks of God one must forget all idols of space and time, or our greatest care is in vain.

Secondly, I can just as little conceal that Jacobi does not agree with the conception which I now have of Spinoza's

---

* This is seen even more satisfactorily in two articles in Lessing's posthumous writings. (Lessing's *Leben und Nachlass,* Th. 2. S. 164. u. f.) They show beyond any doubt the clear and pure conception which Lessing had of Spinoza's system, and put the jests of his conversation in their proper place. [n. 2nd ed.]

system, and about which we agreed point by point. I also took up Mendelssohn's "Morning Hours," and saw that we were more or less in agreement on the historical fact of what Spinoza's system really was. (A1) (B1) Thus you can easily see that I cannot agree with the conclusions* that: "Spinozism is atheism. The Leibniz-Wolffian philosophy is no less fatalistic than the Spinozistic. All demonstration ends in fatalism," and so on. According to my conviction, Spinozism as Spinoza conceived it is not atheism, nor, in Spinoza's drastic expression, is the necessity of the Leibniz-Wolffians the same as the Spinozistic.** Then, too, it seems to me that the word "fatalism" should frighten us no more than any other word. (A1) [509] There is a blind and a seeing, a pagan, a Mohammedan and a Christian fate.*** The latter lies in the unalterable con- [510] ception of the highest power, wisdom and goodness. It can, therefore, become nothing else but the aim and end [511] of every true demonstration, for things arbitrary never permit of proof.

THEOPHRON: But what have you to say about his principle of all human knowledge and activity, belief?**** (B1)

PHILOLAUS: I wish he had explained himself more clearly on that matter. As it is, I fear that he will be badly misunderstood. His principle of human knowledge and activity is obviously, on the one hand, the inner law of thought, or, if you wish, the inner sense; and on the other, the right use of all the external senses, that is, the rule of experience. Now indeed, it is belief when one trusts one's senses or reason, only the expression is rather uncommon among German philosophers.

---

* p. 170, 172.
** On this matter, see Wolff's *Refutation of Spinozism*, Part II, of his *Natural Theology*, para. 671 ff., with which is printed the German translation of Spinoza's *Ethics* (1744). [n. 2nd ed.]
*** On all this, Leibniz defended himself against Clarke.
**** p. 172.

But belief on another's testimony, or even on the testimony of tradition, perhaps of an anonymous legend, is an entirely different thing, the value of which must also be assessed according to different rules, from which I should not like to omit reason.

THEOPHRON: All very good, Philolaus. But I am sorry that you have clung to and scrupled at our author's words, which Haller calls, "the garment of sense." For the truth which he [512] wants to establish with these expressions still seems to me, if impartially weighed, very worthy of acceptance. You will have found that in his conversation with Lessing too, he concludes "that subtle reasoning is not the whole essence, not the whole condition of man." Substance, existence, lies at the basis of all, including the noblest forces of our nature. It cannot be resolved into over-subtle reasoning, let alone argued away by it. Without existence, and a series of existences, man would not think as he does. Therefore, the purpose of his thought cannot be to dream fantasies and to play with illusory ideas and words as if with a self-made reality, but rather, as he says, "to disclose Existence," to take it as something given, or, in his words, "as a revelation of God" beyond and behind which one cannot get. One must, then, purify and sharpen the senses through experience, the inner sense through love of truth, order and coherence in thought, and renounce all compounding of arbitrary, non-existent, illusory ideas, which is to say, inert, dead nothingness. Instead one must learn what exists in the attributes and relations in which it exists. Such knowledge, in union with the inner feeling for the truth, is alone true. It alone illumines the spirit, nurtures the heart, [513] brings order and regularity into all the spheres of our life. As against this, that metaphysical hair-splitting, which does not pre-suppose an external Existence and internal laws of truth, makes the mind barren and the heart empty. (A1) Is not this principle of thought completely convincing to you also?

PHILOLAUS: No philosopher will ever have doubted it.

THEOPHRON: Not in theory, but perhaps more than one of them has in practice. However in my opinion, it would be doing the open-hearted, honest author an injustice if one took these rules to be a principle opposed to Mendelssohn's philosophy.

Mendelssohn was a clear and serene thinker. I could wish many more like him for the philosophy of our country. Like Leibniz, Wolff, Shaftesbury, Lessing, Kästner (B1) and, indeed, like every philosopher deserving of the name, he loved precise ideas, which he carefully sought to distinguish from various conceptions of nonentity, from empty phantoms of an idly speculating imagination. That human knowledge without and before all experience, those sensuous perceptions without and before all sensation of an object, ordered according to implanted forms of thought which no one had implanted, were chimeras to him, as they must also be to every intelligent thinker. Thus, in this principle, Mendelssohn, Jacobi, and, I might say, everyone who but apprehends his own exist- [**514**] ence, are agreed. I at least, my friend, feel so enervated by every philosophy which plays with that type of symbolical words without ideas and without objects, that I cannot soon enough return to nature, to existence, just to become aware again that I am alive. We, too, Philolaus, in our discussion have often had to use the name of God as a mere symbol. How would it be if we interrupted it now, and you played to me, in your expressive way, a gentle song or a hymn by which our soul might be refreshed again?

PHILOLAUS: I desire the same. (B1)

Praise ye the mighty, the merciful Lord,
    Ye worlds of His All-being.
Hosts of the Sun, flame ye to glorify Him,
    Earth forces sing His praise.

Let Echo praise Him and let Nature's choir
    Sing Him a paean of joy.
And thou, lord upon earth, O Man, outpour
    A wondrous harmony.

Thee more than any other being did He bless:
    He gave to thee a soul
Which through the whole great system seeks
    The springs which Nature move.

Exalt Him then for *thine own* blessedness
    He needs no praise for joy.
All lower inclinations, sins take flight
    When thou mov'st up to *Him*.

May ne'er the sun mount from its radiant flood
    And ne'er descend therein,
That thou fail'st to unite thy voice in song
    With Nature's voice itself.

Praise Him in rainfall and in time of drought
    In sunshine and in storm.
[515]   In snows, when frosts build bridges o'er the streams
    And when the Earth is green.

In time of flood, in war or pestilence
    Trust Him and sing His praise.
He'll keep thee safe, for all the human race
    Created He for joy.

And with what love He also cares for me!
    In place of fame or wealth
He gave me pow'r to recognize the Truth,
    Friendship and Harmony.

Preserve for me, O Lord, that which Thou gav'st,
    No more need I for joy.
With holy awe I'll praise Thee to eternity, or
    Else be powerless indeed.

In darkest forests ever will I seek
 For Thee alone.
And sigh aloud and e'er look for the sky
 Which through the branches peers.

Wander will I to the sea's shore and see
 Thee there in every wave,
And hear Thee in the storm, admire Thee
 On every meadow's floor.

Enraptured I will climb on cliffs and search
 Through tattered clouds,
And seek Thee through the day, till in the night
 I'm lulled in holy dreams.

THEOPHRON: Thank you, Philolaus. Through your harmonious singing you have inwardly refreshed me with Kleist's thoughts. I should like to say of music what Vanini said of [516] his straw. "If I were so unfortunate as to doubt of the existence of God, and had music, then it alone would be proof enough for me."

PHILOLAUS: There you persist in a very ancient way of thinking, Theophron. For in recent times, it has been made very clear that there neither is, nor can be any demonstration of God. (B1)

THEOPHRON: And I, for my part, would maintain that without the conception of God, there would be no reason, much less a demonstration. For even if one does not take into consideration the source of the forces which think, act and work, the tremendous number of which the transcendental philosopher, that is, one who overreaches himself, can never deny to be present in our world, yet the manner alone in which all these forces work according to their nature, is for me proof enough of God, that is, of an essential ground of inner truth, harmony, goodness and perfection which includes its existence in itself. (A1) The fact that there is, for example, a truth, that is, something capable of being thought, and that what can be thought can be related according to inner laws, and that by means of innumerable relations of this kind, harmony and order are revealed, is to me in itself the profoundest proof of God, even were I an unhappy egoist or idealist who imagined himself to be the only thinking being in the world. Between every [517] subject and predicate there stands an "is" or "is not," and this "is," this formula of equation and coincidence between different ideas, the mere sign =, is my proof of God. For I repeat, there is a reason, a relating of that which can be thought in the world according to immutable laws, and consequently there must be an essential basis of this relating, even supposing there were only a single thinking being. (A1) No one has arbitrarily conceived the law of this relation any more than any thinking being determined by space and time obeys it arbitrarily. It is the necessary basis of his, as of all thoughts, and is in the world of minds what the principle of equilibrium is among bodies. It carries its inner necessity with it. There is, thus, such an inner necessity, that is, a self-dependent truth.

PHILOLAUS: But where does this self-dependent truth reside?

THEOPHRON: In God; and by derivation it may reside objectively or subjectively in all to which He gave reality. Our knowledge is drawn from the senses and experience. We must therefore at first only observe and bring together many similarities, purify and abstract more general ideas from individual differences. All this is a method which renders errors in observation, in the abstraction, combination and distinction of ideas, not only possible but almost unavoidable. It is the necessary lot of mankind. But the law according to which we observe, abstract, infer and relate is a divine law. Even in error [518] we have acted according to it, and would have to act according to it even if all objects of thought were illusory. Consider the truths of geometry! For our senses there is perhaps no perfect circle in nature. But even if none did exist, the imagined mathematical circle with all that is assumed, abstracted and proved in it according to inner necessity, would be the most perfect demonstration of a self-dependent divine truth. It proves to me, namely, that there is a mathematical reason in the world. And since our senses alone prevent us from knowing and applying it everywhere in nature, this very reason by its essence tells us that if there are thinking beings who observe the world with finer senses, they nevertheless think according to exactly the same unique, necessary laws. Thus the **Being** which is the source of my reason and every other reason, must know the same inner laws of thought in the highest sense, and could do nothing else than make its effects into fundamental principles of existence. Do I make myself clear, Philolaus?

PHILOLAUS: Quite, only your proof is merely hypothetical: "If there is a reason, then there must also be a basis for it, and indeed a basis necessary in itself, because the laws of reason are necessary in themselves." I see very well that there only remains to be subsumed, "but there is a reason; [519] and therefore—" But what if there be none?

THEOPHRON: Then there would be none, and a philosopher who gives up or denies his reason, can indeed have no proof of God. Q.E.D. But as soon as he recognizes it and makes clear to himself what reason is, then in the idea of reason itself he is given proof of God, that is, of an essential necessity in the relation of truths. My friend, I make free to say that this is the only essential proof of God, (and there cannot be several which are essential) recurring in all proofs, but which nowhere appears so exact and pure as in the laws of our reason. For example, all proofs from nature where we observe necessary laws of motion and rest and of the persistence of things according to a relation of their inner forces and so on, presuppose as their basis the same rule that we perceive most purely in our reason, namely:—"That each thing is what it is, that its nature rests upon forces, its persistence upon an equilibrium of those forces, its activity upon the relations of these same forces to other things. All this is not through arbitrary purposes, which we set entirely aside, but through inner laws of necessity from which issue persistence [520] and destruction, combination and dissolution, motion, rest and activity." Every true physico-theology thus exhibits nothing but divine reason and power according to eternal necessary laws in the structure of creatures and in their entire interrelation in place and time. Everywhere it involves one and the same inference, or rather one and the same insight, in a thousand examples and objects, from the most vanishingly minute to the most unsurveyably great. The music, for example, with which you charmed me, is a formula of necessary, eternal harmony even if my ear did not exist and if I, excluding all its sensuous enjoyment, merely counted and measured it with my mind. That my ear, my sensibility, is musical, and that music affects so many beings like me in the same way, all this makes the proof of the indwelling harmony and beauty in it more vivid, but it adds nothing to its demonstrative value. For even if there were no ear in the world, and the nature of music were merely conceived by a reckoning mind, the proof would then already be complete.

PHILOLAUS: But what if there were no reckoning mind at all?

THEOPHRON: My friend, why should we repeat an absurdity? If there is no reckoning mind, then there is nothing reckoned, and hence also no harmony and order, which is [521] only a consequence of mind. If we do away with all thinking, then there is no object of thought, with all reality, then nothing real. But where do such sophistries get us; and are they worthy of a philosopher? If you trample the eternal principles of reason under foot and reduce them to suppositious tissues of words which have no existence and no necessary knowledge of an inner truth, then certainly no proof whether of one, or of any existence is possible. Yet what have you done thereby but destroyed Existence, the basis of all thought? And furthermore, how is a sound philosophy then possible? If even my senses in their way, that is in an obscure and confused way, convince me of Existence, why should not my reason be able to convince me of Existence in its way, that is, through clear comprehensive ideas? But if I ask reason to give me its ideas as sensuous perceptions without any perceptions by the senses, or to demonstrate the existence of sense objects which do not belong to its province at all as pure truths of reason, and condemn reason because it will not or cannot do so, then my condemnation has no more basis than if I wanted to hear colors, taste light and see noise. Let us beware, Philolaus, of straying into this region of hypercriticism of the sound understanding in which one builds without materials, exists without existence, knows without experience and works without powers. The concepts of this realm are like the Fata Morgana, illusory nothings, reflected images without substance, duration or true instruction.

PHILOLAUS: Then you do not construct your proof on the idea of cause and effect either? (B1)

THEOPHRON: I derive these ideas from the daily experi-[522] ence of sound reason. But I cannot transplant them to the province of demonstration, because I do not know clearly either what cause or effect is, much less the relation between the two. In no experience can it be demonstrated that this is the effect of that cause, although with sensuous clarity we know, or rather conjecture that it must be, because we often found both together or following one another. You are aware what false conjectures have often been made in this respect, about even the most ordinary things in the course of daily experience. And the reason for it is plainly that every inference from cause to effect, or contrariwise from effect to cause, was never a proof, but always merely a conjecture in the realm of the senses. We do not know what force is, nor how it works. We only see its activity as spectators, and hence construct analogous judgments for ourselves. We can never demonstrate the general laws about it, not even those we find best confirmed. What should we know more intimately than the force which thinks and works within ourselves? However, we know it as little as we know every other force external to us. I do not even understand the thoughts of my mind considered as effects. They are comprehensible to me only when I can bring them under the law of an inner necessity, "as eternal truths belonging to the essence of my reason." Therefore I have limited my proof to this in regard to God also. He who wishes to prove too much runs the risk of proving nothing.

PHILOLAUS: Then you will not give any explanation of the [523] manner of creation either, that is, whether it was a generation, emanation, or something of that sort?

THEOPHRON: How could I, since I do not know what creation or generation is? The ordinary conception is that God conceived the world out of Himself. It seems to be the purest conception because we have no idea of a purer activity than that of the thoughts of our mind. Leibniz and all other clear thinking minds also held this view, because experience afforded them no better image, and speech no better expression. The thoughts of our mind, it is said, are in themselves ineffectual images, but the thoughts of God, accompanied by inherent omnipotence, were in the highest degree effective. He thought and it was so. He willed and it stood accomplished. I believe that there is no more prudent formula than this for a matter which is inexplicable to us.

It does not, however, disclose to us the fundamental nature of activity. Rather we must be careful that we do not carry the deductions from it too far. The crude conception, for example, that after millions of eternities God conceived the world out of Himself as a spider draws its web out of itself, is intolerable to me.

PHILOLAUS: Then the cruder doctrine of emanation would be even more intolerable to you, and yet Spinoza himself is charged with borrowing his system from the Cabbalism of the Jews. (B1)

THEOPHRON: Who put that into your head, Philolaus?

PHILOLAUS: It is a very usual view. (A1)

THEOPHRON: Which has no further basis than the authority of a learned enthusiast whom I respect in every other [524] regard save as a philosopher. Wachter disputed with a Jew and sought to find Spinozism in Judaism. Later he himself became a very confused Spinozist, and sought to unite his own form of Spinozism, and not the doctrine of Spinoza, with the Cabbala. Both attempts were unfortunate. (A1) Spinoza's philosophy is so different from the Cabbala, that it is trouble in vain to seek to interpret the former through the latter. The Cabbala is a conglomeration of rubble good and bad, but on the whole, of visionary and obscure ideas in monstrous images, with which Spinoza's pure clear philosophical sense could have nothing to do. Otherwise he would have remained a Jew. In his entire *Ethics* you find no image, and his few similes virtually fail him. He is the opposite of the Cabbala if ever there was one. (A2) Nor has Spinoza's system any- [525] thing to do with the doctrine of the emanation which was, by the way, no more invented by the Jews than it was improved by them. (A1) Wherever he has to use the words "production," "activity" he uses them without further explaining the kind of production. But his favorite is the word, "expression." "The world expresses attributes, that is, powers of God in infinite number, in infinite ways." (A2) It seems to me that this manner of speaking is philosophical, pure and noble. (A3) Of "emanations" from God, Spinoza never speaks. Such figures are not favorites with a mathematical mind. In order to explain the activity of God, Leibniz once used the expression, "fulgurations" which was based on the beautiful image of the sun's rays. (B1) In Kästner* you can read how absurdly the image was subsequently taken up. Thus when we speak of God, let us rather use no images! This is our first commandment in philosophy as well as in Mosaic law.

PHILOLAUS: (A4) And yet the Hebraic Cabbalists heaped so many images on God?

THEOPHRON: Because for the most part they were as poor philosophers as they were poor disciples of Moses. Their God was called Jehovah, that is, "I am that I am, and shall be that [526] I shall be." This conception embraces the highest, completely incomparable Existence, even as it excludes all emanations. (A1) Spinoza remained true to this high, unique conception, and for this reason too I value him. There is no more absolute, more pure, more fruitful conception in human reason, for nothing can exceed the eternal, self-existing, most perfect Being, through which all is determined and in which all is given.

PHILOLAUS: Then the image of the World-Soul will not be overly pleasing to you either?

THEOPHRON: It is a human image, and if it is used prudently a great deal concerning the inherently indwelling power of

* Kästner's *Miscellaneous Writings,* Part 2, p. 11 ff.

God can be illustrated clearly by means of it. Nevertheless it remains an image, which, without the greatest care, immediately misleads one. Read, for example, the passage describing how Lessing conceived the image.

PHILOLAUS: "If Lessing wanted to conceive of a personal Deity, he thought of it as the Soul of All."*

THEOPHRON: Mark, "if he wanted to conceive of a personal Deity." But he himself had protested earlier against this "personal," and furthermore how could one call the soul in the body, a "person"?

PHILOLAUS: "And the whole he conceived after the analogy of an organic body. That soul of the whole would thus also be, as all other souls are according to all possible systems, as soul, merely an effect."

THEOPHRON: Reflect now upon the monstrous conse- [527] quences of a deceitful image. God the soul of the whole is an effect, nothing but an effect of the world. All other souls according to all possible systems are, as souls, merely effects. Probably then, they are only effects of a unification without a unifier. The body, that is to say, the world, becomes the creator, God a creature. Can you imagine any worse consequences of a facile explanation? If it were valid, everyone with his own conception of the soul, would attribute to God whatever he conceives or fancies the soul to be. (A1) (B1)

PHILOLAUS: "The organic context of this same soul, could not itself be conceived after the analogy of the organic parts of the context, insofar as it could be related to nothing which exists external to it, from which it could take, and to which it could give back."

THEOPHRON: Thus, God as soul of the world here acquires an organic context and parts of this context. He must be in

* *On the Doctrine of Spinoza*, p. 34.

relation to something which exists outside of Him, from which He could take and to which He could give back. O Spinoza! (A2) How far thou art even with all thy most difficult expressions, from such a catachresis of an image, as the "World-Soul"!

PHILOLAUS: "Thus, in order to sustain Himself in life, God must in some way withdraw into Himself from time to time, uniting death and resurrection with the life within Him. One could represent the economy of such a being in many ways," and so on. Probably all this was merely a joke on Lessing's [528] part, as his friend himself directly afterwards says,* that he used the idea of the World-Soul now in jest and now in earnest.

THEOPHRON: And thus Lessing himself demonstrates the deceptiveness of the whole image which could be turned this way and that, in earnest or in jest. You know Lessing's way of turning things in such a manner as to show the absurdity in the absurd. (A1)

PHILOLAUS: Nevertheless, my friend, we still thirst for a way of conceiving the world-all. Our mind cannot be satisfied with the particular, and if the whole, as I can well understand, can be no leviathan, "who struggles against the void, draws Himself into Himself with frightful contortions, expands Himself again, and thus creates life and death in order that the eternally living One may but keep Himself alive from time to time," — if all this is certainly not so, then what conception shall I form for myself of the world-all?

THEOPHRON: Not a sensuous conception, Philolaus! The endless has no image, much less the absolutely infinite and eternal One. Observe how our poet Haller summons up all the powers of his imagination in order to depict the endless. He cannot do it: (B1)

* p. 35.

Infinity!
O who can scan, who measure Thee, for Whom
Whole worlds are days and men a moment's flash.
Mayhap e'en now a thousandth sun may wheel
And thousands yet remain. Rolling apace
A sun like some vast timepiece animate
With balanced weight, hastens inspired by might
Of God. Its springs run down, another strikes.
But Thou, Infinity, Thou remainest
And dost not count their sum.

[529] With the last line the poet has himself destroyed his whole picture. He does the same with his even more beautiful picture of Eternity.

Time, sound and winds, e'en wings of light are slow
Compared with that swift flight of thought which tires
And loses hope of shore when it surveys Thee.
Prodigious numbers I compile. I heap
The mountainous millions, and time on time,
World upon world amass. But when I look
Up from the fearsome height once more to Thee,
All power of number, even magnified
A thousandfold is no fragment of Thee,
Subtract them all and yet I find
Thee whole before me.

Thus let us learn even from a philosophical poet to renounce metaphysical phantasms and vain intuitions of an endless space and an endless time, not to mention images of the indivisible, eternal Being. Whoever does not do so, brings monsters into philosophy, at which, as is just, the inventor is the first to shudder.

PHILOLAUS: Well then, I should like to learn without any images, the natural laws of God's economy, the symbols expressive of the highest reality, of a necessary goodness and wisdom. A clarification or a recapitulation of these eternal

ideas in the divine mind, would afford as much joy to you,
Theophron, as to me. (A1)

THEOPHRON: We shall devote the evening hours or tomor-
[530] row to it. Are you already acquainted with this Hymn?
It indeed gives you no image of God, but perhaps something
better than images. (B1)

GOD*

The One Alone, He who is All in All,
He is our God. Ye creatures, worship Him
The uncreated One, the One Alone
The Primal Being. Creatures, worship Him!

And thou, His great, His broad and lovely world
With all thy orbs of fire burning bright,
Thou wert not, thou becamest and thou art
In all thy splendor. Creatures, worship now!

Ten thousand of His suns came into being
And everlastingly go their great way.
Ten thousand of His worlds came into being
And everlastingly go their great way.
Ten thousand myriad spirits stand around
About His throne. Around about His throne?
Hence with His throne! He does not sit nor stand.

He is no king, no caliph, He. He is
The Being of all Beings. He is God,
He is our God! Ye creatures worship Him!

Whom has He ever to His workplace called,
To enter and to see, to see—
Him at His work? How He the sea
In supple fealty holds, so that
Of all its waters not a single drop
Seeks to leave its deep: How He
With silken thread the moon doth tie
[531] And holds it swinging in the azure sky; How He

* See Gleim's *Halladat*, III. [n. 2nd ed.]

Ten thousand million solar systems scans
And yet no single mote of dust is lost!
Who is like Him? Upon His earth there lives
No spirit more devoted, more sublime
And none looks from His cloud-course nor
His dawning sky, to tell me
How He does it! There is no seer of God,
No holy one, no devotee who knows of this.

From thee, thou little globe, whence we can see
But glimm'rings of ten thousand million globes a-far,
From thee up to the fiery sun, and thence to Sirius,
Which, a million times as great as thou, is yet
To poor earthdwellers' sight, the merest speck.
From tiny beetle to the eagle proud
Who in his flight dwarfs Caucasus;
From thee, O little snail, whose blood
Must tint the garb of humans proud,
To thee, sly ape, who paints his jowls
In beauty's mimicry; and thence
To spiritual man who would
Conceive of God the Being of all beings—

Ah what steps! What grades are there
In all these million things!
In all the dead, in all the quick,
In all the light, and heavy!—God
The One Alone, He who is All in All,
He is our God! Ye creatures, worship Him!

Fifth Conversation

THEANO: (B1) My friends, allow me to become your visi-
[532] ble auditor today, as thus far I have listened invisibly.
Much of your conversations I have not understood, and I do
not demand to understand everything today either. It will
suffice me if I but follow the sense of your discussion as a
whole. Do not let my presence disturb you. I shall do my work
in silence and accompany you only with my thoughts.

THEOPHRON: You are welcome to our conversation, Theano.
Philolaus, you have no objection to Theano listening to us, have
you?

PHILOLAUS: I should object very much if she intended to
do so only silently. You must mix in our conversation, and
when it wanders into empty metaphysics, help it back to the
human scene. Do you promise to do this, Theano?

THEANO: I shall interrupt you as little as possible, and
instead, shall help you now to start the conversation. Yesterday, Philolaus, you wished to know the laws of God's regimen
in the world, or, as you put it, the symbols expressive of His
reality, power, wisdom and goodness. But how is it possible
that Theophron should draw so few drops out of the ocean
which flows around us? Yesterday I heard almost with disgust
how you expressed views as if the existence of God were un-
knowable, and I was astonished Theophron, that you could
[533] wish to engage in these petty subtleties. It seems to me
that the existence of a being can be known only through being
and the observation of it, and not through arbitrary conceptions and empty words, any more than it can be eliminated by
the latter. There is a saying that we become neither rich nor

162

satisfied through dreams, and just as little do we become so through words. We are human beings, and as such, it seems to me, we must learn to know God as He has really offered and revealed Himself to us. Through ideas we apprehend Him only as an idea, through words only as a word, but through observations of nature, through the use of our powers, through the enjoyment of life, we enjoy Him as a real Existence full of force and life. If you call this enthusiasm, then I shall gladly be an enthusiast, for I would rather see and enjoy the real rose than dream with barren racking of my brains, of an imagined or painted rose.

THEOPHRON: Bravo, Theano! Yet you see the rose which you enjoy and you would not blindfold your eyes because of that enjoyment. And what are you working at there? Why, you are embroidering the flower yourself. You are then imitating the art of nature, which only your seeing eye made visible to you, and which now your mind's eye, your lively memory as it were, is tracing for the needle. Do not, therefore, exclude thought from any feeling or from any enjoyment of the creation. It is as necessary to our observation of God, as the image of the sketch in your mind is necessary to your working needle. He would misunderstand humanity who sought only to taste and feel the Creator without seeing or apprehending Him.

THEANO: Do not accuse me of that, Theophron, for I am [534] warning Philolaus against exactly the same sort of error of one-sided discrimination. I love philosophy heartily if it confines itself to objects of nature and brings them to light. I was very happy when you called your friend's attention to the beauty, goodness, and truth which is not arbitrarily affixed to objects, but which lies in every being as its own reality and constitutes that being. Since then I have taken pains to discover this aspect of pure necessity in all that is about me, and

I always perceive truth, goodness and beauty in it. I wish I could arrange my whole life, all my affairs, my least art, yes, even this insignificant flower, in such a way that the weaving Minerva herself would have to say, "Other than thus it could not be done." How much comfort and sweetness there is in the word "necessity," especially for our sex which is allowed so little free-will through the ordinance of nature and the decrees of men. I thank the good Adrastea for allowing us so little, for it is our own sex which strives most for arbitrariness. I now love this daughter of gracious wisdom, and hate all caprice. That I relinquish to the men who imagine themselves to be the arbitrary lords of the earth.

THEOPHRON: Do not think too highly of these arbitrary [535] lords, dear Theano. The less intelligence one has, the more one is and loves to be arbitrary. I should like to know the man who, in whatever small affair of life it might be, could accomplish it equally well in innumerable ways, and thought it possible that the selection of one of these ways could be left to his blind choice. The most beautiful and difficult aim of a man's life is to learn duty from his youth on, to practice it in the easiest and best way in every moment of life as though it were not duty, and so to attain every time the highest point of art, the law of the uniquely best, of pure and beautiful necessity. This is not compulsion, not internal or external pressure, although it seems so to an inexperienced, lazy and capricious person. Its yoke is gentle and its burden light when once one is accustomed to it. Woe to him who becomes hardened in evil habits! But joy to every intelligent active person whose duty, and the best performance of it, becomes his nature, that is, his necessity. He has in himself the reward of the good angels of whom religion says that they are secure in goodness, and can fall no more nor want to fall, because their duty is their nature, because their virtue is their heaven and their blessedness. We, too, my friends, shall strive to enjoy the inward reward of these blessed beings. Nay, why should we stop with them since all around us in nature we are guided by the example of our Father Himself, who acts in the smallest and largest things entirely without weak arbitrariness, but with the whole beauty and goodness of a self-dependent reason, truth and necessity.

I see, Philolaus, that you are getting your notebook ready. First, however, you, with our friend Theano, must help me to discover the propositions which you want to set down.

PHILOLAUS: Gladly, as soon as you show me the way!

THEOPHRON: Very well, my friends! God Himself will aid [536] us since we are striving to unfold the nature of His being and of His works as the wisest, best necessity. In producing beings in a way incomprehensible to us, is there anything higher which He could give them than that which is highest in Himself, namely existence? In God it is the essence and ground of all enjoyment, the root of all His infinite forces, and it is no less so in every existing thing. Despite all our dependence, we too are, or think ourselves to be, substances, and we feel our existence with such inner certainty, with such tranquil love and joy, that we are not merely reluctant to think of the destruction of our existence, but try as we will, cannot conceive of it. It is the nature of the thinking mind that it has absolutely no conception of nothingness, and it requires a strange barrenness of mind even to imagine that nothingness is a conceivable idea. The mind can conceive a sign for nothing, "O" or "$\sqrt{-1}$," and when it recognizes two things as contradicting one another, it can negate one through the other. That is to say, it can clearly understand that while it conceives the one it cannot at the same time conceive the other also to be so. But thereby it has nothing so little as an idea of absolute nothingness. For example, instead of the full

[537] space of the world, it can imagine a tremendous, black, empty space, but still it does not thereby imagine nothingness. In short nothingness is nothing, and it is thus also a nothing that is completely inconceivable to every being that exists, let alone to the sum of all reality, God Himself. Do you see, Philolaus, what rests upon this inherent necessity of the idea of existence for every thinking being?

PHILOLAUS: The most beautiful truth rests upon it, namely that there is no void in nature, that there never was any nor ever will be, because a nothing is something inconceivable. Consider this line:

> Pregnant with the power of the essence-laden word,
> The ancient Void gives birth. . . .

Or:

> While new Creation still strove with the inane
> And from the night of ancient nothingness
> The stream of light first flowed. . .

As these descriptions of the poet, like the expression, "to create something out of nothing," have no meaning other than a poetic one, so our mind has equally little idea of what it means to annihilate something, or to transform something into nothing. Again, when the poet sings:

> When nothingness again entombs the world
> When of the All itself, nought but its place
> Remains. . . . .,

if the place of this world continues to exist, and therewith (B1) a place for new worlds, then nothing prevails so little [538] as nothingness. I cannot tell you, my friend, how abhorrent all these false expressions and empty specters of an obscure imagination are to me now. When many metaphysicians do away with everything conceivable, the world, God Himself, and find this monstrous nothingness very conceivable as the purest object of their reason, and find it entirely natural that with all the powers of reason, nothing, neither God nor the world can be demonstrated out of nothingness. . . .

THEANO: Please, Philolaus, have done with this horrible "nothingness."

PHILOLAUS: Or, when even the existence, the joyful necessary existence of God seems horrible to them,—"Pure necessity," they say, "as the final support of all things, is an abyss for reason. Even Haller's Eternity does not make the mind swoon so much as does the necessary existence of God; for the former, though it measures, cannot support anything. We cannot bear the thought that a Being which moreover we conceive as the highest of all possible beings should, as it were, say to itself, 'I am from eternity to eternity. Outside of me there is nothing except that which is something through my will alone. But whence am I?' Here, they say, everything falls from under us and the greatest perfection like the smallest, wavers without support, defenseless before speculative reason, which suffers no loss in allowing the one like the other to disappear without the slightest interference."*

THEANO: Save me, Theophron, from the barren concep-[539] tions which Philolaus quotes. I am a woman, and since I have listened to your last conversations, I shall think neither of Haller's Eternity as a measuring one, nor of the wisest necessity as a support, nor yet of the Highest as the proud unknowing One, who vaingloriously speaks with Himself, and foolishly asks, "Whence am I?" I do not know whether among philosophers an obscure feeling wins the decision over clear ideas, or whether it is a triumph of reason to allow the greatest perfection like the smallest to disappear before it, arbitrarily

* Kant, *Critique of Pure Reason.* (2nd ed.) p. 641. "If we say 'there is no God' neither the omnipotence nor any other of its predicates is given; they are one and all rejected, together with the subject, and there is therefore not the least contradiction in such a judgment." Ibid. p. 623. [Kemp Smith trans.]

and without the slightest interference; but I do know that according to my idea there can be no higher, more blessed Being than that through whom all is, through whom all enjoy and live. If the existence of everything rests upon an inherent necessity of His highest wisdom and goodness, He cannot laboriously support anything. Everything supports itself as a sphere rests upon its center of gravity; for all existence is grounded in His own eternal essence, in His power, wisdom, and goodness. You have, indeed, warned us against images, Theophron, but is it really intolerable to think of the root as supporting the tree? It would die and be no root if it did not have to support that beautiful creation, the trunk, with its branches, twigs, blossoms and fruit. So God, the eternal root [540] of the immeasurable tree of life which is entwined throughout the universe, He, the infinite source of existence, that greatest gift which only He could give. . . .

THEOPHRON: And what security this gift affords, my friends, for the perpetuation of our lives! Existence is an indivisible conception, an essence. It can no more be reduced to nothingness than there can be a nothingness, or than God could annihilate Himself. I am not now speaking of appearances, of any compound forms in what we call space and time. All that appears must also disappear. Every flower of time carries within itself the seed of decay, which provides that it does not last forever in its appearance. What is compounded becomes dissolved, for precisely this composition and dissolution itself is the world-order, and the ever-active life of the World-Spirit. Nor am I at present speaking of the immortality of the human soul, and I am not at all willing to describe to you any phantoms of the imagination, such as how it will take on other organs, and renew the exercise of its soul-forces in space and time, that is, in the great world-order. What we are speaking about it a simple idea, Existence, in

[541] which the lowest as well as the highest being has a part. Nothing can perish, nothing can be annihilated, else God would have to annihilate Himself; but everything compounded is dissolved, everything which occupies place and time migrates. Hence, since everything which can be and is, lies in the infinite existence, how endless the world becomes, my friend, endless in space and time and in-itself-enduring. God has bestowed the basis of His own blessedness on beings, of which the smallest and the largest like Him enjoy existence, and to use your comparison, Theano, like branches draw from His eternal root the eternal sap of life.

I think therefore, Philolaus, that we shall write down the first natural law of divine necessity.

PHILOLAUS: I. The highest Existence knew of nothing higher than existence to give His creatures.

THEOPHRON: But, my friend, simple as the idea is, one existence and another are very different in their conditions. Philolaus, what do you think constitutes their gradations and differences?

PHILOLAUS: Nothing else than forces! We found no higher conception in God Himself. All His forces, however, were but one. The highest Power could be nothing but the highest Wisdom and Goodness eternally-living, eternally-active.

THEOPHRON: Now you yourself see, Philolaus, that the Highest, or rather the All (for God is not the Highest in a gradation of things like Him), could reveal itself as active [542] in nothing else than in All. Nothing could be dormant in Him, and what He expressed was Himself, an indivisible wisdom, goodness and omnipotence. The world of God is thus the best, not because He selected it from among the less good, but rather because neither good nor bad existed without Him, and He, according to the inner necessity of His existence could effect nothing bad. Therefore all forces exist which could exist, all together forming an expression of the All-wise, All-good and All-beautiful. He is active in the smallest and in the largest, in every point of space and time, that is, in every living force of the universe. For space and time are only phantoms of our imagination, conditions of measurement for a limited mind which must acquaint itself with things one after another and side by side. For God there is neither space nor time, but all is an eternal connection. He is before all and all exists in Him. The whole world is an expression, an appearance of His eternally-living, eternally-active forces.

THEANO: And oh, how glad we should be that insignificant appearances though we are, there yet dwells in us an expression of the three highest forces of God and the universe: power, reason and goodness. I can imagine no other, let alone [543] higher attributes. For what I see of the divine in all the works of nature, leads back to these three of which one explains the other, and whose highest essence and source is in God. Thus we also have the essential law of God in us, namely, to order our limited power according to ideas of truth and goodness, as the Almighty Himself practices them in accordance with His most perfect nature. He thereby bestowed upon us something essential to Himself and made us into images of His perfection, in that it lies within the nature of a divine force to work, not blindly, but with the highest reason and a goodness which makes nothingness an impossibility. But how far do we depart from this law with every arbitrary, unreasoning and unrighteous use of these forces!

THEOPHRON: Do not worry, Theano, for if it lies within the essence of every divine force to work not blindly but rather according to wisdom and goodness, then this apparent shadow in creation will also clear up for us. (A1) I think, Philolaus, that we can now set down the second great principle of divine necessity.

II. The Deity in whom there is but one essential force [544] which we call power, wisdom and goodness could produce nothing else than a living impression of the same, which is itself therefore, power, wisdom and goodness, and which must inseparably form the essence of every existence appearing in the world.

PHILOLAUS: I have set down the principle and understand it from the nature of God. I wish, however, that you would illustrate it for Theano and myself with particular examples. The grades of perfection in the world are so innumerably manifold that the lowest of them seem imperfections to us.

THEOPHRON: Could it be otherwise, Philolaus? If everything possible exists and must exist according to the principle of an infinite divine force, then the least as well as the highest perfection must exist in this All, only they are all bound together by the highest goodness, and even in the least there is no nothingness, that is, nothing which is essentially evil. Forgive me, Theano, if I must use this expression again, although it is an absurdity which destroys itself. You know, Philolaus, what great things Leibniz claimed for his simple substances. "They are mirrors of the universe endowed with powers of perception to represent and reflect the universe, each according to its point of view. The Infinite sees the All in the smallest and the smallest in the All." (B1)

Sublime as this idea was, and necesssary as it is when one regards the world as an activity of the highest perfection connected in all its parts, it was falsely understood by many people, and especially the infinitesimal simple mirrors of the [545] universe were unworthily interpreted. Let us therefore dispense with this deceptive image, because images do not belong to philosophy, and say instead that, "Every substantial force is in its essence an expression of the highest power, wisdom and goodness as this has been able to present and reveal itself in such and such a place in the universe, and in relation, that is, with all other forces." In order to understand this, we need only observe how each one of these substantial forces functions in the world. You agree with me, do you not, Philolaus, that it functions organically?

PHILOLAUS: Entirely. For I am ignorant of any force which evinces itself outside of bodies, that is, without organs, although I am just as ignorant of how these forces and these organs have come together.

THEOPHRON: Because of their reciprocal nature, Philolaus. In the interconnected realm of the most perfect power and wisdom they could do nothing else. For what do we call body, what do we call organs? In the human body, for example, nothing is without life. From the tips of the hair to the end of the nails everything is pervaded by one sustaining and nourishing force and as soon as this leaves the smallest or largest member, that member separates itself from the body. Then it is no longer in the realm of the living forces of our humanity, but it never escapes from the realm of natural forces. [546] The dead hair, the cast-off nail, now enters another region of the world-nexus in which it again acts or is acted upon only in accordance with its present nature. Now examine the wonders which the physiology of the human being or of any animal unfolds for us. You see nothing but a realm of living forces, each fixed in its place, producing by its activities the connection, structure and life of the whole, and each the consequence of its essential nature. So the body forms and sustains itself. So it spends itself daily, and finally spends itself entirely. All that we call matter is thus more or less imbued with life. It is a realm of active forces which form a whole, not only as a phenomenon for our senses, but in accordance with their nature and their connection. One force dominates, otherwise there would be no unity, no whole. Many serve on the most different levels. But all of these differences, each of which is perfectly determinate, have, however, something in common, dynamic, interactive, otherwise again, they could form no unity, no whole. Now since in the realm of the most perfect power and wisdom, the all is connected in the wisest manner, for nothing in it can combine, support and form itself except in accordance with inherent, necessary laws of things themselves, we therefore see everywhere in nature innumerable organizations of which each in its way is not only wise, good and beautiful, but a perfection, that is, a replica of wisdom, goodness and beauty as it was able to reveal itself in a particular combination. Thus, nowhere in the world, in no leaf of a tree, in no grain of sand, in no fibre of our body, [547] does arbitrariness rule. Everything is determined, fixed and ordered by forces which work in every point of creation, in accordance with the most perfect wisdom and goodness. Examine, my friend, the history of the miscarriages, wastes and monstrosities when the laws of nature seem to be upset through alien causes. The laws of nature were never upset. Every force acted true to its nature, even when another disturbed it; for even this disturbance itself could produce no effect save that the disturbed force sought to compensate itself in another way. I have made extraordinary observations on such compensations in a system of disturbed forces which we can discuss some other time. But on every hand, even in the apparently greatest chaos, I have found constant nature, that is to say, immutable laws of a highest necessity, goodness, and wisdom, active in every force.

PHILOLAUS: I am happy, Theophron, that you have cleared up the obscure conception of matter for me. For although I gladly accepted the system of Leibniz which said that it could be nothing but a phenomenon of our senses, an aggregate of substantial monads, yet the so-called "ideal connection between such substances," in this system remained an enigma to me. Leibniz compared matter to a cloud which is made [548] up of rain drops and only seems a cloud to us, or even to a garden full of plants and trees, to a pond full of fish, and the like. (B1) But by those means I was still unable to explain to myself the existence of this appearance, the connection of these forces. The raindrops in the cloud, the plants in the garden, the fish in the water have a connecting medium, and what could such a medium between the forces constituting matter be, except the forces of the substances themselves, through which they act upon one another? In this way, then, are organs formed; for the organ itself is also a system of forces which in their inner connection serve a single ruling one. Matter no longer remains for me merely an appearance in my idea, or something connected only through the ideas of perceiving creatures, but exists itself through its nature and truth, through the inherent connection of active forces. Nothing is isolated in nature, nothing is without cause, nothing without effect. And since everything possible exists, and exists in connection, nothing in nature therefore is without organization. Every force is connected with other forces which either serve or rule it. Hence, if my soul is a substantial force and its present realm of activity is destroyed, then it can never lack a new organ in a creation in which there is no gap, no leap, no island. New serving forces will come to its aid and form its sphere of activity in its new connection with a world in which all is connected.

THEOPHRON: And from this, dear Philolaus, what a necessary duty results, to see to it that the soul departs thence, [549] well-ordered within, in the system of its forces; for only as it is, can it work. Its external form can appear only in accord with the form of its inherent forces. Our body is only an instrument, a mirror of the soul. Every organization is an external replica of internal efforts which give its appearance stability.

PHILOLAUS: I am reminded by this of many beautiful observations of Spinoza's, which he made about the connection between body and soul; for, although in accordance with the Cartesian system he had to regard both as entirely independent of one another, like thought and extension, nevertheless a keen spirit like his could not fail to reflect upon the harmony of the two. He makes the conception of body the essential form of the human soul, and excellently reasons from that to the condition, the modifications, the perfection and imperfection of this conception. A physiognomy could be developed from his principles which would, to a great extent, set in order the usual chaos of our physiognomical dreams, and refer them back to a definite truth. It especially pleased me that he sets such great store by the process of life, that is, by the modifications in the condition of the body and that he sets parallel with it, the process of thought, that is to say, the form of the conception of the soul. He does not derive the most versatile and delicate mainsprings of the soul, its capacities and its character, from the contour of a leg or a bone, al-[550] though no one would deny that every little contour of the body also belongs to the analogy of the whole. But you are silent, Theano?

THEANO: Your conversation pleases me very much, my friends. But still, because you once appointed me to remind you again of the path whenever you wandered, I wish that you would leave this endless subject of physiognomy, and return to the more general theme of your discourse. Since I am always satisfied with very little, it is enough for me that every organization is the appearance of a system of inner living forces which, in accordance with laws of wisdom and goodness, form a kind of small world, a whole. I wish I could conjure up the spirit of the rose at my work, so that it would tell me how it made its beautiful form, or, since it is only a daughter of the rose-bush, I wish that its dryad would explain how she animated her little tree from the root up to the smallest twig. Even as a child I often stood still before a tree or a flower and marveled at the extraordinary harmony which reveals itself in every living creature from head to foot. I compared many of them and dreamed away many idle hours in the examination of the leaves, branches, blossoms, stems, and the whole growth of trees and plants. The desire to draw such naturally beautiful forms from the living model sharpened my attention, and often I came into such intimate converse with the flower, the tree, the plant, that I believed its essence, which I had caught, must enter into my small creation. But in vain, my creation remained a dead image, and that beautiful, passing creature stood there in all its fulness and calm self-sufficiency, as it were, in an existence complete [551] in and for itself. Speak more of this matter, and aid my stammering talk of nature.

THEOPHRON: Dear Theano, it will probably always remain stammering. We have no senses that can look into the inner nature of things. We stand outside and must observe. The keener and calmer the gaze with which we do this, the more there is revealed to us the living harmony of nature, in which every thing is the most perfect unity, and yet each is interwoven with every other in such various and manifold ways. Art follows this observation of nature, and the modern, more watchful natural science is her sister. It observes in every thing just what it is, how it is constructed, how it acts and is acted upon. It has stored up treasures of information about plants, trees, minerals, animals and so on, about their origin, growth, maturity, and decay, about diseases, death and life, which show us a world of self-existing harmony, goodness and wisdom in every single object. However, this is not to be discussed now. One must see all this on beautiful spring and summer days rather than hear of it now in the twilight talk of evening. What I should like to call your attention to, are the simple laws by which all living forces of nature produce their thousandfold organizations; for everything which the highest Wisdom does, must be in the highest degree simple. The laws, then, seem to me to consist in three words which again are fundamentally only one living conception:

1. Persistence: that is, the inner persistence of every being. [552]   2. The union of likes and repulsion of opposites.

3. Assimilation to self, and reproduction of one's nature in another.

If, to use your expression, Theano, you would also like to hear me stammer about this, then my speech is at your service. We at least, Philolaus, shall thereby crown our discussion of Spinoza, for you know that he himself constructed his moral philosophy on these conceptions.

First, then: Every being is what it is, and has neither any conception of nothingness, nor any desire for it. The whole perfection of a thing is its reality. The awareness of this reality is the inherent reward of its existence, its inner joy. In the so-called moral world, which is also a natural world, Spinoza sought to refer all the passions and strivings of man back to this inner love for existence and for persistence therein. In the physical world, there have been various names, in part unworthy, given to the phenomena which follow from this law of nature. Now it is called the "force of inertia," since everything remains what it is and does not change without a cause; and then again it is called, though from another point of view, the "force of gravity," according to which every thing has its center of gravity upon which it rests. Like their opposite, motion, inertia and gravity are only appearances, since space and body themselves are only appearances. The true essential in every thing is persistence, continuation of its existence, which it neither can nor wants to disturb. That every thing thus strives after a condition of persistence, its structure itself [553] shows, and you, Theano, as a sketcher of nature, will be able to explain much in the form of things if you pay attention to this. Let us take the easiest example from the system of those things which combine the greatest homogeneity with the greatest mobility and which can thus, as it were, elect a form. We call this class, fluid things. Very well, then, Philolaus, what form is assumed by all fluid things whose parts tend to work unhindered toward homogeneity with one another?

PHILOLAUS: The form of a drop.

THEOPHRON: And why a drop? Should we perhaps assume a drop-forming principle in nature which arbitrarily prefers this form?

PHILOLAUS: By no means! The drop is a sphere. In a sphere all the parts homogeneously surround a central point in harmony and order. The sphere rests upon itself; its center of gravity is in the middle. Its form is thus the most beautiful state of persistence of homogeneous entities which enter into connection around this middle point and counterbalance one another with equal forces. Thus a world comes into being in the drop according to necessary laws of harmony and order.

THEOPHRON: Consequently, dear Philolaus, in the law by which the drop is formed, you have at the same time the law by which our earth, the sun, and all heavenly systems are formed. For our earth, too, once emerged from the fluid state and was collected in a drop. So the sun and that whole system [554] in which it rules with attracting power, is a greater drop. Everything tends to gravitate toward a center and is only maintained in its revolution by other forces. Thus the revolution of all planets must more or less approximate a circle. The sun in its system, together with a million other suns, again forms a circle or an ellipse in which they all move about a common middle- or focal-point, as is shown by the Milky Way and by those systems of suns, the Nebulae. All are bright drops out of the ocean of the Deity, which sought their state of persistence according to inherent eternal laws of harmony and order in their structure and motion, and found it. Not otherwise than in the form of the sphere and in revolution, the product of opposite forces, could they find it; not through arbitrariness, but in accordance with inherent laws of homogeneously working forces in fluidity, in spherical form, in elliptical revolution. The little tear, Theano, which you find of a morning in the calyx of a rose, shows you the law by which earth, suns, and all solar, yes, even world-systems took form. For if we permit our fancy the vast flight of conceiving the entire universe, the result is not a colossus but a sphere which rests upon itself.

THEANO: Thank you, Theophron, for this immeasurably expansive view which rests on such a simple self-supporting law [555] of nature. But come back to our earth, or at least to our solar system, for I do not like to fly so high. You spoke of a second law of nature, that likes attract, and opposites repel each other. Won't you give examples of this?

THEOPHRON: I shall keep to my fluid drop. You know, do you not, Theano, the stone of hate and love in the natural world?

THEANO: You mean the magnetic stone?

THEOPHRON: None other, and although the theory of it is still very obscure, the experiences with it are by comparison the more plain. You know, then, its two poles and their friendly or inimical activity?

THEANO: I know them, and I also know that there is a point of greatest love and a point of complete indifference on its axis.

THEOPHRON: Then you know all that I need for my example. Consider the magnet as a round drop in which the magnetic force is distributed so homogeneously and evenly, that its opposite ends form the north and soul poles. You know that one cannot come into being without the other.

THEANO: I know that, and also that if one changes one, one changes both.

THEOPHRON: Then you have in the magnet the most beautiful image of what hate and love in nature are, and I am sure [556] that the identical thing will be found in many, and perhaps in all fluids.

PHILOLAUS: And that identical thing is—?

THEOPHRON: That wherever a system of homogeneous forces acquires an axis, they so dispose themselves about it and about their middle point, that every like force flows to the like pole; and from it they are ordered according to geometrical laws through all the grades of progression to a culmination, and then through the point of indifference to the opposite pole. Every sphere would in this way be a union of two hemispheres with opposite poles, as every ellipse with its two foci. And the laws of this construction would according to fixed laws lie in the active forces of the system which is thus formed. Just as there cannot be a north pole without a south pole in a sphere, so too in a regularly formed system of forces there can be no structure in which the friendly and the inimical are not likewise separated; and hence it forms a whole precisely through the counterbalance which the two effect with one another according to increasing and diminishing grades of the union. There could probably be no system of electrical forces in the world, if there were not two electricities [557] in opposition to one another, which have, moreover, actually been found by experience. It is the same with heat and cold, and probably the same with every system of forces which can maintain unity only through variety, and union only through opposition. Empirical natural science, which is still so young, will one day advance so far in all this, that it will finally banish from the world all blind arbitrariness, in which everything would fall apart and all the laws of nature would cease. For you must concede to me, my friends, that if the magnet, electrical force, light, heat and cold, attraction, gravity and so on, function arbitrarily, if the triangle is no triangle, and the circle no circle, then we could declare all the observations of physics and mathematics to be nonsense, and wait for arbitrary revelations. But if it is certain that we have already found mathematically exact laws of nature in so many forces, who will dare to set the limits where they are no longer to be found, and where the blind will of God begins? In Creation, everything is connection and order. Thus if only a single natural law exists anywhere in it, natural laws must prevail everywhere, or else Creation would fall apart like a chaos.

THEANO: But, my friend, you are getting away from the [558] law of hate and love, whereby, according to your system, the one cannot be without the other.

THEOPHRON: Because everything exists in the world that can exist, opposites must also exist, and a law of the highest Wisdom must everywhere form a system out of this opposition, out of this north and south pole. In every region of nature there is the table of the thirty-two winds, in every ray of sunlight the whole color prism, and it is only a question of which wind blows now and then, which color appears here and there. As soon as the solid emerges from the fluid, everything is crystallized and formed in accordance with the inner laws which lie in our system of active forces. Everything attracts, repels, or remains indifferent to everything else, and the axis of these active forces is continuous throughout all gradations. The chemist institutes nothing but marriages and divorces; nature does so in a much richer, deeper way. Everything seeks and finds its mutual love, and natural science itself could not help adopting the expression, "elective attrac-[559] tion" for the combinations of bodies. Opposites repel one another and are brought together in the point of indifference. Often the forces interchange rapidly, whole systems behaving differently, as do the individual forces of the system among themselves. Hate can become love, love hate—all for one and the same reason, that every system seeks to persist in itself and orders its forces to that end. Thus you see how cautious one must be with analogies between external phenomena, since merely because we find several similar laws in them, one is not immediately justified in considering magnetism, for example, to be the same as electricity. The systems of forces can be very different from one another and yet function in accordance with the same laws, because finally everything in nature must be interconnected, and there can be but one principal law, according to which even the most different forces are ordered.

THEANO: Your law of persistence, of hatred and love, in my opinion, comes very close to this principal law; for it appears everywhere regardless of all the innumerable differences and opposed phenomena in nature. I should like to be a higher spirit for a few minutes, that I might observe this great workshop from the inside.

THEOPHRON: Do not wish that, Theano! The spectator from the outside has perhaps a better, or at least a more agreeable view than an observer from inside who could never survey the whole either. The spectator in front of the stage is more com-[560] fortable than he who peeps from the wings. The search for truth has the greater charm; the possession of it may make one satiated and indolent. To pursue nature, first to conjecture her lofty laws, then to observe, test and confirm them, then to find them verified a thousandfold and to apply them anew, finally, to perceive everywhere the same wisest law, the same divine necessity, to come to love it and make it one's own— all this gives human life its value. For, good Theano, are we merely spectators? Are we not ourselves actors, participants in nature, and her followers? Do not hate and love reign also in the kingdom of man? And are not both equally necessary for the formation of the whole? He who cannot hate, cannot love either, only he must learn to hate rightly and love rightly. There is also a point of indifference amongst men, but praise God! in the whole magnetic axis, this is but one single point.*

PHILOLAUS: Now I must remind you, Theophron, that you still owe us your third part of the great law of nature, namely: "How beings assimilate one to another and form a continuous series in the reproduction of their kind."

THEANO: I need not leave at this point, need I, Theophron?

THEOPHRON: In the name of all the Graces, no, Theano! For we are discussing the most hallowed and certainly divine law. All things that love one another, become assimilated the one to the other. As two colors flow together so that a third [561] intermediate one is produced, so in a wonderful manner, human souls, yes, even facial expressions and features, the subtlest shades of thought and action, become like one another through mutual intercourse. Insanity, illnesses, fanaticism, fear and all passions, are infectious evils not because of that which is evil or nothingness in them, but because of the strength of their active forces. How then should not the activity of regular forces, that is, order, harmony and beauty extend and impart itself to others with much more vital power? We saw that organizations come into being only because

---

* The analogy of these examples will be discussed elsewhere. [Omitted in 2nd ed.]

stronger forces attract weaker ones into their province, and cast them into a form according to the implanted laws of a necessary goodness and truth. All goodness imparts itself. It has the nature of God, who could do nothing else but impart Himself; it has also His infallible efficacy. The laws of beauty for example, urge themselves upon us, they shine upon us, they pass over into us imperceptibly, and this is precisely the secret of the universally connected, active, self-existent creation. The friendly intercourse of human souls makes them similar to one another without compulsion, without words. As Leibniz assumed an ideal influence of the monads upon one another, so I should like to make this ideal influence the secret bond of creation, which we observe irrepressible and indestructible in thinking and acting beings. Let no one despair of the efficacy [562] of its existence. The more order there is in it, and the more it acts conformably to the laws of nature, the more infallible is its activity. Like God, it works omnipotently, and cannot do otherwise than bring order into a chaos around it, and dispel darkness so that there will be light. It makes similar to its beautiful form all that is in agreement with it, yes, more or less, even that which is in opposition to it.*

THEANO: A comforting, beautiful truth, Theophron! It already bears the seal of truth in speaking to our heart and by recalling to me a thousand experiences of my life. There is an unnamable force in the existence of a person, in the way in which his active, calm example works. Everything good in me became mine in this manner. Your way of thinking, Theophron, pleases me because it makes present in all that is about me the all-active One who, according to essential laws of harmony and beauty, acts upon us through the existence of His crea-

* On these general laws of nature, and especially on the affinity and assimilation of beings, see the excellent remarks in the *Observations of the Universe* (Erfurt. 1777) (B 1).

tures themselves. Now I feel that everything living in His [563] realm should become like God, yes, if I may say so, must become like Him. His nature, His thoughts and activities force themselves upon us as immutable laws, even against our will, in thousand upon thousand proofs of His order, goodness and beauty. He who does not wish to follow, must follow; for everything compels him; he cannot escape the all-powerful chain. Happy he who follows willingly! He possesses the sweet, illusory reward that he is forming himself, although God unremittingly forms him. In that he obeys intelligently and serves with love, all creatures and events stamp him with the imprint of the Deity. He becomes intelligent, good, orderly, happy. He becomes like God.—But let us return to the physical economy of things. Is there not compulsion in the fact that one force overthrows another, attracts it to itself and unites it with its nature? When I observe that all the life of creatures depends upon the destruction of other species, that man lives on animals, animals on one another, or only on plants and fruits, then, to be sure, I see organic wholes which form themselves, but which at the same time destroy others. That is to say, I see murder and death in creation. Is not a blade of grass, a flower, the fruit of a tree, and finally an animal which becomes the food of another, just as beautiful an organization as that which destructively converts it into itself? Theophron, drive away this cloud for me, which is drawn like a veil over my view of the sun beaming from every created thing!

THEOPHRON: It will flee, Theano, when you observe that without this apparent death in creation, all would be real [564] death, that is, an inactive quiescence, an empty realm of shadows in which all true, active existence would die. Just now you spoke like a disciple of Plato. Have you not found in your teacher, that in the changing, all is change, that on the wing of time, all is process, haste and migration? Stop but one wheel in creation, and all wheels stand still. Permit one point of what we call matter to be dead and inactive, then death is everywhere. Philolaus, you are not under the unphilosophical illusion that there is, for example, an absolutely solid body in nature, are you?

PHILOLAUS: How could I be? All motion would thereby be frustrated, and, however small it might be, it would stop the wheels of all creation.

THEOPHRON: Very well then! If there can be no absolute rest, no complete impenetrability, solidity, inertia, which would be an all-vitiating nothingness and hence a contradiction, then, my friends, we must venture in our thoughts upon Plato's stream, where everything mutable is a wave, where everything temporal is a dream. You are frightened, Theano? Do not fear! It is the wave of a river which is all existence itself, the dream of a self-dependent, essential truth. The Eternal who wanted to become revealed in temporal phenomena, the Indivisible who wanted to become visible in spatial structure, could not do otherwise than give to each form the shortest and at the same time the longest existence which its appearance demanded in accordance with the image of space and time. All that appears must disappear. It disappears as [565] soon as it can, but it also stays as long as it can. Here, as everywhere, the two extremes fall together, and are, as a matter of fact, one and the same. Every finite being, as a phenomenon, brings the seed of destruction with it. With unremitting pace it hastens to its apogee so that it may hasten down and become, to our senses, the most minute. You observe that this is implied even in the structure of the line which I draw for you here.

THEANO: Sad observation!

THEOPHRON: Observe the flower, how it hastens to its bloom. It draws sap, air, light and all elements to itself, and fashions them so that it grows, prepares vital fluid, and puts forth a blossom. The blossom exists and disappears. It has applied all its force, its love and life to become a mother, to leave images of itself behind, and to multiply its potent existence by propagation. But now its appearance too is ended. It has consumed it in the indefatigable service of nature, and one can say that it worked towards its destruction from the beginning of its life. But what is destroyed in it save an appearance which could no longer maintain itself, which, when it had attained the apogee of the line, in which the form and degree of its beauty consisted, hastened down again? It did not do this, now that it was dead, as if to make place for younger, living appearances. That would be a sad picture. But rather, during its life, with all the joy of existence, it brought the latter into being, and left it in a seed of the wisest, most beautiful form for the ever-blooming garden of time in which it too had bloomed. For it itself did not die with this appearance. [566] The force of its root continues. It will wake again out of its winter sleep and arise in new beauty of spring and youth with the daughters of those beings which are now its friends and sisters, standing beside it virginal and fair. There is thus no death in creation. It is a hastening away of that which cannot remain; it is the working of an eternally young, indefatigable, enduring force, which in accordance with its nature cannot be inactive, mctionless, or unoccupied for a moment. It works incessantly in the richest, most beautiful way toward its own and as many other existences as it can produce and impart. In a world in which everything changes, every force is in eternal activity, and hence in eternal metamorphosis of its organs. For this transformation itself is the expression of its indestructible activity, replete with wisdom, goodness and beauty. As long as the flower lived, it worked toward its own bloom, and toward the reproduction of its existence. Through its own organic powers it became a creator, the highest thing a creature can become. When it died, it withdrew a spent appearance from the world. The inner living force which produced and maintained it drew back into itself, in order to reveal itself once more to the world in rejuvenated beauty. Can you imagine a more beautiful law of wisdom and goodness in what is called change, Theano, than that everything presses on in [567] the greatest haste to new life, to new youth and beauty, and therefore changes every moment?

THEANO: I see a beautiful glimmer, Theophron, but I do not yet see the dawn.

THEOPHRON: Then think of all the forces of nature in this incessant work, in this haste to change on the wing of time. Not the smallest part of a leaf can be inactive for a moment, or there would be death in creation. It attracts, it repels, it respires. For that reason, Theano, the leaf is formed with its two sides so different. The forces dwelling in it are eternally changing their organic dress. Life, thus, is movement, activity, the activity of an inner force, united with the deepest enjoyment of, and striving for persistence. And since nothing can remain unchanged in the realm of change, and yet everything wants to and must maintain its existence, everything is in this state of incessant motion, this eternal palingenesis (B1) so that it will last eternally and appear eternally young.

THEANO: But is this change also progress?

THEOPHRON: Supposing it were not! It would still be the only means of escaping death, and an eternal death. That is, [568] it would maintain our living force in continual activity, in an inwardly-felt existence. It would then be as desirable a benefit as an eternal life is more desirable than an eternal death. But then, Theano, can you very well conceive of an unceasing life, a continually operative force without continual operation, that is, an advance without advancement?

THEANO: It seems a contradiction.

THEOPHRON: And it is one! Every force which takes on appearances in space and time must indeed keep the limits which space and time give it. But with every activity it makes its subsequent activity easier. And, since it cannot do this otherwise than by implanted, internal laws of harmony, wisdom and goodness which, as you have yourself remarked, are benevolently forced upon every creature, impressed upon it, and which assist it in every one of its activities, therefore you see everywhere a progress out of chaos into order, an inner increase and enhanced beauty of forces in ever-widening limits according to ever more observed laws of harmony and order. Every blind force is infused with light, every lawless power with reason and goodness. None of its operations, no activity in creation was in vain. Thus there must be progress, advance in the realm of God, since there can be no standstill, and still less a regress. Moreover, our eye need not be repelled by the forms of death, for if there is no death in creation, then there is no form of death. Whatever this be called, decay, ailment, trituration, it is the transition to new young organization, the old outworn silkworm spinning its cocoon so that it will appear [569] as a new creature. Are you content, Theano?

THEANO: I am, and I resign myself to the wisest, highest goodness which brought me here and gave me undeservedly, but certainly not for nothing, so many powers, and which surrounds me with a thousand forces full of love and goodness with which to order my reason, my heart, my actions according to one eternal law of necessary self-grounded wisdom and goodness.—But Philolaus, you are silent and let me speak, who should and wants to be silent. You even forget your notebook.

PHILOLAUS: I shall catch up and put down at once a list of conclusions which seem to me to follow incontestably from

Theophron's system of a truth and goodness necessary in itself. I left off at the second principle. Thus, to continue:

III. All the forces of nature function organically. Every organization is nothing else than a system of living forces, which serve a principal force in accordance with eternal laws of wisdom, goodness and beauty.

IV. The laws according to which the one rules and the others serve, are: Inherent persistence of every being; union of likes and separation of opposites; finally, assimilation to self and reproduction of one's nature in another. They are activities through which the Deity has revealed Himself, and no other, nor higher ones are conceivable.

V. There is no death in creation, but metamorphosis. Metamorphosis in accordance with the wisest, best law of necessity [570] by which every force in the realm of change seeks to maintain itself ever-new and ever-active, and thus through attraction and repulsion, through friendship and enmity, incessantly changes its organic garb.

VI. There is no rest in creation, for an inactive rest would be death. Every living force is active and continues active. Thus, with every continuation of activity, it progresses and perfects itself according to inner eternal laws of wisdom and goodness, which are urged upon it and inherent in it.

VII. The more it augments itself, the more it works upon others, enlarges its limits, organizes and impresses them with the image of the goodness and beauty that dwells in it. Thus in the whole of nature one necessary law rules, to the effect that order emerges from chaos, that active forces emerge from dormant capacities. The activity of this law is not to be restrained.

VIII. Thus nothing evil which could have reality exists in the realm of God. All that is evil is a nonentity. But we call evil that which is limitation, or opposition, or transition, and none of the three deserves this name. Theophron, I thirst to discuss this point with you. I have in mind a Theodicy of wise necessity. (A1)

IX. But, as limits appertain to the measure of every existence in space and time, and, as in the realm of God where everything exists, opposites must also exist, so it appertains [571] to the highest goodness of this realm that opposites themselves help and need each other; because only through the union of the two does a world come into being in every substance, that is to say, an existing, whole being, complete in goodness as well as in beauty.

X. The errors of men also are good to an intelligent mind, for they must soon show themselves as errors to him, and thus help him, by way of contrast, to more light, to purer goodness and truth. Nor is this all arbitrary, but according to eternal laws of reason, order and goodness.

Are you content with my conclusions, Theophron?

THEOPHRON: Entirely! Your keen mind always hastens on ahead of me, Philolaus, like a noble steed for which we only need to open the race-course, and it flies to the goal. I thank the shade of Spinoza for having provided me with such pleasant hours of conversation with you; for opportunities to discuss matters of this sort are rare with me, and yet they singularly elevate the mind and educate it to clear, keen, unique, necessary truth. In addition, these conversations with you afford me a second enjoyment, namely they bring back to me my youthful ideas, with which I spent and surely more than dreamed away many sweet hours at the feet of Leibniz, Shaftesbury and Plato.

THEANO: The better would it please me, Theophron, if you would write down something consecutive on this matter. A con- [572] versation fades away, and even a written conversation on matters of this sort always seems to lack something. One is drawn on and is at the end before one realizes it. One always feels, however, an inclination to retrace one's steps.

THEOPHRON: Then retrace the steps, Theano, until the conversation itself, as it were, flows from the soul. Among its many defects, it yet has the merit of keeping us from learning by heart, and true philosophy must never be learned by heart.

THEANO: I wish my brother knew that rule. For some time he has been held captive by a philosophy which confuses both his head and mine as soon as he discusses it. (B1) I wish, Theophron, that you would take leave of Spinoza, Descartes, Leibniz and whomever else it may be, and write down only your own thoughts.

THEOPHRON: I am glad to tread in footsteps which already lie before me, Theano. I still lack a great deal to be able to conceive a work on which necessary, eternal Truth would set her seal. (A1)

Appendix A

Revisions in the Text of the Second Edition

FIRST CONVERSATION

The changes in this conversation, though numerous, are of an exclusively literary character. Since this appendix confines itself to the more important revisions in the thought, they have been omitted.

SECOND CONVERSATION

[**442**] (1) We do not know what Substance, that is, a persistent principle of force, is, or how force acts; still less do we know what the All-powerful is, or how it produced, and still produces everything and imparts its nature to all things.

[**445**] (1) . . . . between the infinitely unending and the Infinite-in-itself, which is determinate in the highest degree.

(2) Eternity in the pure sense of the word. . . .

[**447**] (1) Instead of "Spinoza struggled [**447**]" to "Infinite has revealed Himself" [**448**], the Second Edition reads:

Spinoza saw the inadequacy of this Cartesian explanation as well as we do. Read his letters.* Thus, when in his *Ethics* he took matter, that is, body, as equivalent to extension, that is, space, and set it over against thought, an entirely different kind of thing, he himself was aware that this conception was not illuminating as an explanation of the nature of bodies. He was likewise aware, and he says repeatedly, that thought and extension have nothing to do with one another. He finds fault

---

* Letters 69, 70, 71, 72 [olim]. He expressly says in these letters that matter is badly defined by Descartes as extension, that the multiplicity of things cannot be derived from extension, and he even goes to the extent of calling the Cartesian "principles of natural things" not only useless but absurd.

with Descartes for wanting both to set the body in motion and to restrain the affections by means of the pineal gland. For him, extension was a pure conception of the intellect, indivisible in itself, divisible only through the medium of the imagination. Thus, though he was often asked about it, Spinoza left unanswered the question of why, from among an infinite number of other attributes which in their totality express a highest Reality, just these conceptions, thought and extension, should be the only two attributes through which the Infinite reveals Himself to us.

[**449**] (1) Philolaus' speech: "There, my dear Theophron" to "well-reasoned system" is revised as follows:

Philolaus: There, my dear Theophron, you dispel a troublesome fog for me. For this infinitely extended God, as it was customary to call Spinoza's God, was wholly unthinkable to me.

Theophron: It was just as much so to that clear-minded philosopher Spinoza. He did not call God an extensum (on the contrary, he firmly maintained His indivisibility), but rather it was the material world (*res extensas*) which he called "an attribute which expresses one infinite aspect of the self-dependent Substance, as the world of thought expresses another of its infinite aspects." Any cruder formulas, or fanciful images entirely destroy his conception.

Philolaus: It astonishes me that I did not perceive this, when such obvious passages in his letters point directly to it. I did see that Spinoza wanted to avoid the divisibility of an infinitely extended and yet simple being by his use of the notion of mathematical space, inasmuch as physical bodies cannot be derived from mathematical lines and planes. Hence, even though Spinoza seems to value it as highly as matter, and calls it an attribute of God, mathematical space, since it too is merely an abstraction of the imagination, a condition of those truths which cannot be thought of save in a spatial context, can at the most give us information through which the multiplicity of physical, that is, real bodies, is to be explained. And in that regard, according to Spinoza himself, it gives us no information whatever. I wish the philosopher had avoided an expression which most people have crudely misused, and which, as you justly remark, makes half of his well-reasoned system obscure for others.

[**451**] (1) Does any expression occur to you which escapes the Cartesian dualism, that abrupt distinction between spirit and matter, and which indicates the nature of bodies more fecundly than the empty word "extension" or the crude word "matter"?

(2) PHILOLAUS: I know of none except "organic forces."

[**452**] (1) . . . . makes an infinite power known to us.

THEOPHRON: Fine, Philolaus! This goes to the very heart of the Spinozistic system. In it power is an essential reality. For this system all attributes and modifications of it, are manifestly presented, real and effective activities. In the spiritual world, power is thought, and in the material world, motion. I can think of no other substantive which could include both with so little constraint as the conception of force, power, organ, from which every activity in the physical and mental world proceeds. The internal and the external, the mental and the physical, are indicated simultaneously by the term "organic forces." For, as there is no force without organ, so no mind is or acts without a body. Nevertheless, it too is only an expression for we do not understand what force is, nor do we pretend to have explained the term "body" by means of it.

PHILOLAUS: With respect to the inner unity of the world, it seems to me that the expression entails some fine consequences. . .

[**457**] (1) . . . on which Spinoza's whole system depends.*

---

* See his noteworthy 29th letter. *Opp. posth.* p. 465.

[**458**] (1) Who distinguished more than he between the conceptions of *natura naturans* and *natura naturata?*

[**462**] (1) Instead of "Theophron; Don't you know" to "exactness in proof and organization [**464**]" the second edition reads:

THEOPHRON: He? Where?

PHILOLAUS: Everywhere, it seems to me. His two attributes, thought and extension or motion, stand side by side; each must be conceived in itself. Neither can be explained through the other. But each expresses the reality of the Eternal through itself.—Is this not harmony? The harmony of two expressions of the highest Reality, which impart nothing to one another? Since they have their eternal basis in that Reality, why should one not be allowed to call them a harmony?

THEOPHRON: Certainly not a pre-established harmony, and least of all in Leibniz's sense. Spinoza's system contains nothing of that. It contains no infinite number of individual substances whose harmony is pre-established. It knows only One independent nature which expresses itself in infinite ways, and to us in two great attributes. According to Spinoza, they both express one essence. But, as he conceives them, the one cannot be explained from the other. Thus the law that, if two things are united in a third they are one in themselves, does not apply here, else both attributes would merge, and since they express one essence in different ways, they would become one. Matter would become mind, and mind matter, to be distinguished only in our imagination, an identity which Spinoza strongly opposes. You see, his system here makes no attempt at explanation. It postulates and assumes precisely that which we want to have explained, namely: how the eternal Monad reveals itself in attributes as a dyad, as an internal power of thought and an external power of motion. Spinoza does not expound the harmony between this "internal" and "external" since he postulates it as an identity, as one in a distinct two. In the connection between body and soul in human beings, he also assumes it without explanation. If one wished to call this a harmony, one could call it only a symbolical harmony. Extension, with all the active forces, such as motion which it includes, would then be an external representation of the internal and eternal power of thought, as our body is the expression, or as he calls it, the object of the soul. Does this mystical harmony take us any further than we were?*

PHILOLAUS: I hope we shall never get any further, nay, I do not see why it is necessary to get further. Metaphysics is after-physics. The former should never depart from physics, but always accompany it. It then perceives everywhere how force cannot act without organ, or at least could not be observed by us without it; how everywhere the external must link itself with the internal, how the latter must be revealed through the former, and the former express the internal. In a word, it then perceives how nature everywhere is organized. This is a philosophy which, by dispensing with mystical verbiage, can proceed vigorously on its way, and can complete the speculation which, at times in the garb of mathematics itself, has since Descartes rushed on ahead of true philosophy, that is, ahead of the knowledge of nature.

THEOPHRON: Do not be in too great a hurry yourself. That garb, my friend, was useful to it. It prepared the language of philosophy for a calculus of observation and thought. For does it not encourage definiteness of ideas, exactness of proof and

* "According to Spinoza" says Lessing, "the soul is nothing but the body thinking itself, the body nothing but the soul extending itself." (*Lessings Leben und Nachlass.* Th. 2. S. 170 [XI, 113 L].) Precisely! "Leibniz merely got the hint of the pre-established harmony from Spinoza." p. 167. But through what other Cartesians or earlier philosophers might he not have come upon it? And why through an earlier philosopher at all? Does his hypothesis, when it is freed from all arbitrariness, express anything else than a law of experience?

organization? To be sure, the dress could not change, or take the place of, the thing which it clothed.

[464] (1) . . . . An arbitrarily assumed conception, like Substance, attribute, or mode, necessitated a host of other elucidations of a One which reveals itself in two attributes, and so on, which his excellent synthetic method could not remedy, though it could conceal them in a very deceptive manner.

THIRD CONVERSATION

[473] (1) . . . Of the nature of God which is revealed to us, yes, which is expressed in its essence in and around us, in all the highest laws of nature!

[474] (1) . . . . that on the one hand, Spinoza invites objection in these doctrines too, only because he spoke in the Cartesian language and most definitely wanted to speak in it; and that on the other hand he has been interpreted still more harshly than he ever expressed himself.

(2) But if we change the Cartesian expressions into others more familiar to us. . . .

(3) For how else, since all is only through and in Him, could there be thoughts. . . .

[479] (1) "Why did Spinoza" to "system." Omitted in second edition.

(2) Thank you for rending with one stroke the veil which deprived me, rather than Spinoza, of the light. In the Cartesian terminology, thought and extension stood opposed as two attributes each incapable of being explained through the other. Thought . . . .

(3) . . . . both were included, and that was (what else could it be?) power, that is, real activity, active being.

[480] (1) . . . . When the conception of power is developed in the same way as the conception of matter and thought, all

three, according to this system, are synthesized in the conception of a Primal Force which is as infinitely active in matter, the organ of conceptions, as in thought itself. Power and thought also thereby become one. For thought is power, and indeed the most perfect, absolutely infinite power, for it is and possesses everything in itself which pertains to infinite, self-dependent, self-expressing power.

[482] (1) . . . . and would not be God.

THEOPHRON: Do you perceive that? Spinoza says precisely the same thing.

PHILOLAUS: I perceived that quite well, now I read on: *

[484] (1) PHILOLAUS: So much the worse for his followers! For, since they did not separate the kernel from its husk, Leibnizianism meant to them what, for Leibniz himself, was only poetical ornament or accommodation. However, he very strongly asserted his opposition to Spinoza's doctrine of necessity.

[486] (1) "Those who" to "and," omitted in second edition.

(2) PHILOLAUS: It is a question whether Bayle would have had nothing to answer to that. Liebniz was forced. . . .

FOURTH CONVERSATION

[497] (1) . . . . personal cause of the world, and on that matter he sought to discover something new.

THEOPHRON: Did he find it?

PHILOLAUS: The expression "person" is, as you yourself say, merely anthropomorphic, even when it is applied to God by the theologians who do not, however, oppose this "person"

---

* ". . . since in eternity there is no 'when' nor 'before' nor 'after,' it follows from the perfection of God alone that He neither can decree nor could have decreed anything else than that which He has decreed. . . . God has not existed before His decrees, and can never exist without them. If He changed them, then He would change His intellect and will, that is, would be a different God." *Ethics* Prop. XXXIII Schol. 2. [Hale White trans.]

to the world, but take it as a distinction in the nature of God; for the theologian does not say "God is a person," but "in God there are persons."

THEOPHRON: Let us dispense with the language of theologians and speak of the word "person" in its philosophical meaning.

PHILOLAUS: First, then, we should surely discuss what the [498] word means in established usage. Person ($\pi\rho o\sigma\omega\pi o\nu$) meant "mask," then "theatrical character" and from that, the peculiar nature of a character in general by which it is distinguished from another. Thus the word passed into common speech. "So and so" one says, "portrays his 'person,' he puts his 'personality' into the thing," etc. Thus "person" was set against "thing," always meaning something which sets apart, something distinctively characteristic. Then it was introduced into legal language, in the distinction of "the estates." Can we apply anything of this *prosopopoeia* to God? He is neither a face nor a mask, neither a legal personality, nor a distinct character who exists among others and acts beside them. Let us have done with these personalizations which always lead if not to something false, assumed or imputed, then to something distinctive in form, figure, or differentiation from others, to position, rank, and that sort of thing, and hence carry us away from the pure conception of an entirely incomparable essence and truth. God no more portrays a "person," or affects personal qualities, or has a personal way of thinking which is distinct from, and in contrast to other ways, than He resembles a person. He is. None is like unto Him.

THEOPHRON: But does not "the highest intelligence" demand the term "person," in that "unity of self-consciousness" would involve "personality"?

PHILOLAUS: I do not see why. On the contrary, "personality" always remains a strange and superficial term for this conception. Locke and Leibniz also regarded it as such, and sought to explain it by means of more definite expressions.* So too is it regarded in the usage of language, which plays with the words "person" and "personality" as if with an appearance. The most intimate consciousness of self forgets the appearance of person (the *personnel* and the *personage*) so completely, that one as it were drives it out of one's self in pronouncing a word of judgment on personal appearance. All this Lessing knew better than we do.—I read on: "Lessing hears of an intelligent cause of the world."

THEOPHRON: Did he make himself explicit on the matter?

PHILOLAUS: He had not the time to do so. He was probably completely in agreement with Spinoza on this matter also. We saw that the latter distinguished understanding, insofar as it belongs to the *natura naturata,* from that primal power of thought [499] which is the basis of things themselves. The created intellect can only understand what lies before or in it, i.e., what is given to it. To the original power of thought nothing is given but itself. Everything follows therefrom. In

---

* "Person, as I take it, is the name of this Self. Wherever a man finds what he calls Himself, there I think another may say is the same Person. It is a forensick term, appropriating Actions and their Merit, and so belongs only to intelligent Agents capable of a Law, and Happiness and Misery." Locke: *Essay on Human Understanding,* Vol. I, Bk. 2, Ch. 27.

"Le soi fait l'identité reelle et physique; et l'apparence du soi accompagnée de la verité, y joint l'identité personnelle. Si Dieu changeoit extraordinairement l'identité reelle, la personelle demeureroit, pourvu que l' homme conservât les apparences d'identité tant les internes, (c'est à dire de la conscience) que les externes comme celles que consistent dans ce qui paroit aux autres. Ainsi la conscience n'est pas le seul moyen de constituer l'identité personelle; le rapport d'autrui ou même d'autres marques y peuvent suppleer." Leibniz, *Oeuvr. Philosoph.* p. 195–6.

On the usage of the word "person," "personality," etc. open what dictionaries one will—Latin, German, French, Italian, Spanish, English, and all say in the aggregate, that these words indicate a "peculiar character" or "particular" under a certain appearance—which accessory notion does not apply at all to the Infinite as opposed to the world, but rather obscures the notion of the One, Non-portraying.

this sense the highest, that is, primitive intellect knows only itself, and therein everything possible as effect.

THEOPHRON: But does this sense of the word also conform to common speech?

PHILOLAUS: And what if it did not! It does, however, in every language in which there is philosophizing. When Locke calls his "understanding," "power of perception" and even compares it with a dark room into which light streams by means of the senses,* then such a dark chamber into which light streams by means of the senses cannot be attributed to God. When, to the more precise Leibniz, understanding is "a clear perception united with the capacity for reflection,"** who would wish to make the highest Being into a school-boy and attribute to Him such "capacity to perceive and then to reflect"? Language itself struggles against this. In several languages the word "understanding" expresses a "grasping" and "sorting out" of objects (*intellectionem*). What strange object given Him to understand, did and does God "sort out"?

THEOPHRON: Please read on.

[502] (1) "It seems to me that Lessing said too much." is omitted.

(2) What if I named for you from Spinoza's own work, not indeed a single higher force, or genus of forces, but the exact conception. . . .

(3) THEOPHRON: Actuality, reality, active existence. It is the chief conception in Spinoza, the ground and sum of all forces. Actuality, reality, existence. . . .

[503] (1) THEOPHRON: But which is also beyond all conception? This observation lies completely beyond *my* conception, that is to say, I cannot think what it means.

(2) . . . . that it is blind power, which can neither fulfill

---

* Locke, *Essay on Understanding*, Bk. 2, Ch. 21 § 5; Ch. 11 § 17.
** Leibniz, *Oeuvre phil.* (Raspe), p. 132.

itself nor make use of itself, which lacks the most intimate and true reality.

[**504**] (1) But his *Theodicy,* as well as many of his letters, show that he thought out his system precisely in order not to be a Spinozist.

(2) . . . . All this was only to escape from the Spinozistic Necessity which seemed to him mechanistic, and rather than which he chose the more prudent expression "moral necessity." He chose the middle way by which he thought that he could pass between Bayle's skepticism and Spinoza's drastic expressions. He did it with great skill, but Bayle and Spinoza were no longer alive, and could not answer him.

[**505**] (1) THEOPHRON: Listen to what Lessing says elsewhere on this point: "However prejudiced in favor of his own philosophy one can, or wants to conceive Leibniz to have been, yet one cannot truly say that he sought to adjust it to the prevailing doctrines of all factions. For how could that have been possible? [**506**] How, to repeat an old saying, could he take it into his head to make a dress for the moon? Everything which he ever did in the interest of his system was just the opposite. He sought to adjust the prevailing doctrines of all factions to his own system. These two are anything but the same. In his search for the truth, Leibniz never paid any consideration to the accepted opinions, but, firmly convinced that no opinion could be accepted which in one respect or another was not true in some sense, he indeed was often obliging enough to turn such an opinion this way and that, until he succeeded in revealing this particular aspect, or in making that particular sense clear. He struck sparks from flint, but did not hide his fire in the flint.*

[**507**] (1) "What things my friend is not one often delighted with in discussion?" The remainder of Theophron's speech is

* Lessing: *Sämmtliche Schriften.* Th. 7; p. 23, 24. [*Schriften.* ix. p. 159.]

omitted. Instead: "Lessing did not regard this portrayal as the system of Spinoza."

[508] (1) "I also took up Mendelssohn's 'Morning Hours,'" to "really was" is omitted in second edition.

[509] (1) "There is a blind and a seeing" to "in his conversation with Lessing he concludes." [512] is omitted. Instead, the second edition reads: Let us hear Spinoza himself on this point.*

"For in no way do I subject God to fate, but I conceive that everything follows with inevitable necessity from the nature of God just as all conceive that it follows from the nature of God Himself that He should understand Himself. Certainly no one denies that this follows necessarily from the divine nature, and yet no one conceives that God is compelled by any fate to understand Himself, but that He does so absolutely freely, although necessarily.

"Next, this inevitable necessity of things does not do away with either divine or human laws. For moral precepts, whether they do or do not receive the form of law from God Himself, are nevertheless divine and salutary, and whether we receive the good which follows from virtue, and the love of God from God as Judge, or whether it proceeds from the necessity of the Divine nature, it will not on that account be more or less desirable, just as, on the other hand, the evils which follow on wicked actions and feelings will not be less to be feared merely because they follow from them necessarily. Lastly, whether we do what we do necessarily or contingently, we are nevertheless led by hope and fear.

"Further, men are inexcusable before God for no other reason than that they are in the power of God Himself as clay in the hands of the potter who from the same lump makes vessels, some unto honour, others unto dishonour."

* Epist. 23 [olim] *Opp. posth.* 453. [Wolf trans.]

THEOPHRON: Doubtless you have reflected on how it came to pass that Spinoza prepared for himself the extraordinary fate of being misunderstood even by his friends.

PHILOLAUS: I have indeed, and I have always returned to the same causes which you indicated to me at the very first.

In the first place, it is the drastic expressions in a work which was not prepared for publication, which appeared after the death of the author and which should be compared with other works, or at least interpreted in a more moderate sense. For example, Spinoza calls the human mind, insofar as it conceives things in accordance with the truth a part of the Divine Intellect, and calls these clear ideas in it, "ideas of God, not insofar as He is infinite, but insofar as He is expressed through the nature of the human mind, and makes up its essence, or insofar as He thinks other [510] ideas with it." One had only to leave out those "insofars" and one was on the threshold of a misunderstanding which entirely destroys his system. Body and mind were thus conceived as parts of Him who according to Spinoza is indivisible. One added up bodies, summed up human thoughts and said "Lo! Spinoza's God! His Infinite Intellect is nothing but the sum of all human thoughts including the thoughts of the thief and the fool." If one had reflected that thoughts and ways of thinking are not capable of being added, that added up they produce no power which is indivisible in itself, and in every one of the activities which represent it; if one had reflected that according to Spinoza it is one original power, and that one living idea is in it which includes within itself and actively expresses the order and connection of all ideas and their consequences, and hence the connection and order of all things; if one had thus reflected, then would one have ascribed to him the nonsense which is most antipathetic to his system, and objectionable to every intelligence? The cause of it was a few awkward verbal formulations which expressed as they were in a language not native to him, might have been forgiven him.

Equally harmful to him has been the fact that he did not explain some of his most pregnant words, on whose precise meaning so much depended. Thus, for example, "if each of the infinite attributes of his God should express an infinite eternal essence in all of its modes and changes," what does the pregnant word "express" mean here? Are these "modes" mere symbols or expressive characters? Are they representations and reproductions of an eternal Being, who constitutes their essence and being? To him who *wants* to understand, Spinoza said enough, for his work is a single idea from beginning to end. But he who wanted to quarrel about words, found all the more to quarrel about.

Finally, as for his synthetical method which in itself was excellent, it was not suitable in this place. At the least it forced him to make postulates and formulas which, had they been discovered through analysis would not have been at all startling. For example, "substance," "attribute," "mode" et cetera. Would you not venture, Theophron, to present entirely unobjectionably the whole of Spinoza's system in analytical form?

THEOPHRON: Lessing would certainly have done it. Philolaus, if Spinoza returned once more, what do you think he would say to those who regard him as an atheist, pantheist, divider of God, summator of God and so on?

PHILOLAUS: It [511] seems to me that he would say very modestly and decisively: "What are you making of my system whose very basis, a single eternal idea, you are disturbing? Are modifications conceivable without an inner reality? Is expression conceivable without something which expresses itself? Are modes of thought conceivable without an unlimited active power of thought? When, in a language not native to me, I did all that I could in order to make conceivable for you the pure idea and enjoyment of an indivisible power which in its innermost self, potently feels, effects, and presents all things in and through and out of itself; when by analogy, I described this essence in you yourselves in order thereby to direct you to the highest joy and blessedness; how then do you wish to charge me with making the One into nothing, the most active Being into an empty bag and a collective name for shadows which could not even be shadows without light; so you charged me with extinguishing the sun in order to fabricate a mock-sun out of the sparks of glow worms. I beg of you, read other writings than mine, which are imperfect, not in thought, but in expression. . . ."

THEOPHRON: Enough! You spoke of the estimable features which you found in this little book.*

PHILOLAUS: The most estimable was the manner of thought of the author, who in his conversation with Lessing too, comes to the excellent conclusion that subtle reasoning is not the whole essence, not the whole condition of the human power of thought.

[513] (1) The passage following the "Hymn" reads:

THEOPHRON: Excellent! That human knowledge apart from and prior to all experience, those sensuous perceptions without and before all sensation of an object, which act according to implanted forms of thought which no one had implanted, are chimeras which make barren the mind of everyone who is aware of his own existence. We too Philolaus in our discussion, have often had to use the divine name as a mere symbol. How would it be if we interrupted the promenade now? You know and speak the refreshing language of music—well then— here is your instrument.

* *On the Doctrine of Spinoza* (Breslau, 1786).

[516] (1) . . . . the philosopher who overreaches himself. The connection of these forces, the manner in which they all work in accordance with their natures and are united in my mind, is proof enough of an essential basis of inner truth, agreement and perfection, which includes its existence within itself.

[517] (1) "Supposing that" to "one single thinking Being" is omitted in second edition.

[523] (1) . . . . usual view which Spinoza himself provokes* and above all Wachter made current.

[524] (1) THEOPHRON: Wachter was a learned man whom I respect in every regard save as a philosopher. As an itinerant young man of about twenty years of age, he quarrelled with a Jew and sought to find Spinozism in Judaism; some years later he was himself a friend of the Cabbala, and, pursuing his first idea, he sought to unite the doctrine of Spinoza with it.**

(2) From this point of view he is at the antipodes of the Cabbala—natural though it would be, if he, who had grown up in Judaism, a student of the famed Morteira, had, as it were, brought a Hebraic view of things into the Cartesian philosophy. Our first form of thought never entirely leaves us, and since Spinoza entered the Cartesian system through the medium of a strange language, it was natural then, that he made that language conform to his own, and for that same reason he began synthetically with the essential idea of God.

[525] (1) But with the actual Cabbala, and still less with its

* "Omnia in Deo esse et in Deo moveri cum Paulo affirmo, auderem etiam dicere cum antiquis omnibus Hebraeis, quantum ex quibusdam traditionibus, tametsi multis modis adulteratis, coniicere licet." Epist. 21. *Opp. posth.* p. 449.

** The first work was called: "Spinozism in Judaism, or the Deified World of Present-Day Judaism and the Secret Cabbala. The German Moses Exposed and Refuted." (*Der Spinozismus im Judenthum, oder die von dem heutigen Judenthum und dessen geheimen Kabbala vergötterte Welt. An Mose Germano befunden und widerlegt* von J. G. Wachter: Amst., 1699.)

The second: *Elucidarius Cabbalisticus s. reconditae Hebraeorum philosophiae recensio, epistomatore,* J. G. Wachtero, Rom., 1706. He finds 20 similarities between Spinoza's system and Cabbalism.

emanations, which are no more the discovery of the Jews than they are a part of their theology, Spinoza's system has nothing in common.

(2) This way of speaking is mathematical rather than Cabbalistical.

(3) PHILOLAUS: He who so severely judged the imagery of the ancient writings of his nation, surely kept himself free from the rubbish of the Cabbala. However, it is enough that his philosophy did not start from the Cartesian. "I think therefore I am," but rather from the divine name of his forefathers: "I am that I am and shall be that I shall be."

[526] (1) . . . . excludes all emanations. Spinoza needed only to develop it and the greater part of his desire lay before him.

[527] (1) THEOPHRON: Consider: "God, the Soul of the whole (is) an effect! All other souls, according to all possible systems, (are) effects!" Effects of what? Of what is God an effect? Of the whole? Of the organic body? And this is what all souls, according to all possible systems are—effects?*

(2) "O Spinoza . . . ." to the end of Theophron's speech is omitted.

[528] (1) THEOPHRON: You know Lessing's way of turning things in such a manner. "It is raining. Perhaps I am doing that."** And so on. Obviously he thereby sought to exaggerate the image in the worst possible way, that is, to ridicule it.

[529] (1) . . . . goodness and wisdom. For, Theophron, the Gordian knot in Spinoza's system still lies before me, namely the riddle: "If only one substance deserves that name, how did the illusion or the truth of many innumerable particular substances arise?"

* For an explanation of this expression see, in the 2nd ed. of *On the Doctrine of Spinoza*, p. 46 ff.
** p. 35.

[**543**] (1) THEOPHRON: "Do not worry." to "clear up for us," omitted in second edition.

[**570**] (1) "I thirst . . . . necessity." omitted in second edition.

[**572**] (1) The following ending was added in the second edition.

PHILOLAUS: May I now present my reservations, Theophron? Your first proposition was:

"The highest Being gave His creations what is highest: actuality, existence." It is said that just this is lacking in the system of our philosopher. According to him there is no existence. There is but one Substance. We are mere modifications.

THEOPHRON: Modifications of what? Of Existence in the highest sense. The one faction is angry because Spinoza conceded too much to us, the other because he conceded too little. Perhaps both can come to an agreement in a no more suitable expression than his own. We are modes of Existence. These we call individualities. Each has and is his own mode, that is, his own individuality. Do you know a better expression?

PHILOLAUS: But just the opposite is believed: "Spinoza has taken our individuality from us. From this point of view, his system is most vulnerable to decisive attack and destruction."

THEOPHRON: Just as it is also believed that he had stolen existence, and consciousness of self from the highest Existence: "Dead is Osiris, his sundered limbs dangle here and there as modifications. Modifications without essence, radii without center; contrariwise, the most active center without radii, the most real essence without presentations of its reality." Think of this self-contradictory nonsense! Theano shall come to our aid. What in you is self-dependent, actively constant and constantly active? What are you yourself, Theano?

THEANO: My form belongs to me, but I am not my form.

That the picture of my childhood tells me. That my mirror tells me in joy and sorrow, in health and sickness.

THEOPHRON: And yet in this change of circumstances you were, and are always the same, the same individual.

THEANO: Not in my fancy. That changed with the years. Nor in what we call taste, love, affections. They too are garments which we imperceptibly change. Towards the end our memory tires and falters . . . but let me not think of that dreary season of human life. May it come late for all of us.

THEOPHRON: Thus, if the center of selfhood does not lie in the realm of sense, of fancy, taste and desires, where does it lie?

THEANO: In myself. It seems to me that the word does not allow [574] of further dissection, either as idea or as feeling. I was a child and grew up, was ill and recovered, slept and awakened. In all these changes which befell me, internally and externally, not only was I called, but I felt myself and called myself, the same.

THEOPHRON: The principle of selfhood then did not depend on you, as though it were caused by reasoning, and had to be maintained by reflection; as though it depended upon this and without it would disappear.

THEANO: How could this be? That in spite of all changes, my body and spirit do not remain the same, but I remain the same, a self does not depend on my reasoning. When I am awake, I do not reason overmuch, and when asleep not at all. In the magic realms of dreams I was often another. While awake I reflect upon myself, and I find my small self divided. I myself divide it artificially.

THEOPHRON: Thus the conviction of our selfhood, the principle of our individuation, lies deeper than our understanding, our reason, or our fancy can reach. You have hit it, Theano! As feeling and idea it lies in the word "self" itself. Self-consciousness, self-activity make up our actuality, our existence. Upon them rests the ladder of all our developed and undeveloped powers, inclinations, and actions, which reaches from earth to heaven. Do you believe then, Theano, that the principle of individuation (we may call it "feeling of self," "consciousness of self," or otherwise), is active and efficient in the same degree in all that exists?

THEANO: Certainly not. A living rose and this embroidered one, the rosebush and the nightingale which sings upon it, the butterfly which hangs upon the rose, can have neither the same kind nor degree of the feeling of selfhood, of self-consciousness, and hence of existence. And then we humans?

THEOPHRON: Thus they and we are different "modes of existence" with different kinds and grades of self-consciousness, modifications of reality going lower and lower, and higher and higher. And we humans! Do you believe all of our race have an equally deep feeling of selfhood, and an equally active self-consciousness, and hence are equally possessed of existence within?

THEANO: Not in the least. There is many a human organization which one would scarcely compare as to inner self with a flower, a bird, or even many a wild beast.

THEOPHRON: Perhaps not compare; but he always remains within [575] the sphere of human feelings, for no individual can deny the basis of his race. Which do you think is the highest, purest, most beautiful individuation?

THEANO: There is no doubt there! The form of all forms, that which includes all, whose activity pervades all. The more it can include, the more it can impart, why the more it must have, that is to say, be.

PHILOLAUS: Enough my friends. Every additional word would be superfluous. I see the one and eternal principle of individuation developed in the system of our philosopher, along a line which leads into our innermost self. The more life and reality, that is, the more rational, powerful and perfect energy a being has for the maintenance of a whole which it feels belongs to itself, to which it imparts itself inwardly and entirely, the more it is an individual, a self. In accordance with this, Spinoza determined the excellences and qualities of the human body, the capacities of the human mind, and conducted everything back to Him, through whom all lives, in whom we live and of whom we can say, "We are His offspring through consciousness, through the powers which are most proper to us and most powerful in us."

THEOPHRON: And so instead of struggling with empty words let us awaken our true self and strengthen the principle of individuality in us. The more spirit and truth, that is, the more active reality, knowledge, and love of the all to all that there is in us, the more we possess and enjoy God, as active individuals, immortal and indivisble. He alone in whom all is, who comprehends and sustains all, can say: "I am the Self. There is none apart from me."

* * *

Here end our speakers who, as the word "conversation" sufficiently indicates, leave every reader to his own opinion, for they define matters only among themselves and not for others.

There have always been two kinds of philosophers, philosophers from conviction and philosophers from persuasion, thing and word-philosophers. Spinoza was of the first, not of the second kind. He says:

"No one who has a true idea is ignorant that a true idea involves the highest certitude; to have a true idea signifying just this, to know a thing perfectly or as well as possible. No one, in fact, can doubt this, unless he supposes an idea to be something dumb, like a picture on a tablet, instead of being a

mode of thought, that is to say, intelligence itself. Moreover, I
ask who can know that he understands a thing unless he first
of all understands that thing? That is to say, who can know
that he is certain of anything unless he is first of all certain of
that thing? Then, again, what can be clearer or more certain
than a true idea as the standard of truth? Just as light reveals
both itself and the darkness, so truth is the standard of itself
and of the false."*

"I do not presume that I have found the best philosophy,
I know that I understand the true philosophy. If you ask in
what way I know it, I answer: In the same way as you know
that the three angles of a triangle are equal to two right angles:
that this is sufficient, will be denied by no one whose brain is
sound . . . . For the truth is the index of itself and of what
is false." **

A philosopher of that sort has nothing in common with dia-
lecticians to whom it is indifferent whether they establish or
destroy truth, because it merely costs them a word.

And thus nothing gave Spinoza so much concern as the strict
distinction between insight and imagination, comprehension
and invention. His *Tractatus theologico-politicus* shows how
severely he deals with the fictions of the imagination. Many
scholia of his *Ethics,* many of his letters, show how precisely
he distinguished between knowing and dreaming, and in the
former, between the different degrees of knowing, acquaintance
and insight.*** This is shown most clearly in his tractate on the
"Improvement of the Understanding," for the completion of
which one would give a good deal. A philosopher of that sort
could have nothing to do with illusions which, in the form of
schemata, are also supposed to be juggled in speculation and

---

* *Ethic.* P. II, Prop. 43, Schol. [Hale White trans.]
** Epist. LXXIV. [Wolf trans.]
*** For example Schol. I Prop. 40, 43, 44, 49 ff.

lead the conceiving, comprehending, understanding intellect away from itself into error.

"In order to know that I know, I must first know, . . . the mode in which we perceive an actual reality is certainty. . . . For the certitude of truth, no further sign is necessary beyond the possession of a true idea: . . . No one can know the nature of the highest certainty, unless he possesses an adequate idea, ... of a thing: for certainty is identical with subjective essence. Thus, as the truth needs no sign—it being sufficient to possess the subjective essence of things, or, in other words, the ideas of them, in order that all doubts may be removed— . . . . The true method does not consist in seeking for the signs of truth after the acquisition of the idea, but that the true method teaches us the order in which we should seek for truth itself, or the subjective essences of things, or ideas, for all these expressions are synonymous . . . method must necessarily be concerned with reasoning or understanding—I mean, method is not identical with reasoning in the search for causes, still less is it the comprehension of the causes of things: it is the discernment of a true idea, by distinguishing it from other perceptions and by investigating its nature in order that we may thus know our power of understanding, and may so train our mind that it may, by a given standard, comprehend whatsoever is intelligible, by laying down certain rules as aids, and by avoiding useless mental exertion.

". . . Method is nothing else than reflective knowledge, or the idea of an idea; and that as there can be no idea of an idea —unless an idea exists previously—there can be no method without a pre-existent idea. Therefore, that will be a good method which shows us how the mind should be directed, according to the standard of the given true idea.

"Again, seeing that the ratio existing between two ideas is the same as the ratio between the actual realities corresponding to those ideas, it follows that the reflective knowledge which has for its object the most perfect being is more excellent than reflective knowledge concerning other objects—in other words, that method will be most perfect which affords the standard of the given idea of the most perfect being whereby we may direct our mind. We thus easily understand how, in proportion as it acquires new ideas, the mind simultaneously acquires fresh instruments for pursuing its inquiries further. For we may gather from what has been said, that a true idea must necessarily first of all exist in us as a natural instrument; and that when this idea is apprehended by the mind, it enables us to understand the difference existing between itself and all other perceptions. In this, one part of the method consists.

"Now it is clear that the mind apprehends itself better in proportion as it understands a greater number of natural objects; it follows, therefore, that this portion of the method will be more perfect in proportion as the mind attains to the comprehension of a greater number of objects, and that it will be absolutely perfect when the mind gains a knowledge of the absolutely perfect being or becomes conscious thereof. Again, the more things the mind knows, the better does it understand its own strength and the order of nature; by increased self-knowledge it can direct itself more easily, and lay down rules for its own guidance; and, by increased knowledge of nature, it can more easily avoid what is useless.

". . . This is the sum total of method as we have already stated. . . . In order to reproduce in every respect the faithful image of nature, our mind must deduce all its ideas from the idea which represents the origin and source of the whole of nature, so that it may itself become the source of other ideas."*

So thought Spinoza, and all minds capable of true ideas,

* *De emend. intellect.* p. 367, 368. [Elwes trans.]

that is to say, of understanding, thought like him to the extent to which they were thus capable. They foreswore the inventive imagination, and severed themselves from illusions and masks of words. For Spinoza, conceptions which are understood present the essential, the living, the true. Words as pictures are worthless to him. He uses them like algebraical signs.

As for the external form of his method, every one who has ever attempted the strict synthetical method knows its difficulties. Often particular links of the chain have need of a special analysis and deduction, which, when one of these links strikes us as not following from the preceding one, we must patiently institute. But when we cannot do so, we must not therefore deny or discard the link. From one idea, the richest and most complete, Spinoza derives everything. In it he has and enjoys all.

It would be an instructive but too long excursion, to show how far among all nations, in the most different expressions and representations, others took part in this great and simple way of thinking—others who loved simplicity and truth, that is, those in whom the idea of the One and the True was vividly impressed as the norm of all knowledge and method. Jews and Christians, Greeks and Hindus, speculators with heart and head, scholastics, and mystics took part in it. For Spinoza's philosophy existed long before him and will exist long after him. Often those who fought against him, or rather against his misunderstood or poorly chosen expressions, were of his own belief whenever they wished to, or had to explain themselves in better or worse chosen terms of his or their own. That is, they held the intimate belief in one unique vitally-felt all-sustaining idea of the true, good and beautiful, without which all our talk and writing remains vanity. Instead of these manifold witnesses which are being saved for another place, a posthumous piece of Lessing's is adjoined (which at least will show that Spinoza's system was no joke to him), and another of Shaftesbury's, in verse, a "Hymn of Nature."

LESSING

On the Reality of Things Outside God

In whatever fashion I may seek to explain to myself the [**579**] reality of things outside God, I must admit that I can form no idea of it.

If it is called *complementum possibilitatis*, then, I ask, is there an idea of this *complementum possibilitatis* in God, or is there not? Who would maintain the latter? But if there is an idea of it in Him, then all things are real in Him.

But, it will be said, the conception which God has of the reality of a thing, does not destroy the reality of that thing (as existing) outside Him. No? Then the reality external to Him must possess something which distinguishes it from the reality in His conception. That is to say, there must be something in the reality outside Him, of which God has no conception. An absurdity! But if it is not so, if, in the idea which God has of the reality of a thing, everything is to be found which pertains to its reality outside Him, then both realities are one, and everything which is said to exist outside God, exists in God.

Or it may be claimed that "the reality of a thing is the sum of all possible determinations which can be attributed to it." Must not this sum be also in the idea of God? What determinations has that which is real outside God, the archetype of which is not to be found in God also? Thus it follows that this archetype is the thing itself, and to say that the thing exists apart from this archetype as well, is to double the archetype in a way which is as unnecessary as it is absurd.

I believe, indeed, that the philosophers say that to assert

reality of a thing outside God means nothing more than to distinguish this thing from God, and to explain its reality in terms of a kind of being which is different from the necessary reality of God.

But if this is all they want, then why should not the ideas which God has of real things be these real things themselves? They are still sufficiently distinct from God, and their reality becomes not in the least necessary merely because they are real in Him. For would not the contingency which they are supposed to have outside Him also correspond to an image in His idea? And this image is nothing but their contingency itself. What is contingent outside God, will also be contingent in Him, else God would have to have no idea of the contingent outside Himself.—I use this "outside Himself" in the way in which common custom uses it, in order to show by its employment that one should not use it.

But, some will exclaim, this is to attribute contingencies to the unchangeable nature of God!—Well, am I the only one who does this? Has it never occurred to you, who had to ascribe to your God ideas of contingent things, that ideas of contingent things are contingent ideas?

Lessings Leben und Nachlass.

Th. 2 S. 164

(Schriften XI, 111, 112. L.)

Appendix B

Notes to the Translation

FIRST PREFACE

[**403**] (1) The "new circumstances" and the "inducements which the times . . . . offered me" refer to the Jacobi-Mendelssohn controversy over Lessing and Spinoza. See Introduction, p. 28 ff.

(2) It has been suggested by various critics that the "Conversations" grew out of discussions on Spinoza's system between Herder, Goethe and Herder's wife, Caroline, and that Theophron, Philolaus, and Theano (who appears in the final section) represent these persons respectively. See C. Siegel: *Herder als Philosoph* (Berlin, 1907), p. 72, and E. Hoffart: *Herders "Gott"* (Halle, 1918), p. 5. There is no way of verifying this. Theano, however, would seem to resemble Caroline much more than Philolaus does Goethe.

[**404**] (1) Herder planned a work by this name, which was to deal with "Wisdom, Power and Goodness," as the fundamental laws of nature and history. The "Adrastea" which he actually wrote, however, does not fulfill this sub-title, but is concerned more with the history and literature of modern times. *Werke,* Su. XXIII.

SECOND PREFACE

[**405**] (1) Between 1787 and 1800, the dates of the first and second editions of the "Conversations," Kant's *Critique of Practical Reason* (1788), *Critique of Judgment* (1791), Fichte's *Wissenschaftslehre* (1794), Schelling's "Of the Ego

as the Principle of Philosophy" (*Vom Ich als Prinzip der Philosophie*), and "Philosophical Letters on Dogmatism and Criticism" (*Philosophische Briefe über Dogmatismus und Kritizismus,* 1795–6), and the growth of Romanticism, had all contributed to extraordinary changes in German philosophy. Kant and Fichte in particular had attained great influence in the universities.

(2) The reference is to Fichte and Schelling, especially the latter, whose "Of the Ego as the Principle of Philosophy" had appeared in 1795, showing much of this attitude to Spinozism.

(3) This was maintained by Mendelssohn in the Spinoza Quarrel. The point is discussed in the "Conversations," p. 121. [476–7] and note thereto. The other view mentioned here is the more traditional and popular one which had also been strengthened by Jacobi. See Introduction, p. 29.

[406] (1) Horace: *Odes* Bk. I, XXVIII. The translation used here is that of Sir Philip Francis. 1743.

(2) Spinoza: *Ethics* Bk. V, Prop. 42.

[407] (1) Acts 17:28.

(2) The second edition of the "Conversations" had appended to it a versified translation of the "Hymn to Nature" in the last part of Shaftesbury's *Moralists,* thus actually completing the parallelism which Herder had long had in mind. In 1798 he recommended Shaftesbury to his son August as "the author who contained the Spinoza-Leibniz philosophy in the most beautiful and select form." (See Haym: *Herder nach seinem Leben und seinen Werken.* Berlin, 1877–85, II, 269–71.)

FIRST CONVERSATION

[413] (1) Bayle, (1647–1706). His *Dictionnaire historique et critique* first appeared between 1695 and 1697. It contained an article criticizing Spinoza which became the most famous

judgment on that thinker for over a century. He sees Spinoza as an "athée de système et d'une methode toute nouvelle," and calls the *Tractatus theologico-politicus* "un livre pernicieux et détestable." As early as 1755, however, Mendelssohn had defended Spinoza against Bayle's interpretation in his "Philosophical Conversations" (*Philosophische Gespräche*). Herder, in a letter to Jacobi, Feb. 6, 1784, wrote on this point: "Mendelssohn, it seems to me, is right when he says that Bayle misunderstood Spinoza's system. . . . And so it is my opinion that since Spinoza's death, no one has done justice to the system of ἐν καὶ πᾶν (not even Mendelssohn in his conversations on Spinoza). Alas, that Lessing did not do it!" (*Aus Herders Nachlass*, II, 252.)

[414] Moreri (1643–80) was the author of another very popular dictionary. In the introductory chapters of his own work, Bayle pointed out that Moreri's dates are often "absolument chimeriques."

[415] Bayle's work went into many editions and became an extremely popular reference book during the century which followed its publication. Almost every reference to, or judgment upon Spinoza used it as a basis. As late as 1782, a work, translated from the French of de Jariges came out, called *On the System of Spinoza and Bayle's Memorandum Against This System*. For the most part it substantiated Bayle's judgment, differing only by adding to it. (*Mag. für die Philosophie und ihre Geschichte*. Vol. 5.)

(2) Among the philosophers Thomasius, Wolff, Brucker and Korthold were the most prominent.

(3) Excerpts from many of the contemporary judgments on Spinoza's system can be found in E. Altkirch, *Maledictus und Benedictus* (Leipzig, 1924), pp. 15–72.

[419] (1) The reference is, of course, to Kant. For his relation to Herder see Introduction, p. 34 ff.

(2) Korthold (1633–94) Professor of Theology at the University of Kiel. The passage to which Herder refers is probably that in *De tribus impostoribus magnis liber, Cherbury, Hobbes, Spinoza oppositus.* (1700) p. 75: "Benedictus Spinoza, whom one should rather call *Maledictus,* for the thorny earth (*spinoza terra*) which was a consequence of the divine curse, has never carried a more cursed person, nor one whose writings are sown with so many thorns. . . ."

J. J. Brucker (1696–1770) author of a history of philosophy which for those times was excellent: *Historia critica philosophiae,* 5 vols., (Leipzig, 1742). In it he states that "atheism and Spinozism are now names identical in meaning."

[**421**] The following narration is more or less a summary of Colerus' *Life of Spinoza.* It may be found translated in full as an appendix to F. Pollock's *Spinoza, His Life and Philosophy* (London, 1899), pp. 383–418.

(2) Like Spinoza, Acosta was a Jew of Portuguese origin residing in Amsterdam. After many altercations with the Synagogue because of his atheistic tendencies, he finally shot himself in 1647. He left behind him an autobiography *Exemplar humanae vitae.* This was first published in 1687 by Limborch, with a vituperative refutation.

[**422**] (1) Masaniello (Tommaso Aniello) (1622–47) was a popular hero of the seventeenth century. He was a fisherman who led the revolt of Naples against the Spanish rule in 1647, and he was killed at the very threshold of success.

(2) Such a portrait, dated 1749, can be found reproduced in E. Altkirch: *Spinoza im Porträt* (Jena, 1913), p. 97.

[**424**] (1) Epistle XLVII: to Fabritius, the secretary of the Elector Palatine.

[**425**] (1) For the quotation which follows, the Elwes translation of *On the Improvement of the Understanding* has been used.

[**431**] (1) This emphasis upon Spinoza's Cartesian terminology, of which Herder makes a good deal, was first made by Christian Wolff in his refutation of Spinoza's system in the *Theologia naturalis,* 1737, Vol. II.

[**432**] (1) Clauberg (1622–65) was one of the earliest Cartesian philosophers in Germany. One of his best works was a very precise commentary on Descartes' *Meditations.*

(2) The text reads *Giftbaum,* i.e. "poisonous or baneful tree." In the eighteenth century there were many stories rife about the fabulous Upas tree, which was said to exude poisonous vapors which killed all living things within a radius of miles, and it is more than likely that Herder was here referring to it. For a most interesting account of the tree by a Dutch explorer, see Erasmus Darwin's *Loves of the Plants.*

[**434**] (1) By Vanini (1584–1619). See text p. 112 [**465–6**]. The original is in *Amphitheatrum aeternae providentiae divinomagicum christianophysicum Auctore Iulio Caesare Vanino.* Lugduni, MDCXV, p. 334 ff. For a full account of his interesting life see C. Plumptre, *History of Pantheism* (London, 1878), I, 372 ff.

SECOND CONVERSATION

[**439**] (1) Baumgarten (1714–62) was a disciple of Leibniz and Wolff and founder of the science of aesthetics, to which he first gave that name. He and the other men named here are all actual influences in Herder's development. See Introduction.

[**444**] (1) The poetry is from *Gedanken über Vernunft, Aberglauben, und Unglauben,* by Albrecht von Haller (1708–77) ed. Hirzel. p. 57 ff. Haller was a Swiss anatomist and physiologist of repute, who often expressed his scientific conclusions in poetic form.

[**446**] (1) The translation here is somewhat free. Herder actually says: "weil sie sich nie besinnen durfte" but if rendered

"because it could not stop to deliberate (or think)" it would be misleading. Herder himself seems not to have liked the phrase, for it is omitted in the second edition.

[**447**] (1) Christian Wolff, in his *Theologia naturalis* says: "Spinoza has wrongly identified extension with something really existent. This he carried over from his master Descartes." There is no direct evidence that Herder derived his own criticism from this source, but he knew the work well. Although he was in other matters a severe critic of Wolff (see Introduction, p. 8 ff. and text [**450, 459**]) it seems probable that he here was using Wolff's criticism of Spinoza as a starting point for his own interpretation. His tendency to regard Spinoza as afflicted with Cartesian terminology corresponds also to Wolff's view (see text [**431**] and note thereto) and further increases the likelihood of this influence.

[**450**] (1) The three hypotheses referred to are evidently the theory of monads, pre-established harmony, and the doctrine of the moral necessity of God. Herder discusses both of the latter elsewhere and finds them to have shortcomings. (See text [**459–462**] and [**485**] ff.)

(2) R. J. Boscowich (1711–87), an Italian mathematician, natural philosopher and diplomat. For a brief discussion of his atomic theory see Jeans' article "Molecule" in the *Encyclopaedia Britannica,* 11th ed. A translation of his work *A Theory of Natural Philosophy* has been published in this country. (Chicago, 1912.)

[**445**] (1) In a note to this passage, H. Stephan, *Herders Philosophie* (1906) states that the astronomer Herschel is here referred to.

(2) Suphan *Werke.* XVI, 630 has the following note: "*Philosophical Essays* published 1779 (not 1780) in 2 volumes. The verses, freely altered, are from the ode 'God'."

[**457**] (1) Both of these charges had been made by Jacobi in the controversy with Mendelssohn. See Introduction p. 28 ff.

[**459**] (1) In his "Of Perception and Feeling" (*Vom Erkennen und Empfinden der menschlichen Seele*) Herder wrote: "It seems to me that the system of pre-established harmony might very well have been a view alien to the author of the Monad-poem, for, it seems, both do not stand very well side by side," and he goes on to say that the soul as a force, can, and must be conceived as having an effective activity in the whole realm of forces. (Su. VIII, 178.)

[**460**] (1) Arnold Geulincx (1624–69) occupied himself pre-eminently with the Cartesian problem of the relation between body and soul, and came to the conclusion that they operated in harmony like two clocks set by God. He also systematized the doctrine of Occasionalism.

[**462**] (1) The statement that Spinoza's system contained the doctrine of pre-established harmony and that Leibniz got it from that source was first made by Mendelssohn in the first conversation of his *Philosophische Gespräche* (1755). Herder evidently made this view his own in the first edition. However, Lessing's article, *Durch Spinoza ist Leibniz nur auf die Spur der Vorherbestimmten Harmonie gekommen* (1763) and Jacobi's discussion of the same matter in Appendix VI of the second edition of his *Ueber die Lehre des Spinoza* seem to have caused him to modify this view. In the second edition, an interpolation makes this clear. See Appendix A, [**462**].

[**466**] (1) See title of Vanini's work, note to p. 224 [**434**]. His right name actually was Lucilio.

(2) Acts 17:28.

(3) Romans 11:36.

[**467**] (1) Sirach, 43, 29 (Suphan's note). This, and the three following passages are translated from Herder's version.

[**468**] (1) From Sadi's *Gulistan* or "Rose Garden." The

Kama-Shastra Society translation has been used. Herder differs only in minor details. His "prattlers" has been used instead of Kama-Shastra "pretenders."

THIRD CONVERSATION

[**469**] (1) Herder wrote more extensively on the same subject in his "Nemesis, an Instructive Allegory" in Part II of *Zerstreute Blätter,* 1785. Su. *Werke* XV.

(2) J. H. Lambert, see Introduction p. 21.

The full titles of the works here mentioned are: "New Organon, or Thoughts on the Discovery and the Description of the Truth, and Its Distinction from Error and Appearance" (*Neues Organon oder Gedanken über die Erforschung und Bezeichnung des Wahren und dessen Unterscheidung vom Irrthum und Schein.* Leipzig, 1764, 2 vols.), and "Plan for an Architectonic, or the Theory of the Simple and First in Philosophical and Mathematical Knowledge" (*Anlage zur Architektonik oder Theorie des Einfachen und Ersten in der philosophischen und mathematischen Erkenntniss,* Riga, 1771, 2 vols.).

[**473**] (1) See text p. 67 [**404**] and note thereto. Originally, "Adrastea" probably meant "one from whom there is no escape."

(2) Leibniz frequently took pains to distinguish his views from Spinoza's. For example in the *Nouveaux essais* he says: ".... I earlier went a bit too far ... and was very close to allying myself with the Spinozists, who attribute to God only an infinite power without ascribing to Him Perfection and Wisdom, thus paying little heed to final purposes and deriving everything from an unreasoning necessity. But the new understanding which I have since acquired [the *Monadology*] has healed me of this, and since then I call myself a disciple of

Theophilus." Quoted in L. Stein: *Leibniz und Spinoza* (Berlin, 1890), p. 231.

[474] (1) In the second edition of his *On the Doctrine of Spinoza* (p. 347; Appendix V) Jacobi took exception to this statement that Spinoza did not fully understand himself, deeming it far more possible that the inadequacy lay with Herder rather than Spinoza. Herder seems to have capitulated in the second edition to the extent of removing this statement. See Appendix A, p. 198 [474].

[476] (1) Mendelssohn's *Morgenstunden* (p. 186 ff.; 195 ff.) put forth this view that Spinoza's Infinite Substance is nothing but a collective name for all the extensions and thoughts of the world of experience.

[481] (1) This and the following poetry is in J. P. Uz, *Sämmtliche Poetische Werke* (Leipzig, 1768), I, 208 ff.

[483] (1) Haller. See text p. 99 [444] and note thereto.

[485] (1) *Nouveaux essais sur l'entendement humain,* a chapter by chapter criticism of Locke's *Essay on Human Understanding.* Evidently Locke's death prevented publication at the intended time.

[486] (1) The correspondence with Clarke, instigated by Queen Anne, took place during the last few years of Leibniz's life: *Sur Dieu, l'âme, l'espace, la durée.*

[490] (1) There is no indication as to whether the verses are quoted or original. They are typical of a tendency in the last half of the eighteenth century to incorporate the discoveries and truths of science in poetry.

FOURTH CONVERSATION

[495] (1) Jacobi had reported his conversation with Lessing from memory after several years had passed, and, because the charge of Spinozism was considered so serious, it was very important that he should have reported it accurately.

[**497**] (1) Jacobi, in the second edition of his *On the Doctrine of Spinoza* referred to this passage, maintaining that a highest intelligence necessarily implies personality. With this view Herder disagreed, and in the second edition, he substantiated his own view in a long interpolation. See Appendix A [**497**].

[**499**] (1) H. Stephan (*Herders Philosophie*) points out in a note to this passage that this refers rather to Luther's own view (*de servo arbitrio*) than to that of the Lutheran Church, which capitulated in the matter of free-will.

[**502**] (1) Jacobi (*On the Doctrine of Spinoza,* 2nd ed. Appendix V) again attacked Herder accusing him of using Lessing's utterances as an excuse for showing that Lessing was on the way to Herder's own conception of Spinoza. Herder removed the reference in the second edition. See Appendix A [**502**].

[**508**] (1) Herder withdrew this remark from the second edition. He and Mendelssohn can be conceived as in agreement only on the point that Spinoza was not an atheist. In almost every other respect they are at variance.

[**511**] (1) The references to Jacobi's doctrine of Belief were left out of the second edition. See Appendix A [**509–12**]. Jacobi had been greatly offended by the first edition of the "Conversations" and broke off his friendship with Herder. Later, in 1792 some reconciliation was effected, and probably because of this, Herder removed some of the references which had hurt Jacobi.

[**513**] (1) Kästner, A. G. One of a group of Göttingen mathematicians who, in the middle of the eighteenth century promoted English ideas against the Wolffians.

[**514**] (1) The hymn is by Ewald von Kleist (1715–59).

[**516**] (1) The following discussion is aimed at Kant's *Critique of Pure Reason*. See Introduction p. 37.

[**522**] (1) The Humean tone of this discussion of causality

has been pointed out by E. Hoffart, *Herders "Gott"* (Halle, 1918), p. 64–6, who also observes that this view is not consistent with the views of the rest of the work in which Herder of necessity regards causality and the knowledge of it, as real.
[523] (1) Both Jacobi (*On the Doctrine of Spinoza,* p. 223) and Mendelssohn (*Morgenstunden,* p. XIII) make this charge, and quote J. G. Wachter with approval. See Appendix A, p. 208 [523]. (A1) (A2)
[525] (1) *Monadology* § 47.
[527] (1) Herder modified this somewhat in the second edition (see Appendix A, p. 209 [527]) after Jacobi declared that he had misunderstood this passage (*On the Doctrine of Spinoza,* 2nd ed. p. 48). Jacobi also observes that Herder's opposition to the conception of God as the World Soul is astonishing, because that is precisely what Herder has made of the God of Spinoza. Herder himself had earlier declared that this conception of God was to him the highest possible (see Introduction p. 8) but here he is afraid of the anthropomorphism to which it may lead.
[528] (1) These and the following verses are from Haller's "Eternity" (Hirzel's ed.) p. 141–2.
[530] (1) Gleim (1719–1803) was a very intimate friend of Herder, and the author of some very popular Grenadier songs. It was at his home that the Jacobi-Lessing conversation took place.

FIFTH CONVERSATION

[532] (1) Herder's reasons for introducing the character of Theano have aroused speculation among the critics. Kühnemann in his introduction to Vol. IV of *Herders Werke,* p. XXI, maintains that she is brought in to forestall any demand for a justification of Herder's proposition of Active

Being. Haym and all other critics are unanimous in regretting her introduction from the literary point of view.

[537] (1) From Haller's "On the Source of Evil" and "Eternity" (Hirzel, p. 126 f. and 152).

[544] (1) *Monadology* §§ 60–63.

[548] (1) *Monadology* §§ 67–68.

[562] (1) The author is Karl von Dalberg, a Prince of the Catholic Church. In 1787, after reading the "Conversations" he wrote to Herder: "Your God is also mine, and has become more so since I have examined this idea more closely. I cannot imagine the Highest Being in any more estimable fashion.—Spinoza and Christ, only in these two is pure knowledge of God; in Christ, the secret higher way to the Deity, in Spinoza the highest peak to which rational demonstration can attain, and which certainly does not, as Jacobi thinks, lead to atheism. No philosopher, it seems to me, came so near to Christianity, as he did; none sought the truth with purer spirit." [*Herders Reise nach Italien. Herders Briefwechsel mit seiner Gattin von August 1788 bis Juli 1789.* Düntzer, H. und Herder, F. G. von (Giessen, 1859), p. xxx.]

[567] (1) Herder wrote at length on Palingenesis in *Zerstreute Blätter* Part V (Su. XVI) using Lessing's discussion of the same subject in *Erziehung des Menschengeschlechts* § 94 (*Werke* X: 329) as a basis.

[572] (1) Again Kant is referred to.

SELECTED BIBLIOGRAPHY

I. HERDER BIBLIOGRAPHIES:

No complete bibliography of works dealing with Herder exists. Friedrich Ueberweg *Grundriss der Geschichte der Philosophie*. Berlin: Dr. Traugott Konstantin Oesterreich (Ed.), 1923. 12 ed., third part, has a useful, but by no means exhaustive one. Two others of limited range are:

H. D. *Die Herder Litteratur in Deutschland; Vollständiger Katalog von 1769 bis 1851*. Cassel, 1852.

Tronchon, Henri. *La fortune intellectuelle de Herder en France*. Paris: Bibliothèque de littérature comparée, 1920.

II. EDITIONS OF HERDER'S WORKS:

The only complete edition of Herder's works is that by Bernhard Suphan in 33 volumes, Berlin 1877–1913, which supersedes all others. To it the following should be added:

Düntzer, Johann H. J. and Herder, Ferdinand G. von (Ed.). *Aus Herders Nachlass*. 3 vols. Frankfurt a. M., 1856–57.

————. *Von und an Herder: Ungedruckte Briefe aus Herders Nachlass*. 2 vols. in 1. Leipzig, 1861–62.

————. *Herders Reise nach Italien. Herders Briefwechsel mit seiner Gattin von August 1788 bis Juli 1789*. Giessen, 1859. p. xxx.

Herder, Maria Caroline von (geb. Flachsland) and Müller, J. G. *Erinnerungen aus dem Leben Johann Gottfried von Herders*. 3 vols. Stuttgart und Tübingen, 1830. (Another edition, 1820.)

Herder, Emil Gottfried von (Ed.). *Johann Gottfried von Herders Lebensbild.* 3 vols. Erlangen, 1846.

Hoffmann, Otto (Ed.). *Herders Briefwechsel mit Nicolai.* Berlin, 1887.

————. *Herders Briefe an Johann Georg Hamann.* Berlin, 1889.

III. Commentaries and Critical Works Dealing Specifically with Herder's *Gott*:

Dieterle, J. A. "Die Grundgedanken in Herders Schrift 'Gott' und ihr Verhältnis zu Spinozas Philosophie," *Theologische Studien und Kritiken,* Vol. 87 (1914).

Hoffart, Elisabeth. *Herders "Gott."* Halle a. S., 1918; Erlangen, 1917. *Bausteine zur Geschichte der deutschen Litteratur.* Vol. 16.

McGiffert, Arthur Cushman. "The God of Spinoza as Interpreted by Herder," *Hibbert Journal,* III (1904–5), 706 ff.

IV. General Works Relevant to the Setting and Tradition of *Gott*:

Altkirch, Ernst. *Maledictus und Benedictus.* Leipzig, 1924.

Bäck, Leo. *Spinozas erste Einwirkungen auf Deutschland.* Berlin, 1895.

Baumgardt, David. "Spinoza und der deutsche Spinozismus," *Kantstudien Philosophische Zeitschrift,* XXXII (1927), Part I, 182 ff.

Brockdorff, Cay, Baron von. *Die deutsche Aufklärungsphilosophie.* München, 1926. *Geschichte der Philosophie in Einzeldarstellungen.* Vol. 26.

Cassirer, Ernst. *Die Philosophie der Aufklärung.* Tübingen, 1932. (Grundriss der philosophischen Wissenschaften.)

————. *Das Erkenntnisproblem in der Philosophie und Wissenschaft der neueren Zeit.* 2 vols. Berlin, 1906–1907; 1920.

Dilthey, Wilhelm. "Der entwicklungsgeschichtliche Pantheismus nach seinem Zusammenhang mit den älteren pantheistischen Systemen," II, 312 ff. *Gesammelte Schriften.* 12 vols. Leipzig, 1921–36.

Griffing, Harold. "Lambert: A Study in the Development of the Critical Philosophy," *Philosophical Review,* II (1893), 54 ff.

Grunwald, Max. *Spinoza in Deutschland.* Berlin, 1897.

Haym, Rudolph. *Die romantische Schule.* Berlin, 1870–1928.

Heine, Heinrich. *Religion and Philosophy in Germany.* London, 1882.

Hettner, Hermann. *Geschichte der deutschen Litteratur im 18. Jahrhundert.* Braunschweig, 1862. (Another edition, called *Litteraturgeschichte des 18. Jahrhunderts,* 3 vols., Braunschweig, 1881.)

Hibben, John Grier. *The Philosophy of the Enlightenment.* New York, 1910.

Hillebrand, Karl. *German Thought from the Seven Years' War to Goethe's Death.* New York, 1880.

Korff, H. A. *Geist der Goethezeit.* Leipzig, 1923–27.

Krakauer, M. *Zur Geschichte des Spinozismus in Deutschland während der ersten Hälfte des 18. Jahrhunderts.* Breslau, 1881.

Kronenberg, M. *Geschichte des deutschen Idealismus.* München, 1909.

Kroner, R. *Von Kant bis Hegel.* 2 vols. Tübingen, 1921–24.

Lovejoy, Arthur Oncken. *The Great Chain of Being.* Cambridge, Mass., 1936.

Pfleiderer, Otto. *The Philosophy of Religion on the Basis of Its History*. Translated from the German of the second and greatly enlarged edition by A. Stewart and A. Menzies. 4 vols. London, 1886–88. See Vol. I and II: *History of the Philosophy of Religion from Spinoza to the Present Day*. (For the original German see: Religionsphilos. auf geschichtl. Grundl. Aufl. 3, Vol. I.: Gesch. d. Religionsphilos. von Spinoza bis auf die Gegenw., Berlin, 1893.)

Pringle-Pattison, A. Seth. *The Development from Kant to Hegel*. London, 1882.

Randall, John Herman. *Making of the Modern Mind*. New York, 1926.

Richard, Ernst. *History of German Civilization*. New York, 1911.

Royce, Josiah. *Spirit of Modern Philosophy*. New York, 1892.

———. *Lectures on Modern Idealism*. New Haven, 1919.

Scherer, W. *Geschichte der deutschen Litteratur*. 2 vols. Leipzig, 1934; Berlin, 1899.

Schwarz, Hermann. "Die Entwicklung des Pantheismus in der neueren Zeit," *Zeitschrift für Philosophie und philosophische Kritik*, Vol. 157 (1915), Part I, 20–80.

Siegel, C. *Geschichte der deutschen Naturphilosophie*. Berlin, 1890; Leipzig, 1913.

Weiser, Chr. Fr. *Shaftesbury und das deutsche Geistesleben*. Leipzig, Berlin, 1916.

Ziegler, Theobald. *Die geistigen und sozialen Strömungen des neunzehnten Jahrhunderts*. Berlin, 1899, 1901, 1916.

V. The Spinoza Controversy:

Crawford, Alex. *The Philosophy of F. H. Jacobi*. New York, 1905.

Jacobi, Friedrich. *Ueber die Lehre des Spinoza in Briefen an den Herrn Moses Mendelssohn*. Breslau, 1785, (2nd ed., 1789).

Lévy-Bruhl, L. *La Philosophie de Jacobi*. Paris, 1894.

Mauthner, Fritz (Ed.). *Jacobis Spinoza Büchlein nebst Replik und Duplik*. München, 1912.

Mendelssohn, Moses. *Morgenstunden, oder Vorlesungen über das Daseyn Gottes*. Berlin, 1785.

————. *An die Freunde Lessings*. Ein Anhang zu Herrn Jacobis Briefwechsel über die Lehre des Spinoza. Berlin, 1786.

Scholz, H. *Die Hauptschriften zum Pantheismusstreit zwischen Jacobi und Mendelssohn*. Berlin, 1916. (Neudr. selt. phil. Werke, hrsg. v. d. Kantges. Vol. VI.)

Stockum, Theodorus C. van. *Spinoza, Jacobi, Lessing*. Gröningen, 1916.

Wilde, Norman. *F. H. Jacobi*. New York, 1894.

Zirngiebl, Eberhard. *F. H. Jacobis Leben, Dichten und Denken*. Wien, 1867.

————. *Jacobi-Mendelssohn Streit*. München, 1861.

VI. Selected Works on Herder's Life, Thought and Influence

Andress, J. Mace. *Johann Gottfried Herder as an Educator*. New York, 1916.

Bärenbach, Friedrich von. *Herder als Vorgänger Darwins und der modernen Naturphilosophie*. Berlin, 1877.

Barth, Paul. "Zu Herders 100. Todestage," *Vierteljahrsschrift für wissenschaftliche Philosophie und Soziologie*, 27. Jahrgang, Leipzig (1903), p. 429 ff.

Baumgarten, O. *Herders Lebenswerk und die religiöse Frage der Gegenwart*. Tübingen, 1905.

Berger, F. *Menschenbild und Menschenbildung. Die philosophisch-pädagogische Anthropologie Johann Gottfried Herders.* Stuttgart, 1933.

Boor, W. "Herders Erkenntnislehre," *Beiträge zur Förderung der christlichen Theologie,* Vol. 32, Part 6.

Bossert, Adolphe. *Herder; sa vie et son oeuvre.* Paris, 1916.

Bran, Friedrich Alexander. *Herder und die deutsche Kulturanschauung.* Berlin, 1932. (Probleme der Staats- und Kultursoziologie, hrsg. von Alfred Weber, Heidelberg, Vol. 5.)

Burckhardt, G. E. *Die Anfänge einer geschichtliche Fundamentierung der Religionsphilosophie bei Herder.* Halle, 1908.

Bürkner, Richard. *Herder, sein Leben und Wirken.* Berlin, 1904.

De Quincey, Thomas. *The Collected Writings* (Ed. David Masson). 14 vols. (London, 1896–97) IV, 380–394.

Doerne, Martin. *Die Religion in Herders Geschichtsphilosophie.* Leipzig, 1927.

Erdmann, A. H. *Herder als Religionsphilosoph.* Marburg, 1866.

Fischer, Wilhelm. *Herders Erkenntnislehre und Metaphysik.* Leipzig, 1878.

Foerster, K. *Herders Gedanken über Religion, Welt, und Leben.* 1911.

Fries, Martin. *Studier i Herders Religionsfilosofi med Särskild hänsyn till hans ställning till Spinoza.* Uppsala, 1935.

Gemmingen, Otto Freiherr von. *Vico Hamann, und Herder.* Borna-Leipzig, 1918.

Gernhard, A. G. "Herder als Humanist," *Weimarsches Herder Album,* 1845.

Goebel, Louis. *Herder und Schleiermachers "Reden über die Religion."* Gotha, 1904.

Götz, Hermann. "War Herder ein Vorgänger Darwins?" *Vierteljahrschrift für wissenschaftliche Philosophie und Soziologie,* 26. Jahrgang, Leipzig (1902), p. 391 ff.

———. *Herder als Psycholog.* Leipzig, 1904.

Hanssel, O. *Der Einfluss Rousseaus auf die philosophischpädagogischen Anschauungen Herders.* Dresden, 1902; Leipzig, 1900 (Diss.).

Hatch, Irwin Clifton. *Der Einfluss Shaftesburys auf Herder.* Breslau, 1901.

Haym, Rudolph. *Herder nach seinem Leben und seinen Werken.* 2 vols. Berlin, 1877–85.

Heinsius, Th. *Herder nach seinem Leben.* Berlin, 1847.

Jacoby, Günther. *Herder als Faust.* Leipzig, 1911.

Joret, Pierre L. C. R. *Herder et la Renaissance littéraire en Allemagne au 18ᵉ siècle.* Paris, 1875.

Keller, L. *J. G. Herder, seine Geistesentwicklung, seine Weltanschauung.* Jena, 1910.

Kronenberg, Mor. *Herders Philosophie nach ihrem Entwicklungsgang und ihrer historischen Stellung.* Heidelberg, 1889.

Kühnemann, Eugen. *Herders Persönlichkeit in seiner Weltanschauung.* München, 1893.

———. *Herders Leben.* München, 1895.

———. *Herder.* München, 1911–1927.

Lehmann, Rudolf. *Die deutschen Klassiker: Herder, Schiller, Goethe.* Leipzig, 1921.

Litt, Th. *Kant und Herder als Deuter der geistigen Welt.* Leipzig, 1930.

Meyer, H. *Herder und Kant*. Halle a. S., 1904.

Müller, J. G. "Welche Bedeutung hat Herder für die Entwicklung der neueren deutschen Theologie?" *Weimarsches Herder Album*, 1845.

Neumann, Robert. *Herder und der Kampf gegen die kantischen Irrlehren an der Universität Jena*. Berlin, 1911.

Nevinson, Henry. *A Sketch of Herder and His Times*. London, 1884.

Pfleiderer, Otto. "Herder und Kant," *Jahrbuch für protestantische Theologie*, I (1875), 636 ff.

Plantiko, O. *Rousseaus, Herders und Kants Theorie vom Zukunftsideal der Menschheitsgeschichte*. Greifswald, 1895.

Posadzy, L. *Der entwicklungsgeschichtliche Gedanke bei Herder*. Münster, 1906.

Schaede, E. J. "Herders Schrift 'Gott' und ihre Aufnahme bei Goethe," *Germanische Studien*, Part 149 (1934), Berlin.

Schmidt, Ferd. Jac. *Herders pantheistische Weltanschauung*. Berlin, 1888.

Siegel, Carl. *Herder als Philosoph*. Stuttgart und Berlin, 1907.

Stephan, Horst. *Herder in Bückeburg und seine Bedeutung für die Kirchengeschichte*. Tübingen, 1905.

————. *Herders Philosophie; ausgewählte Denkmäler aus der Werdezeit der neuen deutschen Bildung*. Leipzig, 1906. (Philosophische Bibliothek, Vol. 112.)

Suphan, Bernhard. "Herder als Schüler Kants," *Zeitschrift für deutsche Philologie*, IV (1872), 225–237.

Tumarkin, Anna. *Herder und Kant*. Bern, 1896. (Berner Studien zur Philosophie und ihrer Geschichte, Vol. 1.)

Unger, Rudolf. *Herder, Novalis und Kleist*. Frankfurt a. M., 1922. (Deutsche Forschungen, Part 9.)

————. "Zur neueren Herderforschung," *Germanisch-romanische Monatschrift,* I (1909), 145–168.

Vollrath, W. *Die Auseinandersetzung Herders mit Spinoza.* Darmstadt, 1911.

Werner, Aug. *Herder als Theologe.* Berlin, 1871.

Wielandt, R. *Herders Theorie von der Religion und den religiösen Vorstellungen.* Naumberg, 1903; Berlin, 1904.

Witte, J. H. *Die Philosophie unserer Dichterheroen: Lessing und Herder.* Bonn, 1880, Vol. I.

INDEX